Practicable Socialism, New Series

Mrs. S. A. Barnett and S. A. Barnett

Alpha Editions

This edition published in 2024

ISBN 9789361478642

Design and Setting By

Alpha Editions
www.alphaedis.com

Email - info@alphaedis.com

As per information held with us this book is in Public Domain.
This book is a reproduction of an important historical work.
Alpha Editions uses the best technology to reproduce historical work
in the same manner it was first published to preserve its original nature.
Any marks or number seen are left intentionally to preserve.

Contents

INTRODUCTION.	- 1 -
SECTION I. RELIGION.	- 6 -
THE RELIGION OF THE PEOPLE.	- 6 -
CATHEDRAL REFORM.	- 17 -
CONCLUSION.	- 26 -
THE CATHEDRALS AND MODERN NEEDS.	- 28 -
SECTION II. RECREATION.	- 34 -
THE CHILDREN'S COUNTRY HOLIDAY FUN'.	- 34 -
THE RECREATION OF THE PEOPLE.	- 43 -
THE HOPES OF THE HOSTS.	- 54 -
EASTER MONDAY ON HAMPSTEAD HEATH.	- 57 -
HOLIDAYS AND SCHOOLDAYS.	- 59 -
THE FAILURE OF HOLIDAYS.	- 63 -
RECREATION IN TOWN AND COUNTRY.	- 67 -
SECTION III. SETTLEMENTS.	- 72 -
SETTLEMENTS OF UNIVERSITY MEN IN GREAT TOWNS.	- 72 -
THE BEGINNINGS OF TOYNBEE HALL.	- 80 -
TWENTY-ONE YEARS OF UNIVERSITY SETTLEMENTS.	- 89 -
SECTION IV. POVERTY AND LABOUR.	- 97 -
THE ETHICS OF THE POOR LAW.	- 97 -
POVERTY, ITS CAUSE AND ITS CURE.	- 105 -
THE BABIES OF THE STATE.	- 110 -
POOR LAW REFORM.	- 122 -

THE UNEMPLOYED.	- 129 -
THE POOR LAW REPORT.	- 134 -
WIDOWS WITH CHILDREN UNDER THE POOR LAW.	- 147 -
THE PRESS AND CHARITABLE FUNDS.	- 156 -
WHAT IS POSSIBLE IN POOR LAW REFORM.	- 161 -
CHARITY UP TO DATE.	- 166 -
WHAT LABOUR WANTS.	- 173 -
OUR PRESENT DISCONTENTS.	- 176 -
SECTION V. SOCIAL SERVICE.	- 186 -
OF TOWN PLANNING.	- 186 -
THE MISSION OF MUSIC.	- 197 -
THE REAL SOCIAL REFORMER.	- 205 -
WHERE CHARITY FAILS.	- 210 -
LANDLORDISM UP TO DATE.	- 212 -
THE CHURCH AND TOWN PLANNING.	- 215 -
SECTION VI. EDUCATION.	- 219 -
THE TEACHER'S EQUIPMENT.	- 219 -
OXFORD UNIVERSITY AND THE WORKING PEOPLE.	- 224 -
OXFORD UNIVERSITY AND THE WORKING PEOPLE.	- 228 -
JUSTICE TO YOUNG WORKERS.	- 233 -
A RACE BETWEEN EDUCATION AND RUIN.	- 237 -

INTRODUCTION.

THE first edition of PRACTICABLE SOCIALISM was printed in 1888, the second in 1894. Now, twenty-one years afterwards, a new series is issued, but the most important of the two authors, alas! has left the world, and it therefore falls to me to write the introduction alone.

In selecting the papers for this volume, out of a very great deal of material, the principle followed has been to print those which deal with reforms yet waiting to be fully accomplished. It would have been easier and perhaps pleasanter to have taken the subjects dealt with in the previous volumes, and by grouping subsequent papers together, have shown how many of the reforms then indicated as desirable and "practicable," had now become accepted and practised. But so to do would not have been in harmony with our feelings. My husband counted the sin of "numbering the people" as due to a debased moral outlook, and the contemplation of "results" as tending to hinder nobler efforts after that which is deeper than can be calculated. Of him it is truthful to quote "His soul's wings never furled".

The papers have been grouped in subject sections, and though the ideas have for many years been set forth by him in various publications, in most instances the writings here reproduced are under six years old. In a few cases, however, I have used quite an old paper, thinking it gave, with hopeful vision, thoughts which later lost their freshness as they became accomplished facts.

The book begins with *The Religion of the People* and *Cathedral Reform*, for Canon Barnett held with unvarying certainty that—to quote his own words—"there is no other end worth reaching than the knowledge of God, which is eternal life,"—and that "organizations are only machinery of which the driving power is human love, and of which the object is the increase of the knowledge of God". To this test our plans and undertakings were constantly brought. "Does our work give 'life' by bringing men nearer to God and nearer to one another." "In the knowledge of what 'life' is, let us put our work to the test." "Do the Church Services release divine hopes buried under the burden of daily cares?" "Do the new buildings refine manners?" "Does higher teaching tend to higher thoughts about duty?" "Does our relief system help to heal a broken dignity as well as to comfort a sufferer?" "Do our entertainments develop powers for enjoying the best in humanity past and present?"

That the Church should be reformed to make it the servant of all who would lead the higher life, was the hope he cherished throughout many years spent in strenuous efforts to obtain a social betterment. He writes: "The great mass of the people, because they stand apart from all religious communions, may have in them a religious sense, but their thought of God is not worked through their emotions into their daily lives. They do not know what they worship, and so do not say with the psalmist, 'My soul is athirst for the living god,' or say with Joseph, 'How can I do this great wickedness, and sin against God?' The spiritualization of life being necessary to human peace and happiness, the problem which is haunting this generation is how to spiritualize the forces which are shaping the future."

My husband urged that the reform of the Church would tend to solve that problem. "The Church by its history and organization has a power no other agency can wield. If more freedom could be given to its system of government and services, if it could be made directly expressive of the highest aspirations of the people, it is difficult to exaggerate the effect it might have. In every parish a force would be brought to bear which might kindle thought, so that it would reach out to the highest object; which might stir love, so that men would forget themselves in devotion to the whole; and which might create a hope wherein all would find rest. The first need of the age is an increase of Spirituality, and the means of obtaining it is a Reformed Church."

The papers under *Recreation* might almost as well have been placed in the Education Section, so strongly did my husband feel that recreation should educate. Only a few months before his illness he wrote: "The claim of education is now primarily to fit a child to earn a living, and therefore he is taught to read and write and learn a trade. But if it were seen that it is equally important to fit a child to use well his leisure, many changes would be made." And such changes he argued would increase, not lessen, the joy of holidays, an opinion which my experience as Chairwoman of the Country-side Committee of the Children's Country Holiday Fund abundantly supports.

In the Section for *Settlements* and their work, only three papers will be found, for so much has been written and spoken of Toynbee Hall and kindred centres of usefulness, that it seems almost unnecessary to reproduce the same thoughts. Yet in view of the fact that questions are often asked as to the genesis of the idea, I have put in one of the first papers (1884) that my husband wrote after we had had nine years' experience of the work of University men among the poorest and saddest people, in which he suggested the scheme of Toynbee Hall, and also a paper of mine written nine years after its foundation, in which I chat of the *Beginnings of Toynbee Hall*.

Between the first and the third paper there is a stretch of twenty-one busy years, 1884-1905, and the article bears the marks of Canon Barnett's intense realization of the need of higher education, and his almost passionate demand for it on behalf of the industrial classes. "Social Reform," he writes, "will soon be the all-absorbing interest as the modern realization of the claims of human nature and the growing power of the people will not tolerate many of the present conditions of industrial life. . . . The well-being of the future depends on the methods by which reform proceeds. Reforms in the past have often been disappointing. They have been made in the rights of one class, and have ended in the assertion of rights over another class. They have been made by force, and produced reaction. They have been done for the people, not by the people, and have never been assimilated. The method by which knowledge and industry may co-operate has yet to be tried, and one way in which to bring about such co-operation is the way of University Settlements."

So many are the changes which affect *Poverty and Labour*, so rapidly have they come about, and so keen and living an interest did Canon Barnett feel with every step that the great army of the disinherited took towards social justice, that it has been difficult to select which papers on which subject to reprint, but I have chosen the most characteristic, and also those connected with the reforms which most influenced character and life. In this Section also some of the many papers which Canon Barnett wrote on Poor Law Reform have been admitted. I know that the activities of the Fabian Society and the "Break up of the Poor Law" organization have rendered some of the ideas familiar, but many of the Reforms he advocated are not yet accomplished, and to those who are conversant with the subject, his large, sane, unsensational statement of the case, as it appeared to him, will be welcome,—all the more so because for nearly thirty years he was a member of the Whitechapel Board of Guardians, the Founder of the Poor Law Conferences, and had both initiated and carried out large administrative reforms. He also had a very deep and probing tenderness for the character of individual paupers, and a sensitive shrinking from wounding their self-respect or lowering the dignity of their humanity, an attitude of mind which influenced his relation to schemes sometimes made by paper legislators who considered the poor in "the lump" instead of "one by one".

Of the Social Service Section there is but little to say. *The Real Social Reformer* contains guiding principles, *The Mission of Music* is an interesting and curious output from a man with no ear for tune or time or harmony, and *The Church on Town Planning* is but an example of how eagerly he desired that the Church should guide as well as minister to the people. *Where Charity Fails* is another plea that the kindly intentioned should not injure the character of the recipient, and that the crucial question, "Is our aim the self-extinction of our organization," should be borne in mind by the Governors and enthusiastic supporters of even the best philanthropic agencies.

The *Educational* Section might have been much larger, but the papers selected bear on the three sides of the subject which my husband in recent years thought to be the most important. *The Equipment of the Teachers* but carried on the ideals towards which he ever pressed, from the days when as a Curate at St. Mary's, Bryanston Square, he taught the monitors of the Church Schools, through the days when the first London Pupil Teachers' Centre had its birthplace in Toynbee Hall, through the days when he established the Scholarship Committee whose work was to select suitable pupil teachers and support them through their University careers in Oxford and Cambridge, through the days when he rejoiced at the abandonment of the vast system of pupil teachers,—to the days when he demanded that teachers for the poorest children should be called from the cultivated classes, and take their calling as a mission, to be recognized and remunerated, as an honoured profession undertaken by those anxious to render Social Service.

The article *Justice to Young Workers* deals with the vexed question of Continuation Schools, attendance at which Canon Barnett thought should be compulsory, since he believed that economic conditions would more readily change to meet legally established educational demands than was possible, when, in the interwoven complexity of business, one unwilling or ten indifferent employers could throw any complicated voluntary organization out of gear.

The two articles on *Oxford and the Working People* and *A Race between Education and Ruin* only inadequately represent the thought he gave to the matter, or the deeply rooted, great branched hopes he had entwined round the reform of the University,—but for many reasons he felt it wiser to stand aside and watch younger men wield the sword of the pen. So his writings on this subject are few, but that matters less than otherwise it would have done, because the group of friends who have decided to establish "Barnett House" in his memory are among those in Oxford who shared his work, cared for his plans, and believed in his visions, created as they were on knowledge of the industrial workers and the crippling conditions of their lives. So as "Barnett House" is established and grows strong, and in conjunction with the Toynbee Hall Social Service Fellowship will bring the University and Industrial Centres into closer and ever more sympathetic relationship, it is not past the power of a faith, however puny and wingless, to imagine that the reforms my husband saw "darkly" may be seen "face to face," and in realization show once more how "the Word can be made flesh".

In some Sections I have included papers from my pen, not because I think they add much to the value of the book, but because my husband insisted on the previous volumes of PRACTICABLE SOCIALISM being composed of our joint writings as well as illustrative of our joint work, or to use his words in the 1888 volume: "Each Essay is signed by the writer, but in either case they represent our common thought, as all that has been done represents our common work".

HENRIETTA O. BARNETT.

17 July, 1915.

SECTION I.

RELIGION.

<u>The Religion of the People</u>—<u>Cathedral Reform</u>—<u>Cathedrals and Modern Needs.</u>

THE RELIGION OF THE PEOPLE.[1]

By Canon Barnett.

July, 1907.

[1] From the "Hibbert Journal". By permission of the Editor.

THE people are not to be found in places of worship; "the great masses," as Mr. Booth says, "remain apart from all forms of religious communion". This statement is admitted as true, but yet another statement is continually made and also admitted, that "the people are at heart religious". What is meant by this latter statement? The people are certainly not inclined to assert their irreligion. Mr. Henderson, who as a labour leader speaks with authority, says, "I can find no evidence of a general desire among the workers to repudiate the principles of Christianity". And from my own experience in East London I can testify to the growth of greater tolerance and of greater respect for the representatives of religion. Processions with banners and symbols are now common, parsons are elected on public bodies, and religious organizations are enlisted in the army of reform. But this feature of modern conditions is no proof that men and women are at heart religious. It may only imply a more respectful indifference, a growth in manners rather than in spiritual life. Does the statement mean that the people are kind, and moved by the public spirit? This again is true. There is widely spread kindness: rough lads are generous—one I knew gave up his place to make room for a mate whose need was greater; weak and weary women watch all night by a neighbour's sick-bed; a poor family heartily welcomes an orphan child; workmen suffer and endure private loss for the sake of fellow-workmen. The kindness is manifest; but kindness is no evidence of the presence of religion. Kindness may, indeed, be a deposit of religion, a habit inherited from forefathers who drew into themselves love from the Source of love, or it may be something learnt in the common endurance of hardships. Kindness, generosity, public spirit cannot certainly be identified with the religion which has made human beings feel joy in sacrifice and given them peace in the pains of death.

Before, however, we conclude that the non-church-going people are religious or not religious, it may be well to be clear as to what is meant by religion. I would suggest as a definition that religion is thought about the Higher-than-self worked through the emotions into the acts of daily life. This definition involves three constituents: (1) There must be use of thought—the power of mental concentration—so that the mind may break through the obvious and the conventional. (2) There must be a sense of a not-self which is higher than self—knowledge of a Most High whose presence convicts the self of shortcoming and draws it upward. (3) There must be such a realization of this not-self—such a form, be it image, doctrine, book, or life—as will warm the emotions and so make the Higher-than-self tell on every act and experience of daily life. These constituents are, I think, to be found in all religions. The religious man is he who, knowing what is higher than himself, so worships this Most High that he is stirred to do His will in word and deed. The Mohammedan is he who, recognizing the Highest to be power, worships the All-powerful of Mohammed, whom in fear he obeys, and with the sword forces others to obey. The Christian is he who, recognizing the Most High to be love, worships Christ, and for love of Christ is loving to all mankind. Are these three constituents of religion to be found among the people?

1. They are using their powers of thought. There is a distinct disposition to think about unseen things. The Press which circulates most widely has found copy in what it calls Mr. Campbell's "New Theology". The "Clarion" newspaper has published week after week letters and articles which deal with the meaning of God. There is increasing unrest under conditions which crib and cabin the mind; men and women are becoming conscious of more things in heaven and earth than they can see and feel and eat. They have a sense that the modern world has become really larger than the old world, and they resent the teaching which commits them to one position or calling. They have, too, become critical, so that, using their minds, they measure the professions of church-goers. Mr. Haw has collected in his book, "Christianity and the Working Classes," many workmen's opinions on this subject. Witness after witness shows that he has been thinking, comparing things heard and things professed with things done. It is not just indifference or self-indulgence which alienates the people from church or chapel or mission; it is the insincerity or inconsistency which they themselves have learnt to detect. Huxley said long ago that the greatest gift of science to the modern world was not to be found in the discoveries which had increased its power and its comfort, so much as in the habit of more scientific thinking which it had made common.

The people share this gift and have become critical. They criticize all professions, theological or political. They criticize the Bible, and the very children in the schools have become rationalists. They also construct, and there are few more interesting facts of the time than the strength of trades unions, co-operative and friendly societies, which they have organized. Even unskilled labour, ever since the great Dock strike, has shown its power to conceive methods of amelioration, and to combine for their execution. The first constituent of religion, the activity of thought, is thus present amid the non-church-going population.

2. This thought is, I think, directed towards a Higher-than-self; it, that is to say, goes towards goodness. I would suggest a few instances. Universal homage is paid to the character of Christ. He, because of His goodness, is exalted above all other reformers, and writers who are bitter against Christianity reverence His truth and good-will. Popular opinion respects a good man whatever be his creed or party; it may not always be instructed as to the contents of goodness, but at elections its votes incline to follow the lead of the one who seems good, and that is sometimes the neighbouring publican whose kindness and courtesy are experienced. In social and political thought the most significant and strongest mark is the ethical tendency. Few proposals have now a chance of a hearing if they do not appeal to a sense of justice. Right has won at any rate a verbal victory over might. In late revivals there has been much insistence on the need of better living, on temperance, on payment of debts and fulfilment of duty, and the reprints which publishers find it worth their while to publish are penny books of Seneca, Marcus Aurelius, and other writers on morals.

People generally—unconsciously often—have a sense of goodness, or righteousness, as something which is higher than themselves. They are in a way dissatisfied with their own selfishness, and also with a state of society founded on selfishness. There is a widely spread expectation of a better time which will be swayed by dominant goodness. The people have thus, in some degree, the second constituent of religion, in that they have the thought that the High and Mighty which inhabits Eternity is good.

3. When, however, we come to the third constituent, we have at once to admit that the non-church-going population has no means of realizing the Most High in a form which sustains and inspires its action. It has no close or personal touch or communion with this goodness; no form which, like a picture or like a common meal, by its associations of memory or hope rouses its feelings; nothing which, holding the thought, stirs the emotions and works the thought into daily life. The forms of religion, the Churches, the doctrines, the ritual, the sacraments, which meant so much to their fathers and to some of their neighbours, mean nothing to them. They have

lost touch with the forms of religious thought as they have not lost touch with the forms of political thought.

Forms are the clothes of thought. Forms are lifeless, and thought is living. Unless the forms are worn every day they cease to fit the thought, as left-off clothes cease to fit the body. English citizens who have gone on wearing the old forms of political thought can therefore go on talking and acting as if the King ruled to-day as Queen Elizabeth ruled 300 years ago, but these non-church-going folk, who for generations have left off wearing the forms of religious thought, cannot use the words about the Most High which the Churches and preachers use. They have breathed an atmosphere charged by science—they are rationalists, they have a vision of morality and goodness exceeding that advocated by many of the Churches. They have themselves created great societies, and their votes have made and unmade governments. When, therefore, they regard the Churches, the doctrines of preachers, and all the forms of religion, not as those to whom by use they are familiar or by history illuminated, but as strangers, they see what seem to them stiff services, irrational doctrine, disorganized and unbusinesslike systems, and the self-assertion of priests and ministers. They, with their yearnings to touch goodness, find nothing in these forms which makes them say, "There, that is what I mean," and go on stirred in their hearts. They who have learnt to think turn away sadly or scornfully from teaching such as that of the Salvation Army about blood and fire, where emotion is without thought. Those who manage their own affairs resent membership in religious organizations where all is managed for them. They want a name for the Most High of whom they think as above and around themselves, but somehow the doctrines about Christ, whom they respect for His work 2000 years ago, do not stir them up as if He were a present power. The working classes, says Dr. Fairbairn in his "Religion in History and Modern Life," are alienated because "the Church has lost adaptation to the environment in which it lives".

Perhaps, however, some one may say, "Forms are unimportant". This may be true so far as regards a few rarely constituted minds, but the mass of men are seldom moved except through some human or humanized form. The elector may have his principles, but it is the candidate he cheers, it is his photograph he carries, it is his presence which rouses enthusiasm, and it is politicians' names by which parties are called. The Russian peasant may say his prayers, but it is the ikon—the image dear to his fathers—which rouses him to do or to die. The Jews had no likeness of Jehovah, but the book of the law represented to them the thought and memories of their heart, and they bound its words to their foreheads, their poets were stirred to write psalms in its praise, and by the emotions it raised its teaching was worked into their daily acts. A non-religious writer in the "Clarion" bears witness to the same fact when he says, "All effective movements must have creeds. It is impossible to satisfy the needs of any human mind or heart without some form of belief." The Quaker who rejects so many forms has made a form of no-form, and his simple manner of speech, his custom of dress or worship, often moves him to his actions.

Mr. Gladstone bears testimony to the place of form in religion. "The Church," he says, "presented to me Christianity under an aspect in which I had not yet known it, . . . its ministry of symbols, its channels of grace, its unending line of teachers forming from the Head a sublime construction based throughout on historic fact, uplifting the idea of the community in which we live, and of the access which it enjoys through the living way to the presence of the Most High."

Mr. Gladstone found in the Anglican Church a form of access to the Most High, and through this Church the thoughts of the Most High were worked into his daily life. Others through the Bible, the sacraments, humanity, or through some doctrine of Christ have found like means of access. Forms are essential to religion. Forms, indeed, have often become the whole of religion, so that people who have honoured images or words or names have forgotten goodness and justice—they wash the cup and platter and forget mercy and judgment; they say "Lord, Lord," and do not the will of the Lord. Forms have often become idols, but the point I urge is that for the majority of mankind forms are necessary to religion. "Tell me thy name," was the cry of Jacob, when all night he wrestled with an unknown power which condemned his life of selfish duplicity; and every crisis in Israelitish history is marked by the revelation of a new name for the Most High. The Samaritans do not know what they worship; the Jews know what they worship,—was the rebuke of Christ to a wayward and ineffective nation. Even those Athenians to whom God was the Unknown God had to erect an altar to that God.

The great mass of the people, because they have no form and stand apart from all religious communions, may have in them a religious sense, but their thought of God is not worked through their emotions into their daily lives. They do not know what they worship, and so do not say with the Psalmist, "My soul is athirst for the living God," or say with Joseph, "How can I do this wickedness, and sin against God?" They have much sentiment about brotherhood, and they talk of the rights of all men; but they are not driven as St. Paul was driven to the service of their brothers, irrespective of class, or nation, or colour. They have not the zeal which says, "Woe is me if I preach not the Gospel". They endure suffering with patience and meet death with submission, but they do not say, "I shall awake after His likeness and be satisfied". The majority of English citizens would in an earthquake behave as brave men, but they have not the faith of the negroes who in the midst of such havoc sang songs of praise.

The three constituents I included in the definition are all, I submit, necessary. Thought without form does not rouse the emotions. Form without thought is idolatry, and is fatal to growth. Emotion without thought has no abiding or persistent force. Religion is the thought of a Higher-than-self worked through the emotions into daily life.

With this definition in mind I now sum up my impressions. The religion of the majority of the people is, I think, not such as enables them to say, "Here I take my stand. This course of life I can and will follow. This policy must overcome the world." It is not such either as keeps down pride and egotism, and leads them to say as Abram said to Lot, "If you go to the right I will go to the left". It does not make men and women anxious to own themselves debtors and to give praise. It does not drive them to greater and greater experiments in love; it does not give them peace. It is not the spur to action or the solace in distress. It has little recognition in daily talk or in the Press. One might, indeed, live many years, meet many men, and read many newspapers and not come into its contact or realize that England professes Christianity.

When I ask my friends, "How does religion show itself in the actions of daily life?" I get no answer. There seems to be no acknowledged force arising from the conception of the Most High which restrains, impels, or rests men and women in their politics, their business, or their homes. There are, I suggest, three infallible signs of the presence of religion—calm courage, joyful humility, and a sense of life stronger than death. These signs are not obvious among the people.

The condition is not satisfactory. It is not unlike that of Rome in the first century. The Roman had then forsaken his old worship of the gods in the temples, notwithstanding the official recognition of such worship and the many earnest attempts made for its revival. There was then, as now, something in the atmosphere of thought which was stronger than State or Church. There was then, as now, an interest in teachers of goodness who held up a course of conduct far above the conventional, and the thoughts of men played amid the new mysteries rising in the East. The Romans were restless, without anchorage or purpose. They were not satisfied with their bread and games; they walked in a dense shadow, and had no light from home. Into their midst came Christianity, giving a new name to the Most High, and stirring men's hearts to do as joyful service what the Stoics had taught as dull duty.

In the midst of the English people of to-day there are Churches and societies of numerous denominations. Their numbers are legion. In one

East-London district about a mile square there were, I think, at one time over twenty different religious agencies. Their activity is twofold. They work from without to within, or from within to without—from the environment to the soul, or from the soul to the environment.

1. The work from without to within, resolves itself into an endeavour to draw the people to join some religious communion. The environment which an organization provides counts for much, and influences therefrom constantly pass into the inner life. Membership in a Church or association with a mission often brings men and women into contact with a minister who offers an example of a life devoted to others' service. It opens to them ways of doing good, of teaching the children, of visiting the poor, and of joining in efforts for social reform. It affords a constant support in a definite course of conduct, and makes a regular call on the will to act up to the conventional standard, and it brings to bear on everyday action an insistent social pressure which is some safety against temptation. Sneers about the dishonesty of religious professors are common, but, as a matter of fact, the most honest and reputable members of the community are those connected with religious bodies.

Those bodies have various characters, with various forms of doctrine and of ritual. Human beings, if they are true to themselves, cannot all adopt like forms; there are some men and women who find a language for their souls in a ritual of colour and sound, there are others who can worship only in silence; there are some who are moved by one form of doctrine, and others who are moved by another form. Uniformity is unnatural to man, and the Act of Religious Uniformity has proved to be disastrous to growth of thought and goodwill. Progress through the ages is marked by the gradual evolution of the individual, and the strongest society is that where there are the most vigorous individualities. If this be admitted, it must be admitted also that the growth of vigorous denominations, and not uniformity, is also the mark of progress.

But, it may be said, denominations are the cause of half the quarrels which divide society, and of half the wars which have decimated mankind. This is true enough. The denominations are now hindering the way of education, and it was as denominations that Catholics and Protestants drowned Europe in thirty years of bloodshed. It is, however, equally true to say that nationalities have been the cause of war, and that the way of peace is hard, because French, Germans, and British are so patriotically concerned for their own rights. Nationalities, however, become strong during the period of struggle, and they develop characteristics valuable for the whole human family; but the end to which the world is moving is not a universal empire under the dominance of the strongest, it is to a unity in which the strength of each nationality will make possible the federation of the world. In the same way denominations pass through a period of strife; they too develop their characteristics; and the hope of religion is not in the dominance of any one denomination, but in a unity to which each is necessary.

The world learnt slowly the lesson of toleration, and at last the strong are feeling more bound to bear with those who differ from themselves. There is, however, dawning on the horizon a greater lesson than that of toleration of differences: it is that of respect for differences. As that lesson prevails, each denomination will not cease to be keen for its own belief; it will also be keen to pay honour to every honest belief. The neighbourhood of another denomination will be as welcome as the discovery of another star to the astronomer, or as the finding of a new animal to the naturalist, or as is the presence of another strong personality in a company of friends. The Church of the future cannot be complete without many chapels. The flock of the Good Shepherd includes many folds.

The energy of innumerable Churches and missions is daily strengthening denominations, and they seem to me likely to stand out more and more clearly in the community. One advantage I would emphasize. Each denomination may offer an example of a society of men and women living in reasonable accord with its own doctrine—not, I ask you to reflect, just a community of fellow-worshippers, but, like the Quakers, translating faith into matters of business and the home. Mediaeval Christians sold all they had and lived as monks or nuns. Nineteenth century Christians were kind to their poorer neighbours. Twentieth century Christians might give an example of a society fitting a time which has learnt the value of knowledge and beauty, and has seen that justice to the poor is better than kindness. Every generation must have its own form of Christianity.

The earnest endeavour of so many active men and women to increase the strength of their own denomination has therefore much promise: provided always, let me say, they do not win recruits by self-assertion, by exaggeration, or by the subtle bribery of treats and blankets. Each denomination honestly strengthened by additional members is the better able to manifest some aspect of the Christian life, and, in response to the call of that life, more inclined to reform the doctrines and methods which tend to alienate a scientific and democratic generation.

Such denominations are, I submit, those most likely to reform themselves, and as they come to offer various examples of a Christian society, where wealth is without self-assertion, where poverty is without shame, where unemployment and ignorance are prevented by just views of human claims, and where joy is "in widest commonalty spread," all the members of the community will in such examples better find the name of the Most High, and feel the power of religion. "If," says Dr. Fairbairn, "religion were truly interpreted in the lives of Christian men, there is no fear as to its being believed." "What is wanted is not more Christians but better Christians."

2. The activity of ministers and missionaries is, as I have said, twofold. Besides working from without to within by building up denominations, it also works from within to without by converting individuals. Members of every Church or mission are, in ordinary phrase, intent "to save souls". Their work is not for praise, and is sacred from any intrusion. Spirit wrestles with spirit, and power passes by unknown ways. Souls are only kindled by souls. Conversion opens blind eyes to see the Most High, but it is not in human power to direct the ways of conversion. The spirit bloweth where it listeth. There are, however, other means by which eyes may be opened at any rate to see, if only dimly, and some of these means are under human control. Such a means is that which is called higher education or university teaching, or the knowledge of the humanities.

I would therefore conclude by calling notice to the much or the little which is being done by this higher education. The people are to a large extent blind because of the overwhelming glory of the present. They see nothing beyond the marvellous revelations of science—its visions of possessions and of power, and its triumphs over the forces of nature. They are occupied in using the gigantic instruments which are placed at the command of the weakest, and they are driven on by some relentless pressure which allows no pause on the wayside of the road of life. They see power everywhere—power in the aggressive personalities which heap money in millions, power in the laboratory, power in the market-place, power in the Government; but they do not see anything which satisfies the human yearning for something higher and holier; they cannot see the God whose truth they feel and whose call they hear. Many of them look to the past and surround themselves with the forms of mediaeval days, and some go to the country, where, in a land of tender shades and silences, they try to commune with the Most High.

But yet the words of John the Baptist rise eternally true, when he said to a people anxiously expectant, some with their eyes on the past, and some with their eyes on the future, "There standeth one among you". The Most High, that is to say, is to be found, not in the past with its mysteries, its philosophies, and its dignity of phrase or ritual, and not in the future with its vague hopes of an earthly Paradise, but in the present with its hard facts, its scientific methods, its strong individualities, and the growing power of the State. The kingdom of heaven is at hand; the Highest which every one seeks is in the present. It is standing among us, and the one thing wanted is the eye to see.

Mr. Haldane, in the address to the students of Edinburgh University, has described the character of the higher teaching as a gospel of the wide outlook, as a means of giving a deeper sympathy and a keener insight, as offering a vision of the eternal which is here and now showing its students what is true in present realities, and inspiring them with a loyalty to the truth as devoted as that of tribesmen to their chief. This sort of teaching, he says, brings down from the present realities, or from a Sinai ever accompanying mankind, "the Higher command," with its eternal offer of life and blessing—that is to say, it opens men's eyes to see in the present the form of the Most High. Higher education is thus a part of religious activity.

I am glad to know that my conclusion is shared by Dr. Fairbairn, who, speaking of the worker in our great cities, and of his alienation from religion, says, "The first thing to be done is to enrich and ennoble his soul, to beget in him purer tastes and evoke higher capacities".

I will conclude by calling notice to the much or the little which is being done to open the people's eyes by means of higher education. I fear it is "the little". There are many classes and many teachers for spreading skill, there are some which increase interest in nature; there are few—very few—which bring students into touch with the great minds and thoughts of all countries and all ages—very few, that is, classes for the humanities. For want of this the souls of the people are poor, and their capacities dwarfed; they cannot see that modern knowledge has made the Bible a modern book, or how the bells of a new age have rung in the "Christ that is to be".

For thirty-four years my wife and I have been engaged in social experiments. Many ways have been tried, and always the recognized object has been the religion of the people—religion, that is, in the sense which I have defined as that faith in the Highest which is the impulse of human progress, man's spur to loving action, man's rest in the midst of sorrow, man's hope in death.

With the object of preparing the way to this religion, schools have been improved, houses have been built and open spaces secured. Holidays have been made more healthy, and the best in art has been made more common. But, viewing all these efforts of many reformers, I am prepared to say that the most pressing need is for higher education. Where such education is to begin, what is the meaning of religious education in elementary schools, and how it is to be extended, is part of another subject. It is enough now if, having as my subject the religion of the people, I state my opinion that there is no activity which more surely advances religion than the teaching which gives insight, far sight, and wide sight. The people, for want of religion, are unstable in their policy, joyless in their amusements, and uninspired by any sure and certain hope. They have not the sense of sin—in modern language, none of that consciousness of unreached ideals which makes men humble and earnest. They have not the grace of humility nor the force of a faith stronger than death. It may seem a far cry from a teacher's class-room to the peace and power of a Psalmist or of a St. Paul; but, as Archbishop Benson said, "Christ is a present Christ, and all of us are His contemporaries". And my own belief is that the eye opened by higher education is on the way to find in the present the form of the Christ who will satisfy the human longing for the Higher-than-self.

SAMUEL A. BARNETT.

CATHEDRAL REFORM.[1]

By Canon Barnett.

December, 1898.

[1] From "The Nineteenth Century and After". By permission of the Editor.

CATHEDRALS have risen in popular estimation. They represent the past to the small but slowly increasing number of people who now realize that there is a past out of which the present has grown. They are recognized as interesting historical monuments; their power is felt as an aid to worship, and some worshippers who would think their honesty compromised by their presence at a church or a chapel, say their prayers boldly in the "national" cathedral. A trade-union delegate, who had been present at the Congress, was surprised on the following Sunday afternoon to recognize in St. Paul's some of his fellow delegates. No reformer would now dare to propose that cathedrals should be secularized.

But neither would any one who considers the power latent in cathedral establishments for developing the spiritual side of human nature profess himself satisfied. It is not enough that the buildings should be restored, so that they may be to-day what they were 400 or 500 years ago, nor is it enough that active deans should increase sermons and services.

A cathedral has a unique position. It holds the imagination of the people. Men who live in the prison of mean cares remember how as children their thoughts wandered free amid the lights and shadows of tombs, pillars, arches, and recesses. Worshippers face to face with real sorrow, who turn aside from the trivialities of ritual, feel that there is in the solemn grandeur a power to lift them above their cares.

A cathedral indeed attracts to itself that spiritual longing which, perhaps, more than the longing for power or for liberty, is the sign of the times. This longing, compared with rival longings, may be as small as a mustard-seed, but everywhere men are becoming conscious that things within their grasp are not the things they were made to reach. There is a heaven for which they are fitted, and which is not far from any one of them. They like to hear large words, and to move in large crowds. They see that "dreaming" is valuable as well as "doing". They feel that there is a kinship between themselves and the hidden unknown greatness in which they live. The ideal leader of the day is a mystic who can be practical.

Men turning, therefore, from churches or chapels which are identified with narrow views, and from a ritual which has occupied the more vacant minds, are prepared to pay respect to the cathedral with its grand associations.

And the cathedrals which thus attract to themselves modern hope, and become almost the symbol of the day's movement, are equipped to respond to the demand. They have both men and money. They have men qualified to serve, and a body of singers qualified to make common the best music, and they have endowments varying from £4000 to £10,000 a year.

A cathedral is attractive by its grandeur and its beauty, but it ought to be something more than an historic monument. Its staff is ample, and is often active, but it ought to be something more than a parish church.

Its government, however, is so hampered that it can hardly be anything else, and the energies of the chapter are spent in efforts to follow the orders of restoring architects. The building is cleared of innovations introduced by predecessors, who had in view use and not art. Its deficiencies are supplied, the dreams and intentions of the early builders are discovered, and at last a church is completed such as our ancestors would have desired.

The self-devotion of deans or canons in producing this result provokes admiration from those who in their hearts disapprove. Money is freely given, and, what is often harder to do, donations are persistently begged. The time and ability of men who have earned a reputation as workers, thinkers, or teachers, are spent in completing a monument over which antiquaries will quarrel and round which parties of visitors will be taken at 6d. a head.

The building has little other use than as a parish church, and the ideal, before a chapter, anxious to do its duty, is to have frequent communions, services, and sermons, as in the best worked parishes. In some cases there is a large response. The communicants are many, but, being unknown to one another and to the clergy, they miss the strength they might have derived by communicating with their neighbours in their own churches. The sermons are sometimes listened to by crowded congregations, but the people are often drawn from other places of worship, and miss the teaching given by one to whom they are best known. But in most cases the response is small. The daily services, supported by a large and well-trained choir of men and boys, preceded by a dignified procession of vergers and clergy, often help only two or three worshippers. Many of the Holy Communions which are announced are not celebrated for want of communicants, and the sermons are not always such as are suitable for the people.

There are, indeed, special but rare occasions when the cathedral shows its possibilities. It may be a choir festival, when 500 or 600 voices find space within its walls to give a service for people interested in the various parishes. It may be some civic or national function, when the Corporation attends in state, or some meeting of an association or friendly society, when the church is filled by people drawn from a wide area. On all those occasions the fitness of the grand building and fine music to meet the needs of the moment is recognized, and the citizens are proud of their cathedral.

But generally they are not proud. They think—when they care enough to think at all—that a building with such power over their imagination ought to be more used, and that such well-paid officials ought to do more work. "One canon," a workman remarked, "ought to do all that is done, and the money of the others could be divided among poor curates." The members of the chapter would probably agree as to the need of reform. It is not their conservatism, it is the old statutes which stand in the way.

These statutes differ in the various cathedrals, but all alike suffer from the neglect of the living hand of the popular will which in civil matters is always shaping old laws to present needs. Their object seems to be not so much to secure energetic action as to prevent aggression. Activity, and not indolence, was apparently the danger which threatened the Church in those old days.

The Bishop, who is visitor and is called the head of the cathedral, cannot officiate—as of right—in divine service; he is not entitled to take part in the Holy Communion or to preach during ordinary service.

The Dean governs the church, and has altogether the regulation of the services; but he can only preach at the ordinary services at three festivals during the year.

The Canons, who preach every Sunday, have no power over the order or method of the uses of the church.

The Precentor, who is authorized to select the music and is required to take care that the choir be instructed and trained in their parts, must not himself give instruction and training.

The Organist, who has to train and instruct the boys, has to do so in hours fixed by the Precentor, and in music chosen by him.

An establishment so constituted cannot have the vigour or elasticity or unity necessary to adapt cathedrals to modern needs. It affords, as Trollope discovered, and as most citizens are aware, a field for the play of all sorts of petty rivalries and jealousies. No official can move without treading on the other's rights. Bishops, Deans, and Canons hide their feelings under excessive courtesies. Precentors and Organists try to settle their rights in the law courts, and the trivialities of the Cathedral Close have become proverbial.

The apparent uselessness of buildings so prominent, and of a staff so costly, provokes violent criticism. Reformers become revolutionists as the Dean, Chapter, and choir daily summon congregations which do not appear, and the officials become slovenly and careless as they daily perform their duties in an empty church. Sacraments may be offered in vain as well as taken in vain, and institutions established for other needs which go on, regardless of such needs, are self-condemned.

If the army or navy or any department of the civil service were so constituted, the demand for reform would be insistent. "We will not endure," the public voice would proclaim, "that an instrument on whose fitness we depend shall be so ineffective. It is not enough that the members of the profession are prevented from injuring one another. Our concern is not their feelings, but our protection." It is characteristic of the indifference to religious interests that an instrument, so costly and so capable of use as a cathedral establishment, has been left to rust through so many years, and that the troubles of a Chapter should be matter for jokes and not for indignant anger.

A Royal Commission, indeed, was appointed in 1879. It was in the earlier years presided over by Archbishop Tait, who showed, both by his constant presence and by his lively interest, how deeply he had felt and how much he had reflected on this subject. The Commissioners had 128 meetings, and issued their final report in 1885; but notwithstanding the humble and almost pathetic appeal that something should be "quickly done" to remedy the abuses they had discovered, and forward the uses which they saw possible, nothing whatever has been done. The position of the Cathedrals still mocks the intelligence of the people they exist to serve, and the hopes which the spread of education has developed.

The Commissioners recognized the change which had been going on in the feeling with regard to the tie which binds together the cathedral and the people, and their recommendations lead up, as they themselves profess, to "the grand conception of the Bishop of a diocese working from his cathedral as a spiritual centre, of the machinery there supplied being intended to produce an influence far beyond the cathedral precincts, of the capitular body being interested in the whole diocese, and of the whole diocese having claims on the capitular body".

This conception, apart from its technical phraseology, may be taken as satisfactory. "A live Cathedral in a live Diocese" is, in the American phrase, what all desire. It may be questioned, however, in the light of thirteen years' further experience of growing humanity, whether their recommendations would bring the conception much nearer to realization.

Their recommendations are somewhat difficult to generalize. The peculiarities and eccentricities in the constitution of each cathedral are infinite. Some are on the old foundation, with their Deans, Precentors, Chancellors, and Prebendaries. Some date from Henry VIII, and have only a Dean and a small number of residentiary Canons. Some possess statutes which are hopelessly obsolete, and one claims validity for a new body of statutes adopted by itself. Some are under the control of the chapter only, some have minor corporations. Some have striven to act up to the letter of old orders, some have statutes which are of no legal authority. But the difference of constitution of the several cathedrals was by no means the only difficulty with which the Commissioners had to contend.

There is the difference in their local circumstances. Some, as Bristol and Norwich, are in the midst of large populations; some, as Ely and St. David's, are in small towns or amid village people. St. Paul's, London, stands in a position so peculiar that it does not admit of comparison with any other cathedral in the kingdom.

There is, further, the difference in wealth and the provision of residences for the capitular body; some are rich, and endowed with all that is necessary for the performance of their duties; some are comparatively poor.

The Commissioners have met these difficulties by considering each cathedral separately, and by issuing on each a separate report with separate recommendations. There is, however, a character and a principle common to all their recommendations, by which a judgment may be formed as to how far they would, if adopted, fit cathedrals to the needs of the time.

I.—CENTRAL AUTHORITY.

The Commissioners were at the outset met by the fact that cathedral bodies are stationary institutions in a growing society. They remain as they had been formed in distant days: ships stranded high above the water-line, in which the services went on as if the passengers and cargo had not long found other means of transit. They felt that even if by the gigantic effort involved in parliamentary action the cathedrals were reformed in order to suit the changed society of the nineteenth century, the reforms would not necessarily suit the twentieth century. They saw that there must be a central authority always in touch with public opinion, which would, year by year, or generation by generation, shape uses to needs.

They at once therefore introduced the Cathedral Statutes Bill, by which a Cathedral Committee of the Privy Council was to be appointed. The Bill did not become law, but the provision was admirable. By this means, just as the Committee of Council year by year now issues an Education Code, by which changes suggested by experience or inquiry are introduced into the educational system of the country, so this new Committee of Council was, as occasion required, to issue new statutes to control or develop the use of cathedrals.

A living rule was to take the place of the dead hand. Representative men, and not the authority of an individual or of an old statute, were henceforth to control this State provision for the religious interests of the people, as a similar body, with manifest advantage, controls the State provision for the secular interests. A Committee of the Privy Council made up of the Ministers of the day, being professed Christians, together with some experts, is probably the best central authority to be devised.

But when the Commissioners further proposed that after the expiration of their commission it should remain with Deans and Chapters to submit proposals for reform in the use of their cathedrals, they at once limited the utility of that central authority. Is it to be conceived that Deans and Chapters will promote necessary reforms? Can they be said to be in touch with the people? Will they, if they make wise and far-reaching suggestions, be trusted as representatives?

The Commission aimed to create a living authority, and then proposed to bind it hand and foot; it set up a body of representative men capable of daring and of cautious action, and then limited the sphere of such action by the decisions of Chapters sometimes concerned for inaction.

The obvious criticism is a testimony to the progress of the last few years. Education and the extension of local government have made all parties recognise that the voice of the people ought to be trusted, and can be trusted. Checks and safeguards are no longer thought to be so necessary. Interests once jealously preserved by the classes are now known to be safe in the hands of the masses. The Crown, property, order, are all safe grounded on the people's will.

It seems therefore out of place, in the eyes of the present generation, to safeguard every change in the use of the cathedral by trusting to those proposed by Dean and Chapter. The basis of government must be democratic. The people, and not any class, must have the chief voice in their control. The County Councils, by means of a committee of professed Christians, the Diocesan Council, or any body to which the people of the neighbourhood have free access, should be that empowered to bring suggestions before the central authority. In the Church of England, of which every Englishman is a member, and whose Prayer Book is an Act of

Parliament, there is no new departure in making the County Councils the originating bodies to suggest uses for the cathedral.

With the growing interest to which allusion has been made, it is not hard to conceive that the call for suggestions would evoke deeper thought and remind members of secular bodies that progress without religion is very hollow. Parliament was never more dignified, or better fitted for foreign or home policy, than when it held Church government to be its most important function. County Councils, called on through their committees to submit suggestions for the better use of the cathedrals to the Committee of Privy Council, might be elevated by the call, and at the same time offer advice valuable in itself, and approved by the people as coming from their representatives.

The first essential cathedral reform is therefore a central authority as recommended by the Commission, which, on the initiative of really representative bodies, shall have power to make statutes and publish rules of procedure in the several cathedrals.

II.—THE BISHOP AND HIS CATHEDRAL.

The Commissioners were evidently struck by the need of promoting "earnest and harmonious co-operation between the Bishop of the Diocese and the Cathedral Body". They have endeavoured, as they reiterate, "to define and establish the relation in which the Bishop stands to the cathedral, and have made provision for assuring to him his legitimate position and influence". When, however, reference is made to the statutes by which they carry out their intention, they seem very inadequate: the Bishop, for instance, is to "have the highest place of dignity whenever he is present"; "to preach whenever he may think fit"; "to hold visitation and exercise any function of his episcopal office whenever it may seem good". He is also empowered to nominate a certain number of preachers, and is constituted the authority to give leave of absence to the Dean or Canons. The Dean, however, is left responsible for the services, in control of the officials, and at liberty to develop the use of the church.

It is difficult to see how, by such changes, the cathedral will become the spiritual centre from which the Bishop will work his diocese, and at the same time have harmonious relations with the Dean and Chapter. If he uses his full powers: gathers week by week diocesan organizations for worship, for encouragement, and for admonition; if he is often present at the services, if he arranges classes for the clergy, devotional meetings for church workers; if he institutes sermons and lectures on history or on the signs of the times—what is there left for the Dean and Canons to do? If he does not do such things, how can he make the cathedral the centre of spiritual life?

The Commission was evidently hampered in its recommendation by the presence of two dignitaries with somewhat conflicting duties. The simple solution is to make the Bishop the Dean. He would then have, as by right, all the powers it is proposed to confer upon him; he would exercise them at all times, without fear of any collision, and he would be in name and fact the sole authority in carrying out the statutes, and in controlling all subordinate officials. He would then be able to make the cathedral familiar to every soul in his diocese, associate its building and services with every organization for the common good—secular and religious—with choral societies, clubs, governing bodies, friendly societies, missionary associations, and such like. He would, in fact, make the cathedral the centre of spiritual life, and he would for ever abolish the petty rivalries and jealousies which grow up under divided control, and which bring such discredit on cathedral management. He would be master, and it is for want of a master that each official is now so disposed to magnify the petty privileges of his own office. There must be some one who is really big, that others may feel their proper place.

III.—THE CANONS AND THEIR UTILITY.

The Commission has little to suggest, save that they should be compelled to reside for eight months of the year in the neighbourhood of the cathedral, and during three months attend morning and evening service, each one "habited in a surplice with a hood denoting his degree". They are also, if called on, "to give instruction in theological and religious subjects, or discharge some missionary or other useful work". These functions seem hardly sufficient for men who are to receive £800 a year, and it is difficult to see what virtue there is in mere technical residence, or how daily attendance at service is compatible with the performance of regular duties as citizens or teachers.

The Canons would better help in making the cathedral the centre of spiritual life if they were the Suffragan Bishops of the diocese. They would in this case have to receive appointment by the Bishop, and take duties assigned by him. One might be responsible for the order of the services, for the care of the property of the cathedral, and for the proper control of the officials. He might, indeed, be called the Dean. Another might be a lecturer or teacher for the instruction of the clergy, and the others might assist the Bishop in those functions which now so largely intrude on his time.

The Bishop of the twentieth century looms large in the distance. He has a place not given to any of his predecessors, as a democratic age has greater need of leaders. He is called to new duties and new functions, and the danger is that he who might be lifting his clergy on to a higher plane, meeting them soul to soul, and comforting them by his contagious piety, will be absorbed in organizing, in business, or in the performance of functions. Suffragan Bishops attached to the cathedral would relieve him from "such serving tables," and leave him more free to be a father in God to the clergy.

IV.—THE FABRIC AND FINANCE.

The care of the fabrics is more and more recognized as a national concern. Not long ago there was a proposal put forward by non-Christians for their preservation out of local or national resources. The Commissioners' suggestion that a report on their condition should be published at frequent intervals shows trust in the readiness of a voluntary response, but it is hardly a businesslike recommendation.

The suggestion, already made in this paper, that some local representative body, such as the County Council, should be the body authorized to initiate reforms in the use of the building, would naturally lead to the same body becoming responsible for its proper care. It is not hard to conceive of such a growing interest as would lead to a ready expenditure under the direction of the best advisers. The mass of the people are now shut out from contribution; their pence are not valued, and even if their gift "be half their living," it opens to them no place on the restoration committee.

If the cathedral is to be the people's church, its support must rest on the people, and this is only possible by means of the local bodies which they control.

Finance, as might be expected in a commercial country, takes up a large portion of the report. Failure is again and again attributed to poverty, and a schedule shows what is wanting in each cathedral for the proper payment of officials. The total per annum is an increase of £10,876. The Commissioners' happy thought was, "Why not get this amount from the Ecclesiastical Commissioners, who have profited largely from cathedral property?" They forthwith made application and were duly snubbed.

But the suggestion already made in this paper, for the more harmonious management of cathedrals by the absorption of the Dean's functions in that of the Bishop, at once solves the financial difficulty. The salaries now given to the Deans—probably on an average at least £1000 a year—would then be ready for redistribution, and might follow the lines suggested by the Commissioners, and would supply other gaps due to the depreciation of agricultural values.

Conclusion.

The Commissioners take into view many details connected with the other officials, with the rivalry of Precentor and Organist, with the meeting of the greater chapter, and with the abolition of the minor corporations existing in some cathedrals alongside of the chapter corporation, which are in their way important, but which would all fall into place under a large scheme of reform.

The essentials of such a scheme are, it is submitted, (1) control by a distinguished body, like that of the Committee of the Privy Council, which takes its initiative from a representative body like that of the County Council; (2) the reinstatement of the Bishop as the chief officer of the cathedral, with the Canons as his suffragans.

The cathedrals seem to be waiting to be used by the new spiritual force which, amid the wreck of so much that is old, is surely appearing. There is a widespread consciousness of their value—an unexpressed instinct of respect which is not satisfied by the disquisitions of antiquarians or the praises of artists. Common people as well as Royal Commissioners feel that cathedrals have a part to play in the coming time. What that part is none can foretell, but all agree that the cathedrals must be preserved and beautified, that the teaching and the music they offer must be of the best, offered at frequent and suitable times, and that they must be used for the service of the great secular and religious corporations of the diocese.

Under the scheme here proposed this would be possible. The Bishop, as head of the cathedral, would direct the order of the daily worship and teaching, arrange for the giving of great musical works, and invite on special occasions any active organization. He would have as coadjutors able men chosen by himself, who, by lectures, meetings, and conferences, would make the building alive with use. He would have behind him the committee of the County Councils or other local authority, empowered to suggest changes in the statutes as new times brought new needs, and ready with money as their interest was developed. The scheme, at any rate, has the merit of utilizing two growing forces—that of the Bishop, and that of local government. No scheme can secure that these forces will work to the best ends. That, as everything else, must depend on the extent to which the growing forces are inspired by the spirit of Christ.

A cathedral used as a Bishop would use it would receive a new consecration by the manifold uses. Just as the silence of a crowd which might speak is more impressive than the silence of the dumb, so is the quiet of a building which is much used more solemn than the quiet of a building kept swept and clean for show. Our cathedrals, being centres of activity, would more and more impress those who, themselves anxious and careful about many things, feel the impulse of the spiritual force of the time. Workmen and business-men would come to possess their souls in quiet meditation, or to join unnoticed in services of worship which express aspirations often too full for words.

SAMUEL A. BARNETT.

THE CATHEDRALS AND MODERN NEEDS.[1]

By Canon Barnett.

1912.

[1] From "The Contemporary Review". By permission of the Editor.

THIS generation is face to face with many and hard problems. Perhaps the hardest and the one which underlies all the others is that which concerns the spiritualizing of life. Discoveries and inventions have largely increased the attractions of the things which can be seen and heard, touched, and tasted. Rich and poor have alike found that the world is full of so many things that they ought to be all as happy as kings, and the one ideal which seems to command any enthusiasm is a Socialistic State, where material things will be more equally divided among all classes.

But even so, there is an underlying consciousness that possessions do not satisfy human nature. Millionaires are seen to miss happiness, and something else than armaments are wanted to make the strength of a nation. There is thus a widely-spread disposition to take more account of spiritual forces, and people who have not themselves the courage to forsake all for the sake of an idea speak with sympathy of religion and patronize the Salvation Army. There is much talk of "rival ideals dominating action," and the prevalent unrest seems to come from a demand, not so much for more money as for more respect, more recognition of equality, more room for the exercise of admiration, hope, and love. Modern unrest is, in fact, a cry for light.

The problem which is haunting this generation is how to spiritualize the forces which are shaping the future; how to inspire labour and capital with thoughts which will both elevate and control their actions; how to enable rich and poor to move in a larger world, seeing things which eyes cannot see; how to open channels between eternal sources and every day's need; how to give to all the sense of partnership in a progress which is fitting the earth for man's enjoyment and men for one another's comfort. The spiritualization of life being necessary to human peace and happiness; its accomplishment is the goal of all reformers, and every reform may in fact be measured by its power to advance or hinder progress to that goal.

I would suggest that the cathedrals are especially designed to help in the solution of the problem. Their attractiveness is a striking fact, and people who are too busy to read or to pray seem to find time to visit buildings where they will gain no advantage for their trade or profession, not even fresh air for their bodies. They are recognized as civic or national possessions, and working people who stand aloof from places of worship, or patronize meeting-houses, are distinctly interested in their care and preservation. They have an unfailing hold on the popular imagination, so that it is always easy to gather a congregation to take part in a service, or to listen to a lecture.

"It was not so much what the lecturer said," was the reflection of Mr. Crooks after a lecture in Westminster Abbey on English History, "as the place in which it was given."

The cathedrals have thus a peculiar position in the modern world, and if it be asked to what the position is due I am inclined to answer: to their unostentatious grandeur and to their testimony to the past. They are high and mighty, they lift their heads to heaven, and they open their doors to the humblest. They give the best away, and ask for nothing, neither praise nor notice. They are buildings through which the stream of ages has flowed, familiar to the people of old time as of the present, bearing traces of Norman strength and English aspirations, of the enthusiasm of Catholics and Puritans, of the hopes of the makers of the nation. The cathedrals are thus in touch with the spiritual sides of life, and make their appeal to the same powers which desire before all things to see the fair beauty of the Lord, and to commune with man's eternal mind.

But the cathedrals which make this appeal can hardly be said to be well used. There are the somewhat perfunctory services morning and afternoon, often suspended or degraded during holiday months when visitors are most numerous; there are sermons rarely to be distinguished from those heard in a thousand parish churches; there is a staff of eight or ten clergy who may be busy at good works, but certainly do not make their cathedral position their platform; and there are guides who for a small fee will conduct parties round the church. Among these guides are indeed to be found men who have made a study of the building, and are able to talk of it as lovers, but the guides for the most part give no other information than lists of names and dates, sometimes relieved by a common-place anecdote. The cathedrals are treated as museums, and not so well as the Forum of Rome. The question is: Can they be made of greater use in spiritualizing life? I would offer some suggestions:—

1. Cathedrals might, I think, be more generally used for civic, county and national functions, for intercession at times of crisis, and for services in connexion with meetings of conferences and congresses. The services might be especially adapted by music and by speech to deepen the effect of the building with its grandeur and memories. The use in this direction has increased of late years, and even when the service seems to be little more

than a church parade, those present are often helped by the reminder that their immediate concern has a place in a greater whole. But the use might be largely extended, so that every example of corporate life might be set in the framework which would give it dignity. Elections to civic councils might be better understood if the newly-elected bodies gathered in the grand central building where vulgar divisions would be hushed in the greatness, and the ambitions of parties lifted up into an atmosphere in which the rivals of past days are recognized in their common service to the State. The meetings of congresses and conferences—of scientific and trade societies—of leagues and unions for social reform would be helped by beginning their deliberations in a place which would both humble and widen the thoughts of the members.

Intercessional services, when guided by a few directing words, at which men and women would gather to fix their minds on great ideals—on peace—on sympathy with the oppressed—on the needs of children and prisoners, would gain force from the association of a building where generations have prayed and hoped and suffered. And if, as well as being more frequent, such use were more carefully considered the effect would be much deeper. It is not enough, for instance, that the service should always follow the old form, and the music be elaborate and the sermon orthodox. Consideration might be given so that prayers, and music, and speech might all be made to work together with the influences of the building to touch the spiritual side of the object interesting to the congregation. The soul of the least important member of a civic council or a society is larger than its programme. The cathedral service might be, by much consideration, designed to help such souls to realize something of the vast horizons in which they move—something of the infinite issues attached to their resolutions and votes, something of the company filling the past and the future of which they are members. The cathedrals, by such frequent and well-considered uses, might do much to spiritualize life.

2. There are, as I have said, usually eight or ten clergy who form the cathedral staff. Many of them are chosen for their distinction in some form of spiritual service, and all have devoted themselves to that service. They may be in other ways delivering themselves of their duties, but they as spiritual teachers cannot as a rule be said to identify themselves with the cathedral. They do not use all their powers to make the building a centre of spiritual life.

I would suggest, therefore, that these clergy attached to the cathedral should have classes or lectures on theological, social, and historic subjects. They should give their teaching freely in one of the chapels of the cathedral, and the teaching should be so thorough as to command the attention of the neighbouring clergy and other thoughtful people. They would also, on occasions, give lectures in the nave designed to guide popular thought to the better understanding of the live questions of the day, or of the past.

And inasmuch as many of the clergy have been chosen for their skill in music, which often at great cost holds a high place in cathedral worship, I would suggest that regular teaching be given in the relation of music to worship. Words, we are often told, do not make music sacred, and religion has probably suffered degradation from the attachment of high words to low music. There is certainly no doubt that the music in many churches is both bad in character and pretentious. If teaching were freely given by qualified teachers in the cathedrals, if examples of the best were freely offered, and if the place of music in worship were clearly shown, then music might become a valuable agent in spiritualizing life.

Perhaps, however, the clergy might urge that they could not by such teaching deliver themselves of their obligation to do spiritual work. They would rather wrestle with souls and unite in prayer. But surely if their teaching has for its aim the opening of men's minds to know the truth—the enlistment of men's hearts in others' service and the bringing of the understanding into worship, then their teaching will end in the knowledge of others' souls and in acts of common devotion. The cathedral staff might, through the cathedral and the position it holds in a city, do much to spiritualize life.

3. The great spiritual asset of the cathedral is, however, its association with the past, and its living witness that the present is the child of the past. This may be called a spiritual asset, because it is this conception of the past which, as is evident among the Jews and Japanese, is able to inspire and control action. The people who see as in a vision their country boldly standing and suffering for some great principles and hear the voices of the great dead calling them "children," have power and peace within their reach.

It is, as I have said, because of some dim consciousness of this truth that crowds of visitors flock into the buildings and spend a rare holiday in hanging upon the dry words of the guides. It is easy to imagine how their readily-offered interest might be seized, how guides with fresh knowledge and trained sympathy might make the building tell and illustrate the tale of the nation's growth, how the different styles of architecture might be made to express different stages of thought, how the whole structure might be shown to be a shell and rind covering living principles, how every one might be lifted up and humbled as the building told him of England's search for justice, freedom, and truth. It is easy to imagine how such a living interpretation might be given to the message of the building, but much work would first be necessary.

The cathedral staff would have to be constant learners, and take up different sides of interest. They would themselves frequently accompany parties and individuals, so that in intimate talk they would learn the mind of the people, and they would be continually instructing the regular guides. Their special duty would be to give at certain times short talks on the history, the architecture, and the art, so that visitors might be sure that at these times they would learn what light new knowledge was throwing on the familiar surroundings.

The power of the past is dormant, it is buried beneath the insistent present, but it is not dead, and it is conceivable that thoughtful and devoted effort might rouse it to speak through the buildings which have witnessed the highest aspirations of successive ages. If such effort succeeded, and if the people of to-day could be helped to know and feel the England of old days, they would be conscious of a spiritual force bearing them on to great deeds. They would begin to understand how things which are not seen are stronger than things which are seen. The cathedrals have in themselves a message which would help to spiritualize life, but without interpreters the message can hardly be heard.

4. I would add one other suggestion arising from the monuments which in every cathedral attract so much notice. They are the memorials of men and women notable in national or local history who belonged to various parties and classes, to different forms of faith and different professions representing divers qualities and diverse forms of service.

It would not be difficult for each cathedral to make a calendar of worthies. A lecture every month on one such worthy would give an opportunity for taking the minds of modern men into the surroundings of the past, where they would see clearly the value of character. Familiarity with the lives of Saints has been doubtless a great help to many lonely and anxious souls, but this hardly applies to those who hear sermons on St. Jude, and St. Bartholomew, and other Saints of whom little can be known. If, however, from its great men and women each cathedral selected twelve, for one of whom a day should be set apart each month, the people in the locality would gradually become familiar with their characters and gain by communion with them.

Thoughts are best revealed through lives, and the attraction of personality was never more marked than at the present day. Through the lives of the great dead, and through the persons of those who walked or worshipped within familiar walls, it would be possible to make people understand great principles, and gradually become conscious of the

Common Source from which flows "every good and perfect gift". The dead speak from the walls of the cathedral, but they have no interpreter, and the mass of the people who are waiting for their message go away unsatisfied. A power which would help to spiritualize life is unused.

But perhaps it may be urged that if all were done which has been suggested, if the minds of visitors were kindled to admiration, if the past were made to live and the dead to speak, much more would be necessary to spiritualize life. Certainly the "spirit bloweth where it listeth," and only they who feel its breath are born again and enter a world of power, of peace, and of love.

But it may be claimed that some attitudes are better than others in which to feel this breath, and that people whose pride has been brought low by the beauty of a great building, or whose ears have been opened to the voices of the past, will be more likely to bow before the Holy Spirit than those who have no thought beyond what they can see, hear, or touch.

The age, we sometimes say, is waiting for a great leader—a prophet who will make dead bones to live. It is well to remember that for all redeemers the way has to be prepared, and the coming spiritual leader will be helped if through our cathedrals people have developed powers of communion with the Unseen.

SAMUEL A. BARNETT.

SECTION II.

RECREATION.

The Children's Country Holiday Fun'—Recreation of the People—Hopes of the Hosts—Easter Monday on Hampstead Heath—Holidays and School days—The Failure of Holidays—Recreation in Town and Country.

THE CHILDREN'S COUNTRY HOLIDAY FUN'.[1]

By Mrs. S. A. Barnett.

April, 1912.

[1] From "The Cornhill Magazine". By permission of the Editor.

FIVE thousand two hundred and eighty Letters, 872 Sketches, 199 Collections, all in parcels neatly tied up, the name, age, and sex of the writer, artist, or collector clearly written on the first page of the covering paper. There they lie, all around me, stack upon stack. The sketches are crude but extraordinarily vivid and unaffected; the collections are very scrappy but show affectionate care; the letters are written in childish unformed characters, and are of varying lengths, from a sheet of notepaper to ten pages of foolscap, but one and all deal with the same subject. What that subject is shall be told by a maiden of nine years old:—

"On one Thursday morning my Mother woke me and said, 'To-day is Country Holiday Fun,' so I got up and put my cloes on".

On that Thursday morning, 27 July, 22,624 happy children left London and its drab monotonous streets, and went for a fortnight's visit into the country, or by the sea. Oh! the joy, the preparation, the excitement, the hopes, the fears, the anxieties lest anything should prevent the start; but at last, by the superhuman efforts of all concerned, the Committee, the ladies, the teachers, and the railway officials, the whole gay, glad, big army of little people were successfully got off. It is from these 22,624 children, and 21,756 more who took their places two weeks later, that my 5,280 letters come; for only those who really choose to write are encouraged to do so.

In almost all cases the journey is fully described, the ride in the 'bus, the fear of being late, the parcel and how "it fell out," the gentlemen at the station, the porter who gave us a drink of water "cause we were all hot," the gentleman who gave the porter 6d. because he said: "This 6d. is for you for thinking as how the children would be thirsty". The number that managed to get in each carriage, the boy who lost his cap "for the wind went so fast when my head was outside looking," the hedges, the cows, the big boards with —— Pills written on them, how "it seemed as if I was going that way and the hills and cows and trees were going the other way". It is all told with the fresh force of novelty and youth. The names of the Stations and the mileage is often noted, as well as the noise. "We shouted for joy," writes a boy of eleven. "We told them it was rude to holler so," writes a more staid girl. "I got tired of singing and went to sleep," records a boy of eight; but the journey over there follows the description, often given with some awe, of how,—

"We all went and were counted together, and there were the ladies waiting for us, and the gentleman read out our names and our lady's name and then we went home with our right ladies,"

and then, almost without exception, comes the bald but important statement, "and then we had Tea". Indeed, all through the letters there is frequent mention of the gastronomic conditions, which appear to occupy a large place among the memories of the country visit. Evidently the regularity of the meals makes a change which strikes the imagination.

"I got up, washed in hot water and had my breakfast. It was duck's egg. I then went out in the fields till dinner was ready. I had a good dinner and then took a rest. We had Tea. My lady gave us herrings and apple pie for tea, then we went on the Green and looked about and then came home and had supper and went to bed."

Some letters, especially those written after the first visit to the country, contain nothing but the plain unvarnished tale of the supply of regular food. One girl burns with indignation because

"We girls was sent to bed at 7·30 and got no supper, but the boys was let up later and got bread and a big thick bit of cheese".

A boy of eight chronicles that

"I had custard for my Tea and some jelly which was called corn flour".

One small observer had apparently discovered the importance of meal-times even to the sea itself, for he writes: "The sea always went out at dinner time and came back when Tea was ready". I can see my readers smile, but to those of us who know intimately the lives of the poor, the significance of meals and their regularity occupying so large a place in a child's mind is more pathetic than comic.

From all the letters the impression is gathered of the generosity of the poor hostesses to the London children. For 5s. a week (not 9d. a day) a growing hungry boy or girl is taken into a cottager's home, put in the best bed, cared for, fed three or four times a day, and often entertained at cost of time, thought, or money.

"I like the day which was Bank lolyiday Monday because it was a very joyafull day. My Lady took me to a Flower Show. It was 3d. to go in but she paid, and I had swings and saw the flowers, and then we had bought Tea, and a man gave away ginger beer."

Another girl of eleven writes:—

"My lady took me to Windsor Castle. The first thing I saw was the Thames. I went and had a paddled and then I went in the Castle and saw a lot of apple trees."

The visits to Windsor are modern-day versions of the old story of the Cat who went to see the King and saw only "Mousey sitting under the Chair," for another child records:—

"There were plenty of orchards with apple trees in it. But we would not pick them, or else we would be locked up but I went in the Castle and I saw a very large table with fifty chairs all round it and a piano and a looking glass covered up on the wall."

One boy who was taken to the lighthouse, though only ten, was evidently eager for useful information. He writes:—

"I asked the man how many candlepowers it was but I forgot what he said——"

an experience not unknown to his elders and betters!

This child records that "when playing on the beach I made Buckingham Palace but a big boy came along and trod it and so we went home to bed"—an unconscious repetition of the often-recorded conclusion of Pepys' eventful days.

One of the small excursionists was taken by her hostess to see Tonbridge, and writes: "We went to the muzeam wear we saw jitnoes of different people".

The hospitality of the clergymen and their families and the goodness of doctors is also often mentioned. Some of the children write so vividly that the country vicarage and its sweet-smelling flowers, the hot curate and the active ladies, rise up as a picture, the "atmosphere" of which is kindness and "the values" incalculable. Other children merely record the facts—in some cases anticipating time and establishing an order of clergywomen.

"We asked the Vicar Miss Leigh if we could swim and she said No because one boy caught a cold."

"We all went to the Reveren to a party." "Saturday mornings we went to the Rectory haveing games, swings, sea sawes and refreshments." "The party by the Church was fine." "They had a Church down there called the Salvation Army. I thought there was only one Salvation Army."

One of the Vicars hardly conveyed the impression he intended, for the boy writes:—

"We went to Church in the morning and in the afternoon for a walk as the Clergyman told us not to go to Sunday School as he wanted us to enjoy ourselves".

One wonders if the Sunday School organization and the "intolerable strain" which would be put on it by London visitors was in that vicar's mind.

The letter that is sent by the Countryside Committee to the children before they leave London tells them in simple language something about the trees and flowers and creatures which they will see during their holiday, and asks them to write on anything which they themselves have observed or which gave them pleasure to see. This request is granted, for the children wrote:—

"The trees seemed so happy they danced".

"The wind was blowing and the branches of the trees was swinging themselves."

"The rainbow is made of raindrops and the sun, tears and smiles."

"It was nice to sit on the grass and see the trees prancing in the breeze."

These extracts show, in the four small mortals who had each spent the ten years of their lives in crowded streets, an almost poetic capacity, and the beginning of a power of nature sympathy that will be a source of unrecorded solace. The sights of the night impress many children, the sky seen for the first time uninterrupted by gas lamps.

"When I (aged eleven) looked into the sky one night you could hardly see any of the blue for it was light up with stars."

"I saw a star shoot out of the sky and then it settled in a different place."

"One night I kept awake and looked for the stars and saw the Big Bear of stars."

"At night the moon looked as if it were a Queen and the stars were her Attendants."

"The clouds are making way for the moon to come out."

The sun, its rising and setting, is also frequently mentioned. One child had developed patriotism to such an extent as to write:—

"One day I looked up to the Sky and saw the sun was rising in the shape of the British Isles".

Alas! What would the Kaiser think?

Another of my correspondents expressed surprise that "the moon came from where the sky touched the Earth," an evidence of street-bound horizon.

In other letters the writers record:—

"I saw the sun set it was like a big silver Eagle's wing laying on a cliff".

"When the sun was setting out of the clouds came something that looked like a County Council Steamer".

That must have been a rather alarming sunset, but hardly less so than "the cloud which was like Saint Paul's Cathedral coming down on our heads".

The animals gave great pleasure and created wonder:—

"The cows made a grunting noise, the baa lambs made a pretty little shriek".

"The cows I saw were lazy, they were laying. One was a bull who I daresay had been tossing somebody."

"I heard a bird chirping it was make a noise like chirp chirp twee."

"I saw a big dragon fly. It was like a long caterpillar with long sparkling transparent wings."

"The birds are not like ourn they are light brown."

"There were wasps which was yellow and pretty but unkind."

"I (aged eleven) saw a little blackbird—its head was off by a Cat. I made a dear little grave and so berreyed it under the Tree."

The flowers, of course, come in for the greatest attention and after them the trees are most usually referred to:—

"I (aged nine) know all the flowers that lived in the garden, but not all those who lived in the field".

"Stinging nettles are a nuisance to people who have holes in their boots."

"The Pond is all covered with Rushes. These had flowers like a rusty poker."

"I picked lots of flowers and always brought them home—"

shows influence of the Selborne Society in teaching children not to pick and throw away what is alive and growing.

"The Cuckoo dines on other birds."

"There was one bird called the squirrel."

"Only gentlemen are allowed to shoot pheasants as they are expensive."

"We caught fish in the river some were small others about 2 feet long."

"Butterflies dont do much work."

"The trunk of the oak is used for constructing furniture, coffins and other expensive objects."

But my readers will be weary, so I will conclude with the pregnant remark of a little prig, who writes:—

"I think the country was in a good condition for *I* found plenty of interesting things in it."

One or two of my small correspondents show an early disposition to see faults and remember misfortunes.

"There was no strikes on down there but there was a large number of wasps," was the reflection of one evidently conscious of the fly in every ointment. Another (aged ten) writes:—

"DEAR MADAM,—When I was down in the country I was lying on the couch and a wasp stung me. As I was on the common a man chased me, and I fell head first and legs after into the prickles, and the prickles dug me and hurt me. . . . I was nearly scorched down in the country. . . . One day when I fed the Pigs the great big fat pig bit a lump out of my best pinafore. One morning when I was in bed the little boy brought the cat up and put it on my face. When I was down in the country the Common caught a light for the sun was always too hot. So I must close with my love."

Was there ever such a catalogue of misfortunes compressed into one short fortnight? Still, in the intervals she seems to have noticed a considerable number of trees, of which she makes a list, and adds: "I did enjoy myself". Poor little maiden! Perhaps her elders had graduated in the school of misfortunes, and she had learnt the trick of complaining.

A good many children, both boys and girls, were very conscious of the absence of their home responsibilities.

"I did not see a babbi. I mean to mind it all the time."

"The ladys girl dont mind the baby as much as me at home. It stops in the garden."

It opens up a whole realm of matters for reflection: the baby not dragged hither and thither in arms too small and weak for its comfort, and then plumped down on cold or damp stones while its over-burdened nurse snatches a brief game or indulges in a scamper; the clouding of the elder child's life by unremitting responsibilities, and the effortful labour which sometimes wears out love, though not so often as could be expected, so marvellous is human nature, and its capacity for care and tenderness. "I didn't have to mind no twins," writes one small boy of nine, "I think thems a neusence. I wish Mother had not bought them." But the baby left in a garden! opening its blinking eyes to the wonders of sky and flowers and bees and creatures, while its elder brothers and sister do their share of work and play. This makes a foundation of quiet and pleasure on which to build the strenuous days and anxious years of the later life of struggle and effort.

The reiteration of the kindness of the cottage hostesses would be almost wearisome if one's imagination did not go behind it and picture the scenes, the hard-worked country woman accepting the suggestion of a child guest with a lively appreciation of the usefulness of the 5s.'s which were to accrue, but that thought receding as the enjoyment of the town child became infectious, until the value given for the value received became forgotten, and generous self-costing kindnesses were showered profusely.

"My lady she was always doing kind to me." "Mrs. P. washed my clothes before I came home to save Mother doing it." "My lady told Mr. S. to shake her tree for our apples." "The person that Boarded me gave me nice thing to bring back."

In some cases the thrifty, tidy ways of the country hostesses conveyed their lessons.

"She use to make browan bread and She use to make her own cakes and apple turn overs and eggloes and current cake." "The wind came in my room and blew me in the night." "We always had table clothes where I was." "I washed myself well my lady liked it." "We cleaned our teeth down in the country ever morning."

Sometimes examples on deeper matters were observed and approved of.

"Every morning and dinner and tea we say grace." "The lady told us Sunday School was nice and we went." "We had Church 3 times. Morning noon and night"—

is not reported with entire approval, but the letter ends:—

"I loved my holidays very much and hope that I can go next year to live with the same lady".

A boy writes:—

"The lady was very kind she never said any naughty words to me".

And another lad reports:—

"I was fed extremely well and treated with the best respect".

One little girl had clear views on the proper position of man.

"My ladie," she writes, "had a big pig 4 little ones, 2 cats. some hens a bird in a cage a apple tree a little boy and a Huband."

Sometimes the history of the place has been impressed on the children.

"I (aged eleven) was very glad I went to Guildford because Sir Lancelot and Elaine lived there but its name was then Astolat."

"When I (aged eleven) reached Burnham Thorp I felt the change of air and I heard the birds sing—and then I knew that I should see the place where our great English sailor Lord Nelson was born,"—

he being a character so indissolubly associated with innocent country joys.

The letters both begin and end in a variety of ways, for though I do not write all the letters which are issued to the children by the Countryside Committee of the Children's Country Holiday Fund, it is considered better for me as Chairwoman to sign them, so as to give a more personal tone to the lengthy printed chat, which the teachers themselves open, kindly read and talk about to the children, and a copy of which each child can have if it so wishes. Thus the reply letters are all sent to me, and the vast majority begin "Dear Madam"; but some are less conventional, and I have those commencing, "Dear Mrs. Barnett," "Dear Country Holdday Site

Commtie," "Dear friend," "Dear Miss," while the feeling of personal relation was evidently so real to one small boy that he began his epistle with "Dear Henrietta"—I delight in that letter! Among the concluding words are the following: "Your affectionate little friend," "Your loving pupil," "From one who enjoyed," "Yours gratefully," "Yours truly Friend".

Some of the regrets at leaving the country are very pathetic:—

"I wish I was in the country now". "I shall never go again; I am too old now." "I think in the fortnight I had more treats than ever before in all my life." "The blacking berries were red then and small. They will be black now and big." "I wish I was with my lady's baker taking the bread round." "I enjoyed myself very much, I cannot explain how much. Please God next year I will come again. As I sit at school I always imagine myself roaming in the fields and watching the golden corn, and when I think of it it makes me cry."

And those tears will find companions in some of the hearts which ache for the joyless lives of our town children, weighted by responsibilities, crippled by poverty, robbed of their birthright of innocent fun. The ecstatic joy of children in response to such simple pleasures tells volumes about their drab existence, their appreciation of adequate food, their warm recognition of kindness, represent privation and surprise. In a deeper sense than Wordsworth used it, "Their gratitude has left me mourning".

I know, and no one better, the countless servants of the people who are toiling to relieve the sorrows of the poor and their children, but until the conditions of labour, of education, and of housing are fearlessly faced and radically dealt with, their labour can only be palliative and their efforts barren of the best fruit; but articles, as well as holidays, must finish, and so I will conclude by another extract:—

"We had a bottle of Tea and cake and it was 132¾ miles. I saw all sorts of things and come to Waterloo Station and thank you very much."

HENRIETTA O. BARNETT.

THE RECREATION OF THE PEOPLE.[1]

By Canon Barnett.

July, 1907.

[1] From "The Cornhill Magazine". By permission of the Editor.

WORK may, as Carlyle says, be a blessing, but work is not undertaken for work's sake. Work is part of the universal struggle for existence. Men work to live. But the animal world early found that existence does not consist in keeping alive. All animals play. They let off surplus energy in imitating their own activities, and they recreate exhausted powers by change of occupation. Man, as soon as he came into his inheritance of reason, recognized play as an object of desire, and as well as working for his existence, and perhaps even before he worked to obtain power and glory, he worked to obtain recreation. A man, according to Schiller's famous saying, is fully human only when he plays.

Work, then, let it be admitted, is undertaken not for work's sake but largely for the sake of recreation. England has been made the workshop of the world, its fair fields and lovely homesteads have been turned into dark towns and grimy streets, partly in the hope that more of its citizens may have enjoyment in life. Men toil in close offices under dark skies, not just to increase the volume of exports and imports, and not always to increase their power, or to win honour from one another; they dream of happy hours of play, they picture themselves travelling in strange countries or tranquilly enjoying their leisure in some villa or pleasant garden. Men spend laborious days as reformers, on public boards or as public servants, very largely so as to release their neighbours from the prison house of labour, where so many, giving their lives "to some unmeaning taskwork, die unfreed, having seen nothing, still unblest".

Recreation is an object of work. The recreations of the people consume much of the fruit of the labour of the people. Their play discloses what is in their hearts and minds and to what end they will direct their power. Their use of leisure is a sign-post showing whether the course of the nation is towards extinction in ignorance and self-indulgence, or towards greater brightness in the revelation of character and the service of mankind. By their idle words and by the acts of their idle times men are most fairly judged.

The recreation of the people is therefore a subject of greater importance than is always remembered. The country is being lost or saved in its play, and the use of holidays needs as much consideration as the use of workdays.

Would that some Charles Booth could undertake an inquiry into "the life and leisure of the people" to put alongside that into their life and work! Without such an inquiry the only basis for the consideration which I invite is the impression left on the minds of individuals, and all I can offer is the impression made on my mind by a long residence in East London.

People during the last quarter of a century have greatly increased their command of leisure. The command, as Board of Trade inspectors remind us, is not sufficient as long as the rule of seventy or even sixty hours of work a week still holds in some trades. But the weekly half-holiday has become almost universal, some skilled trades have secured an eight or nine hours' day, many workshops every year close for a week, and the members of the building trades begin work late and knock off early during the winter months. There is thus much leisure available for recreation. What do the people do? How do these crowds who swarm through the streets on Saturday afternoons spend their holiday?

Many visit the public-houses and try to drink themselves out of their gloom. "To get drunk," we have been told, is "the shortest way out of Manchester," and many citizens in every city go at any rate some distance along this way. They find they live a larger, fuller life as, standing in the warm bright bar, they drink and talk as if they were "lords". The returns which suggest that the drink bill of a workman's family is 5s. or 6s. a week prove how popular is this use of leisure, and they who begin a holiday by drinking probably spend the rest of it in sleeping. The identification of rest with sleep is very common, and a workman who knows he has a fair claim to rest thinks himself justified in sleeping or dozing hour after hour during Saturday and Sunday. "What," I once asked an engineer, "should I find most of your mates doing if I called on Sunday?" His answer was short: "Sleeping".

Another large body of workers as soon as they are free hurry off to some form of excitement. They go in their thousands to see a football-match, they yell with those who yell, they are roused by the spectacle of battle, and they indulge in hot "sultry" talk. Or they go to some race or trial of strength on which bets are possible. They feel in the rise and fall of the chance of winning a new stirring of their dull selves, and they dream of wealth to be enjoyed in wearing a coat with a fur collar and in becoming owners of sporting champions. Or they go to music halls—1,250,000 go every week in London—where if the excitement be less violent it still avails to move their thoughts into other channels. They see colour instead of dusky dirt, they hear songs instead of the clash of machinery, they are interested as a performer risks his life, and the jokes make no demands on their thoughts. The theatres probably are less popular, at any rate among men, but they attract great numbers, especially to plays which appeal to generous impulses. An audience enjoys the easy satisfaction of shouting down a villain. The same sort of excitement is that provided on Sunday mornings in the clubs, where in somewhat sordid surroundings, a few actors and singers try to stir the muddled feelings of their audience by appeals, which are more or less vulgar.

There is finally another large body of released workers who simply go home. They are more in number than is generally imagined, and they constitute the solid part of the community. They are not often found at meetings or clubs. Their opinions are not easily discovered. Large numbers never vote. They go home from work, they make themselves tidy, they do odd jobs about the house, they go out shopping with their wives, they walk with the children, they, as a family party, visit their friends, they sleep, and they read the weekly paper. All this is estimable, and the mere catalogue makes a picture pleasant to the middle-class imagination of what a workman's life should be. The workers get repose, but from a larger point of view it cannot be said they return to work invigorated by new thoughts and new experiences, with new powers and new conceptions of life's use. Repose is sterilized recreation.

These, it seems to me, are the three main streams which flow from work to leisure—that towards drink, that towards excitement, and that towards home repose.

There are other workers—an increasing number, but small in comparison with those in one of the main streams—who use their leisure to attend classes, to study with a view to greater technical skill or to read the books now so easily bought. There are some who take other jobs, forgetting that the wages which buy eight hours' work should buy also eight hours' sleep and eight hours' play. There are many who bicycle, some it may be for the excitement of rapid motion, but some also for the joy of visiting the country and of social intercourse. There are many who play games and take vigorous exercise. There are a few—markedly a few—who have hobbies or pursuits on which they exercise their less used powers of heart or head or limb.

Such is the general impression which long experience has left on my mind as to the recreations of the people. It is, however, possible to give a closer inspection to some popular forms of amusement.

Consider first one of the seaside resorts during the month of August. Look at Blackpool, or Margate, or Weston. On the Saturday before Bank Holiday £100,000 was drawn out of the banks at Blackburn and £200,000 from the banks at Oldham, to be spent in recreation, mostly at Blackpool. How was it spent?

The sight of the beach of one of these resorts is familiar. There is the mass of people brightly coloured and loudly talking, broken into rapidly changing groups. There are the nigger singers, the buffoons, the acrobats; there are the great restaurants and hotels inviting lavish expenditure on food. There are bookstalls laden with trashy novels. There are the overridden beasts and the overworked maid-servants; there is the loafing on the pier, and the sleep after heavy meals. Nothing especially wicked, much that shows good-nature, but everything so vulgar—so empty of interest, so far below what thinking men and women should enjoy, so unworthy the expenditure of hundreds of thousands of pounds earned by hard work.

Consider again the music hall. Mr. Stead has lent his eyes. "If," he says, "I had to sum up the whole performance in a single phrase I should say, 'Drivel for dregs'. For three and a half hours I sat patiently listening to the most insufferable banality and imbecility which ever fell on human ears. There was neither beauty nor humour, no appeal to taste or to intelligence, nothing but vulgarity and stupidity to recreate the heirs of a thousand years of civilization and the citizens of an empire on which the sun never sets." And in one year there are some 70,000,000 admissions to music halls in London! Consider, too, the football fields or the racecourses. The crowd of spectators is often 100,000 to 200,000 persons. What can they find worthy the interest of a reasonable creature? Would they be present if it were not for the excitement of gambling, the mind-destroying pleasure of risking their money to get their neighbours' money? "If," as Sir James Crichton-Browne says, "you would see the English physiognomy at its worst, go to the platform of a railway station on the day of a suburban race meeting when the special trains are starting. On most of the faces you detect the grin of greed, on many the leer of low cunning, on some the stamp of positive rascality."

Consider once more the crowds who go to the country in the summer. "One of the saddest sights of the Lake District during the tourist season," says Canon Rawnsley, "is the aimless wandering of the hard-worked folk who have waited a whole year for their annual holiday, and, having obtained it, do not know what to do with it. They stand with Skiddaw, glorious in its purple mantle of heather, on one side and the blue hills of Borrowdale and the shining lake on the other, and ask 'Which is the way to the scenery?'" The people, according to this observer, are dull and bored amid the greatest beauty. The excursionist finds nothing in nature which is his; he reads the handwriting of truth and beauty, but understands not what he reads.

But enough of impressions of popular recreations. There are brighter sides to notice. There is, for instance, health in the instinct which turns to the country for enjoyment. There is hope in the prevalent good temper, in the untiring energy and curiosity which is always seeking something new. There are better things than have been mentioned and there are worse things, but as a general conclusion it may, I think, be agreed that the recreations of the people are not such as recreate human nature for further progress. The lavish expenditure of hardly earned wages on mere bodily comfort does not suggest that the people are cherishing high political ideals, and the galvanized idleness which characterizes so much popular pleasure does not promise for the future an England which will be called blessed or be itself "merrie".

England in her great days was "Merrie England". Many of our forefathers' recreations were, judged by our standard, cruel and horribly brutal. They had, however, certain notable characteristics. They made greater demands both on body and mind. When there were neither trains nor trams nor grand stands people had to take more exertion to get pleasure, and they themselves joined in the play or in the sport. Their delight, too, was often in the fellowship they secured, and "fellowship," as Morris says, "is life and lack of fellowship is death". Our fathers' sports, even if they were cruel—and the "Book of Sports" shows how many were not cruel but full of grace—had often this virtue of fellowship. Their pageants and spectacles—faithfully pictured by Scott in his account of the revels of Kenilworth, were not just shows to be lazily watched; they enlisted the interest and ingenuity of the spectators, and stirred their minds to discover the meaning of some allegory or trace out some mystery.

The recreations which made England "merrie" were stopped in their development by the combined influence of puritanism and of the industrial revolution. Far be it from me to consider as evil either the one or the other. In all progress there is destruction. The puritan spirit put down cruel sports such as bull baiting and cock fighting, and with them many innocent pleasures. The industrial revolution drew the people from their homes in the fields and valleys, established them in towns, gave them higher wages and cheaper food. Under the combined influence work took possession of the nation's being. It ruled as a tyrant, and the gospel of work became the gospel for the people.

In the latter part of the nineteenth century signs of reaction are apparent. Sleary, in Dickens's "Hard Times," urges on the economist the continual refrain: "The people, Squire, must be amused," and Herbert Spencer, returning from America in 1882, declares the need of the "Gospel of Recreation". Recreation has since increased in pace. The right to shorter and shorter hours of labour is now admitted, and the provision of amusement has become a great business. The demand which has secured shorter hours may safely be left to rescue further leisure from work; but demand has not, as we have seen, been followed by the establishment of healthy recreation. A child knows a holiday is good, but he needs also to know how to enjoy it or he will do mischief to himself or others. The people also need, as well as leisure, the knowledge of what constitutes recreation.

The subject is not simple, and Professor Karl Groos, in his book "The Play of Man," has with Teutonic thoroughness analysed the subject from the physiological, the biological, and the psychological standpoints. The book is worthy of study by students, but it seems to me that recreation must involve (1) some excitement, (2) some strengthening of the less used fibres of the mind or body, (3) the activity of the imagination.

(1) Recreation must involve some excitement, some appeal to an existing interest, some change, some stirring of the wearied or sleeping embers of the mind. Routine work, tending to become more and more routine, wears life. It is "life of which our nerves are scant," and recreation should revive the sources of life. Most people, as Mr. Balfour, look askance at efforts which, under the guise of amusing, aim to impart useful culture. Recreation must be something other than repose—something more stirring than sleep or loafing—it must be something attractive and not something undertaken as a duty.

(2) Recreation must involve the strengthening of the less used fibres of the mind and the body; the embers which are stirred by excitement need to be fed with new fuel, or the flames will soon sink into ashes. Gambling and drink, sensational dramas, and exciting shows stir but do not strengthen the mind. Mere change—the fresh excursion every day, the spectacle of a contest—wears out the powers of being. "The crime of sense is avenged by sense which wears with time." On the other hand, games well played fulfil the condition, and there is no more cheering sight than that of playing-fields where young and old are using their limbs intent on doing their best. Music, foreign travel, congenial society, reading, chess, all games of skill, also fulfil the condition, as they make a claim on the activity of heart or mind, and so strengthen their fibres. A good drama is recreation if the spectator is called to give himself to thought and to feeling. He then becomes in a sense a fellow creator with the author, he has what Professor Groos says satisfies every one, "the joy of being a cause," or, as he explains in another passage, "it is only when emotion is in a measure our own work do we enjoy the result". Recreation must call out activity, it fails if it gives and requires nothing. We only have what we give. He that would save his life loses it.

(3) The last and most notable mark of recreation is the use of the imagination. Recreation comes from within and not from without the man. It depends on that a man *is* and not upon what a man *has*. A child grows tired of his toys, a man wearies of his possessions, but there is no being tired of the imagination which leaps ahead and every day reveals something new. Sleary was wrong when he said, "People must be amused". He should have said, "People must amuse themselves". Their recreation must, that is, come from the use of their own faculties of heart and mind. "The cultivation of the inner life," it was truly said in a discussion on the hard lot of the middle classes, "is the only cure for the commercial tyrannies and class prejudices of that class." The Japanese are the best holiday takers I have ever met; they have in themselves a taste for beauty, and they go to the country to enjoy the use of that taste. A man who because he is interested in mankind sets himself on his holiday to observe and study the habits of man; or, because he cares for Nature, looks deeper into her secrets by the way of plants or rocks or stars; or, because he is familiar with history, seeks in buildings and places illustrations of the past; a holiday maker who in such ways uses his inner powers will come home refreshed. His pleasure has come from within; he, on the other hand, who has lounged about a pier, moved from place to place, travelled from sight to sight, looking always for pleasure from outside himself, will come home bored.

If such be the constituents of recreation one reflection stands out clearly, and that is the importance of educating or directing the demand for amusement. Popular demand can only choose what it knows; it could not choose the pictures for an art gallery or the best machines for the workshop, neither can it settle the amusements which are recreative. Children and young people are with great care fitted for work and taught how to earn a living; there is equal need that the people be fitted for recreation, and taught how to enjoy their being. They must know before they can choose. Education, and not the House of Lords, is the safeguard of democratic government.

Mr. Dill's "History of Social Life in the Towns of the Roman Empire during the First and Second Centuries" shows that there is a striking likeness between the condition of those times to that which prevails in England. The millionaires made noble benefactions, there were magnificent spectacles, there were contests which roused lunatic excitement as one of the combatants succeeded in some brutal strife, there was lavish provision of games and great enjoyment in feasting. The amusement was provided by others' gifts, and, as Mr. Dill remarks, the people were more and more drawn from "interest in the things of the mind". The games of Rome were steps in the decline and fall of Rome.

The lesson which modern and ancient experience offers is that people must be as thoughtfully and as seriously prepared for their recreation as for their work.

The first illusion which must, I think, be destroyed is that a holiday means a vacation or an empty time. It is not enough to close the school and let the children have no lessons. It is not enough to enact an eight hours' day and leave the people without resources. If the spirit of toil be turned out of men's lives and they be left swept and garnished, there are spirits of leisure that will return which may be ten times worse. It is a pathetic sight often presented in a playground, when after some aimless running and pushing, the children gradually grow listless, fractious, and quarrelsome. They came to enjoy themselves and cannot. Many a boy for want of occupation for his leisure has taken to crime. It is not always love of evil or even greed which makes him a thief, it is in the pure spirit of adventure that he stalks his prey on the coster's cart, risks his liberty and dodges the police. It is because they have no more interesting occupation that eager little heads pop out of windows when the police make a capture, and eager little tongues tell experiences of arrests which baby eyes have seen. The empty holiday is a burden to a child, and every one has heard of the bus driver who could think of nothing better to do on his off day than to ride on a bus beside a mate. The idea that, given leisure, the people will find recreation is not justified. A kitten may be satisfied with aimless play, but a spark disturbs mankind's clod and his play needs direction.

The other illusion which must be dissipated is that amusement should call for no effort on the part of those to be amused. It is the common mistake of benevolence that it tries to remove difficulties, rather than strengthen people to surmount difficulties. The gift which provides food is often destructive of the powers which earn food. In the same way the benevolence which, as among the Romans, provides shows, entertainments, and feasts, destroys at last the capacity for pleasure. Toys often stifle children's imaginations and develop a greed for possession; children enjoy more truly what they themselves help to create, so that a bit of wood with inkspots for eyes, which they themselves have made, is more precious than an expensive doll. Grown people's amusements to be satisfying must also call out effort.

The shattering of these two illusions leaves society face to face with the obligation to teach people to play as well as to work. It is not enough to give leisure and leave amusement to follow. Neither is it enough to provide popular amusement. James I was not a great King but he was a collector of wisdom, and he laid down for his son a guide for his games as well as for his work. Teachers and parents with greater experience might, like the King, guide their children.

(1) It is not, I think, waste of time to watch infants when at play, to encourage their efforts, to welcome their calls to look, and to enter into their imaginings. This watching, so usual among the children of the richer classes, is missed by the children of the poorer and often leaves a gap in their development.

(2) It would not either be wasted expenditure to employ game-teachers in the elementary schools, who, on Saturdays and out of school hours would teach children games, indoor and outdoor, conduct small parties to places of interest, and organize country walks or excursions such as are common in Swiss schools.

(3) It is, I think, reasonable to ask that the great school buildings and playgrounds should be more continually at the children's service. They have been built at great expense. They are often the most airy and largest space in a crowded neighbourhood. Why should they be in the children's use for only some twenty-five hours a week? Why should they be closed during two whole months? The experience gained in the vacation schools advocated by Mrs. Humphry Ward gives an object lesson in what might be done. During the afternoon hours between five and seven, and in the summer holidays, the children, with the greatest delight to themselves, might be drawn to see new things, to use new faculties of admiration or develop new tastes. Every child might thus be given a hobby. Recreation means, as we have seen, change. If the children ended their school days with more interests, with eyes opened to see in the country not only a nest to be taken but a brood of birds to be watched, with hands capable not only to make things but to create beauty, the limits within which they could find change would be greatly enlarged.

If I may now extend my suggestion to parents I would say that those of all classes might do more in planning holidays for their children. There is now a strong disposition to leave all responsibility to the teachers, and parents are in the danger of losing parental authority. In the holidays is their chance of regaining authority; for every day they could plan occupation, put aside time to join in some common pursuit, arrange visits, and make themselves companions of their own children. The teacher may be held responsible, but his work is often spoiled in the idle hours of a holiday, when bad books are read, vulgar sights enjoyed, low companions found, and habits of loafing developed. But it is not only teachers and parents by whom children are guided. There is a host of men and women who plan treats, excursions, and country holidays. Their efforts could, I think, be made more valuable. The monster day treats, which give excitement and turn the children's minds in a direction towards the excitements of crowds and of stimulants from without, might be exchanged for small treats where ten or twenty children in close companionship with their guide would enjoy one another's company, find new interests, and store up memories of things seen and heard. Tramps through England might be organized for elder boys and girls in which visits might be paid to historic fields and scenes of beauty, and objects of interest sought. Children about to be sent to the country by a Holiday Fund might, as is now very happily done by a committee in connexion with the Children's Country Holiday Fund, by means of pictures and talk be taught what to look for and be encouraged to tell of their discoveries. Habits of singing might be developed, as among the Welsh or the Swiss. And in a thousand ways thought might be drawn to the observation of nature. Good people might, if I may say so, give up the provision of those entertainments which now, absorbing so much of the energy of curates and laywomen, seem only to prepare the children to look for the entertainment of the music halls. They might instead teach children one by one to find amusement, each one in his own being.

The hope of the future lies obviously in the training of the children, but the elder members of the community might also have more chances of growth. Employers, for instance, might more generally substitute holidays of weeks for holidays of days, and so encourage the workpeople to plan their reasonable use. They might also enlarge their minds by informing them about the material on which they work, whence it comes and whither it goes. Miss Addams tells of a firm in Ohio where the hands are gathered to hear the reports of the travellers as they return from Constantinople, Italy, or China, and learn how the goods they have made are used by strange people. In the same firm lantern lectures are given on the countries with which the firm has dealings, and generally the hands are made partners in the thoughts of the heads. "This," as Miss Addams says, "is a crude example of the way in which a larger framework may be given to the worker's mind," and she adds, "as a poet bathes the outer world for us in the hues of human feeling, so the workman needs some one to bathe his surrounding with a human significance." Employers also, following the example of Messrs. Cadbury, might require their young people not only to attend evening classes to make them fitter for work, but also to attend one class which will fit them to ride hobbies, which will carry them from the strain and routine of work into other and recreating surroundings. Municipal bodies have in these latter days done much in the right direction by opening playing fields, picture galleries, and libraries, and by giving free performances of high-class music. They might perhaps do more to break up the monotony of the streets, introducing more of the country into town, and requiring dignity as well as healthiness in the great buildings. Such variety adds greatly to the joy of living, diverts the minds of weary workers, and stimulates the admiration which is one-third of life.

But, after all, improvement starts from individuals, and it is the action of individual men and women which will reform popular reaction. They must, each one as if the reform depended on him alone, be morally thoughtful about the amusements they encourage or patronize, and be considerate in preparing for their own pleasure. Each one must develop his own being, and stir up the faculties of his own mind. Each one must practise the muscles of his mind as a racer practises the muscles of his legs.

The most completely satisfying recreation is possibly in the intercourse of friends, and it is a sad feature in English holidays that men and their wives, who are naturally the closest friends, seem to find so little pleasure in one another's company. They walk one behind the other in the country, they are rarely found together at places of entertainment, and they are seldom seen talking with any vivacity. The fault lies in the fact that they have not developed their own being, they have neither interests nor hobbies nor ideas, and so have nothing to talk about save wages, household difficulties, and the shortest way home.

Enough, however, in the way of suggestion as to what may be done in guiding people towards recreation. Under guidance recreations would take another than their present character. People, having a wider range of interests, would find change within those interests, and cease to turn from sensation to sleep and from sleep to sensation. People having active minds would look to exercise their minds in a game of skill, in searching Nature's secrets, in spirited talk, in some creative activity, in following a thought-provoking drama, in the use, that is, of their highest human faculties. The forms of recreation would be changed. Much of the difficulty about what seems Sunday desecration would then vanish. The play of the people would no longer be fatal to the quiet of the day, or inconsistent with the worship which demands the consecration of the whole being. It is not recreation so much as the form of recreation which desecrates Sunday. This, however, is part of another subject.

As a conclusion of the whole matter I would say how it seems to me that Merrie England need be not only in the past. The present time is the best of times. There are to-day resources for men's enjoyment such as never existed in any other age or country. There are fresh and pure capacities in human nature which are evident in many signs of energy, of admiration, and of good will. If the resources were used, if the capacities were developed, there would soon be popular recreations to attract human longings, and encourage the hope of a future when the glory of England shall not be in its possessions of gold and territory, but in a people happy in the full use of their powers of heart and of head.

SAMUEL A. BARNETT.

THE HOPES OF THE HOSTS.[1]

By Mrs. S. A. Barnett.

January, 1886.

[1] From "The Toynbee Journal".

CERTAINLY a great deal of entertaining goes on in Toynbee Hall. From the half-hours spent in the little room, where its Entertainment Committee meets, there issue some prominent if not exactly big results, and, perhaps, its members are not without a hope that deep consequences as well may follow. This method of helping people has not been without its critics, one of whom uttered the opinion, "that the Toynbee Hall plan was to save the people's souls alive by pictures, pianos, and parties," and though the remark was made derisively, there may be some doubt if it was altogether without truth: only the speaker should have added that it was *one* of the Toynbee Hall plans, instead of using only the definite article.

If the Toynbee Hall aim is to help to make it possible that men should carry out the command given long ago of "Be ye perfect," and if, as a modern lover of righteousness has put it, "the power of social life and manners is one of the great elements in our humanization, and unless we cultivate it we are incomplete"; then it is not an error that "pictures, pianos, and parties" should be pressed into service to fill up some of the incompleteness in the East London dweller's life, and to help him to "save his soul alive".

It is one of the saddest facts of life in this crowded, busy, tiring, and hurried part of London that it is more difficult to keep one's soul (like one's plants) alive than it is in gentler places, where folk get the aid of some of nature's beauties, and some moments of that outside quiet which help to make it possible to fancy "the peace which passeth all understanding". But because Whitechapel is Whitechapel and Toynbee Hall is in its midst, more artificial methods for gaining and keeping life must be adopted.

It is true that the Entertainment Committee prefer those gatherings which can take place out of doors in the country, where the guests gain all that comes from the charm of being graciously entertained under "the wider sky"; but still town parties are not to be despised, and, judging from the glad acceptance of those many who "cannot bid again," they are generally enjoyed.

The method of food entertainment is very simple, so simple that it sometimes wars against the generous instincts of the hosts; but, after careful thought, it has been decided that the object of Toynbee Hall entertainments and parties will be more surely gained if "plain living and high thinking" can be maintained—not to mention the more mundane consideration that more friends can be welcomed as guests, if each is not so expensive. So the pleasure to be gained from rich or dainty food is neglected, and the guests are summoned in order to give them pleasures by increasing their interests. And among the means of doing this may be reckoned the fine thoughts of the great dumb teachers, the artists, of which those who care can learn as they turn over the portfolios, look at the photograph books, or study the gift pictures on the walls. The great in the musical world are called upon for offerings as the musically generous among the friends of Toynbee Hall pass on the plaintive ideas of Schumann, or the grand soul-stirring aspirations of Beethoven and Mozart.

To give pleasure is now almost universally considered to be a righteous duty, and when it is taken into consideration that the homes of most East Londoners are too narrow, their daily labour too great, and their resources too limited to permit them taking pleasure by entertaining in their own houses, it cannot but be considered as a gladdening sight when the Toynbee reception rooms are full of a happy, an amused, and an enjoying company.

To increase interests is not perhaps as yet recognized as so deep a human need, but it may be so, none the less for this; and to the young or to the much tempted, this opportunity of increasing their interests is of untold value.

Most young folk are better educated than their parents, and, with a keen sense of enjoyment, a belief in their own powers of self-guidance, and a happy blank on their page of disappointments, they are eager for "fuller life," and will take its pleasure in some guise, warn their elders never so wisely. To give it them free from temptation, and in such a form that when the first novelty is worn off, it will still be true that "the best is yet to be"; to increase interests, until a self-centred and self-seeking existence shows itself in its true and despicable colours; to increase scientific interests with microscopes, magic lanterns, and experiments; literary interests with talks on books, recitations from the poets, scenes from Shakespeare; to increase musical interests with the aid of glee clubs, string quartettes, and solo and chorus songs; to increase interests on all sides is the aim of the Entertainment Committee, hoping that thus for some "all earth will seem aglow where 'twas but plain earth before".

"The cultivation of social life and manners is equal to a moral impulse, for it works to the same end. . . . It brings men together, makes them feel the need of one another, be considerate of one another, understand one another." So teaches Matthew Arnold. And the introduction of the guests to each other is no neglected feature in the Toynbee Hall gatherings. It is for this reason that guests of all classes are summoned together, that the hand-worker may have sympathy with the head-labourer, that the eager reformer may gather hints from the clear-visioned thoughts of the untried lad, or that the boy living a club life far removed from women's power, may be introduced to a "ladye faire," who may (if she will) become to him a "sheltering cloud by day and a pillar of fire by night," guiding him safely through stonier wastes than ever the old Israelites weathered. It is no slight duty this, to introduce one human being to another—to help them to pass quickly along the dull road of acquaintanceship and out into the sweet valley of knowledge and friendship, and there gain, the comfort, refreshment, and inspiration, without which it almost seems impossible to believe in and hold on to an ideal good.

The highest and noblest thing yet revealed to man is the human creature's soul, "the very pulse of the machine," and if Toynbee Hall parties do something to reveal the depths of one creature to another; if they do a little to keep alive and weld into solidarity the floating hopes and aspirations, which idly live in every human heart, but, alas! so often die from loneliness; if they do something to help people to care for one another and to see the higher vision; and if those thus caring are stirred to take thought for the growth and development of the larger, sadder world, then, perhaps, the "pictures, pianos, and parties" will not so ill have played their part in the work of Toynbee Hall.

HENRIETTA O. BARNETT.

EASTER MONDAY ON HAMPSTEAD HEATH.[1]

By Canon Barnett.

April, 1905.

[1] From "The Westminster Gazette". By permission of the Editor.

BANK HOLIDAY on Hampstead Heath sets moving many thoughts. No drunkenness, no bad temper, no brutal rowdiness—but where are the family parties? Three-quarters of the people seem to be under twenty years of age. Where are the family groups such as are found in France or in the colder Denmark making pleasure by talk, or by gaiety, singing, or dancing, or acting—finding interest in things beautiful or new? There were, indeed, some families at Hampstead, and perambulators were driven through the thickest crowd, every one making room for the baby. But the father often looked bored and the mother worried. They were doing their duty, giving the children pleasure, and getting fresh air. The crowd was a young persons' crowd—boys by themselves, girls by themselves, and a smaller number paired. They had come to be amused, and the caterers of amusement had established by the roadside the shows and shooting-galleries and swings such as are to be found within the reach of most crowded neighbourhoods. Organ-grinders played, sweets were exposed for sale, and the Heath Road was as packed with people as Petticoat Lane on a Sunday morning. The people wandered over the Heath, but while they wandered they seemed listless, or on the watch for anything to occupy their attention. A few children dancing as every day they dance in Whitechapel at once drew together a crowd. Golder's Hill Park, which was never more radiant in its beauty, was comparatively empty. The road outside, where public-houses had provided various attractions, was packed, not by people who were customers but by people watching one another and waiting for something to happen. But inside the park, where the County Council's restaurant had spread its tables for tea, where from the Terrace there is a view of unequalled beauty, where the gardens are rich in flowers, there were only a few scattered groups.

The holiday is not a feast of brutality or drunkenness. No one need have been offended by sight or sound. The Shows, thanks to the County Council regulations, were all decent, and there was everywhere the courtesy of good temper. An observer, thinking of twenty years ago, would say, "What an improvement!" but his next thought would be, "How much better things are possible!" In the first place, the arrangements for the supply of food might be different. In Golder's Hill itself the regulation that no teas should be served on the grass for fear of its injury shows a curious ignorance of relative values when, for the want of very slight protection, boys are allowed to tear away the banks on the side of Spaniard's Road. The injured grass would revive in a month; the torn banks are irreparably damaged. There is no reason why the London County Council's restaurants both on Golder's Hill and in other parts of the Heath should not attract people by the daintiness of their display, and why the people should not be held by music and singing. Family parties would be more likely to frequent the place if the elders could be assured of pleasant resting-places. How differently, how very much better, they manage feeding abroad! People are always hungry and thirsty on holidays, and from the public-house to the whelk-stall, from the tea-gardens to the coffee-stand, there was evidence of English incapacity to supply the most persistent of holiday needs. The first improvement possible is, therefore, more dainty and more frequent provision of refreshment. The next improvement, which especially applies to Golder's Hill, is the addition of objects of interest. There might be an aviary, the greenhouses might be filled with flowers and opened, rooms in the house might be decorated with pictures of the neighbourhood or with a collection of local objects. People who are unconsciously taking in memories through their eyes need some illusion; they must think they are going to see something they understand, if they are to be led to see the better things beyond their understanding. Then, surely, some more care might be taken of the tender places on the Heath—there are acres of grass on which boys may play, who might thereby be kept from scouring the surface of the light sand soil, making highways through the gorse, opening waterways to starve the trees.

These improvements are possible at once. There are others longer in the doing which are also necessary. People must be educated not only to be wage-earners but to enjoy their being. They too much depend on stimulants, on some outside excitement always liable to excess. They might find pleasure in themselves, in the use of their own faculties, in their powers of observation or activity, in their own intelligence and curiosity. They might with better education be "good company" for themselves and for one another. The people possess in Hampstead Heath a property a king might envy, but they only partially enjoy its opportunities.

SAMUEL A. BARNETT.

HOLIDAYS AND SCHOOLDAYS.[1]

By Canon Barnett.

July, 1911.

[1] From "The Daily Telegraph". By permission of the Editor.

HOLIDAYS, as well as schooldays, help to form the minds of the citizens. Habits, tastes, friendships, are fixed in the hours when restraints are relaxed, and the Will takes its shape when it is most free. Our school holidays, when in play we commanded or obeyed, when we learnt to know the country sights and objects, when, with different companions, we travelled to new places, have been largely responsible for such satisfaction as we have found in life.

Men and women are what their holidays have made them, and a nation's use of its holidays may almost be said to determine its position in the world's order of greatness. A nation whose pleasures are coarse and brutal, whose people delight in the excitement of their senses by actions in which their minds take no part, and where solitude is unendurable, can hardly do great things. It is not likely that it will be remembered, as the poets are remembered, by its care for any principle of action. It will hardly be generous in its foreign policy or happy in its homes.

The use of holidays is thus most important, and everywhere there are signs of their increase. The schools for the richer classes lengthen the period of their vacations till they extend, in some cases, to a quarter of the year. The King asked that his Coronation year may be marked by an extra week of exemption from school. Business people shorten hours of business, and workmen's organizations demand more time for holidays. Seaside resorts grow up which live mainly by the pleasures of the people, and a vast and increasing body of workers find employment in the provision of amusement.

More time and more money are being given to holidays. Their use or misuse is a matter of importance, and it is reasonable to demand that more thought should also be given to this subject. People—this fact is often forgotten—need to be taught to play as they need to be taught to earn or to love. Leisure is as likely to produce weariness as joy, and the Devil still finds most of his occupation among the idlers.

The public schoolboy who has eight weeks' vacation, and this year an extra week, will hardly be happy if he acquires habits of loafing at the seaside shows or picks up acquaintance with despisers of knowledge, or comes to think that learning is a "grind," and he certainly will not in after years bless his holiday givers. The workman who obtains holidays and shorter hours will hardly be the better if he spends them in eating and sleeping, or in exciting himself over a match or race where he does not even understand the skill, or in watching an entertainment which calls for no effort of his mind.

Rich people, who can do what they like in the time they themselves choose, add excitement to excitement; they invent new methods of expenditure; they go at increasing speed from place to place; they come nearer and nearer to the brinks of vice; they have what they like; and yet, like the millionaire in the American tale, they are not happy. People need to be taught the use of leisure. The question is, how is such teaching practicable? . . . I would offer two suggestions: one which may be applied to the schools of the rich and of the poor, and the other to the free provision of means of recreation:—

1. As to schools. The authorities may, it seems to me, keep in mind the fact that the children are meant to enjoy life as well as to make a living. Enjoyment comes largely by the use of the power of imagination. We enjoy ourselves before the beauty of nature, before a work of art, in listening to music, and in imagining the life of other climes and countries. How little is done in any school to develop this power of imagination! The great public schools, though often they are established in buildings of much beauty, rarely do anything to develop in the boys any understanding of the beauty. There is but little art in the schoolrooms and little attempt to teach the value of pictures. There are few flowers about the windows and very often the time given to music is grudged by the chief authorities.

The elementary schools have not even the advantage of beauty in their buildings, and although the children may be taught art, they have their lessons in rooms made ugly by decorations, or wearying by untidiness. What wonder is it that boys and girls become destructive of the beauty in the admiration of which they and others might have found pleasure?

The authorities might thus do something by the curriculum to make leisure time a happy time, but they might do more by making holiday arrangements. Richer parents may justly be expected to care for their own children, and many seize the opportunity of becoming their playmates, so that holiday times develop the memories that bind together old and young. But few parents can take themselves from business for eight or nine weeks together, and not all parents have the knowledge or the sympathy to lead the young in their pleasures. A solution might be the arrangement by the school authorities of travelling parties—such as those organized at Manchester Grammar School; or of walking tours with some object, such as the collection of specimens or the investigation of places of interest,—or of holiday homes in the school houses or elsewhere, where, under the guidance of sympathetic teachers, the children could enjoy freer life and more varied interests than are possible in school, or of the interchange of visits between the children of English and foreign homes. Once let it be realized that the long holiday period—if necessary for the teachers—is full of danger for the children, and something will be done to make that period healthy as well as happy.

For the children in elementary schools it is easy to make arrangements. During the three summer months the curriculum might be like that of the Vacation Schools. The buildings, often the only pleasant place in a crowded neighbourhood—would thus be in continuous use, while the children and teachers could get away for their country or foreign holiday, without breaking into any school routine. The children would then go into the country prepared to see and enjoy its interests, not only in the month of August, but at times when they might play in the hayfields, pick the spring flowers, and hear the birds sing. The teachers could have, not four, but six weeks' vacation, in which there would be time for a foreign visit when the hotels were less crowded. The children, at the end of their fortnight in the country, would return, not just to loaf about the streets amid the dirt and the noise and degrading temptation, but to take their places in the open and pleasant surroundings of the school, with its manifold interests.

The end of the summer would, if this arrangement could be carried out, find teachers and children alike refreshed and ready for the hard work of the ordinary school routine; and, greatest gain of all, the children would have learned how to enjoy their leisure. They would have planted memories which would call for refreshment; they would have developed powers of admiration which would need to be used; they would have found interests to occupy their thoughts, and they would look forward to holidays in which to go to the country—not to play "Aunt Sally," or even to find fresh air from town pursuits, but to visit old haunts, discover more secrets of nature and taste its quiet. They would, as men and women, make "good company" for one another, and learn to require some distinction of quiet or beauty to make a British holiday. They would find, in the appreciation of English scenery, new reasons for being patriots.

Satisfying pleasure, it must always be remembered, comes from within, and not from without a man. Outside stimulants always fail at last, whether they be drink, shows, sensational tales, or games of chance; but the pleasures which come from the activity of head, or heart, or of limbs last as long as strength and life last.

This leads to the other practicable suggestion which I would offer. The Community might provide freely the means which would give the people the pleasures which come from culture. Much has been done in this direction. Open spaces in our great towns have been made more common, but their use has not been developed as has been done in American cities, where superintendents teach the children how to play, and the playgrounds become centres of common enjoyments. Museums and picture galleries are sometimes provided, but they are still rare and often dull. Personal guidance is necessary if the objects in a museum are to have any meaning for the ordinary visitor, and the pictures in a gallery need to be changed frequently if attention is to be held. The Japanese wisely, even in their private rooms, have a succession of pictures, relegating those not hung to the seclusion of the "Godown". Music is given in the parks and sometimes in the town halls, but the best is not made common, and much is so poor that it fails to reach or express the thoughts which, if deeply buried, are to be found in the hearts of common people.

No attempts are made to open dull ears, to listen to good music, though teachers in public schools report how it is possible by a few talks to make athletes enthusiastic for Beethoven. The total amount of good free music is very small and certainly not enough to raise the common taste and attract minds capable of thought and admiration.

The duty of the Community to provide means of recreation is recognized, but too often it has seemed enough if it provides amusement which can be measured by popular applause. The duty should, I submit, have for its aim the provision of such recreation as would gradually lead the people in the way of enjoyment, and raise the character of all holidays by making them more satisfying to the higher demands of human nature.

SAMUEL A. BARNETT.

THE FAILURE OF HOLIDAYS.[1]

By Canon Barnett.

May, 1912.

[1] From "The Daily Telegraph," May, 1912. By permission of the Editor.

EIGHT hundred thousand children are every August turned out of the airy and spacious Schools which London has built for their use, and for four weeks they can do what they like. To the people whose opinions form public opinion, "to do what one likes" seems the very essence of a holiday. The forgotten fact is that the majority of these children do not know what they like. All children, indeed, need to be taught to enjoy themselves, just as they are taught to earn for themselves; and children whose parents are without money to take them to the country or the seaside, where nature would give them playmates, and without leisure to be referees in their first attempts at games, miss the necessary teaching. They get tired of trying to find out what they like, tired of waiting for the sensation of a street fight or accident, tired of aimless play in the parks, tired even of doing what they had been told not to do. A few—40,000 of the 800,000—are sent by the Children's Country Holiday Fund to spend a fortnight of the month in country cottages; a few others go to stay with friends or accompany their parents, but the greater number—it is said that 480,000 children never sleep one night out of London during the year—have no other break than a day treat, which, with its intoxicating excitements and its distracting noises, can hardly claim to be a lesson in the art of enjoyment or to be a fair introduction to country pleasures. The August holiday under present conditions, cannot be described as a time in which working-class children store up memories of childhood's joys, nor does it prepare them as men and women to make good use of the leisure gained by shorter hours of labour.

The use of leisure has not, I think, been sufficiently considered from a National point of view. It concerns the happiness, the health, and also the wealth of the nation. If their leisure dissipates the strength of men's minds, leaves them the prey to stimulants, and at the same time absorbs the wages of work, there is a continual loss, which must at last be fatal. The children's August holiday, with its dullness and its dependence on chance excitements, prepares the way for Beanfeasts where parties of men find nothing better to do amid the beauty of the country than to throw stones at bottles, or for the vulgar futilities of Margate sands, Hampstead Heath and the music hall, or for the soul-numbing variety of sport.

The recent report issued by the London County Council tells the result of an experiment in a better use of the holiday by means of Vacation Schools. The word "School" may suggest restraint, and put off some of my readers, who are apt to think of "heaven as a place where there are no masters". They will say, "Let the children alone". But they do not realize what "letting alone" means for children whose homes have no resources in space or interests. They do not remember that the schoolhouse is the Mansion of the neighbourhood, and that the Vacation School curriculum includes visits to the parks and to London sights, such as the Zoological Gardens, Hampton Court, and the Natural History Museum; manual occupations in which really useful things are made, painting and cardboard modelling, by which the children's own imaginations have play; lessons on nature, illustrated by plants and by pictures, readings from interesting books, about which the teachers are ready to talk, and organized games. When relieved from the trouble of having to choose at what to play, the children find untroubled enjoyment. Vacation Schools thus understood have no terror, but let the children themselves give evidence whether they prefer to be let alone.

In a Battersea Vacation School there was an average attendance of 91·6 per cent, and on one day 153 children out of 154 on the roll voluntarily attended. "The high rate of actual attendance at the Vacation Schools, which compares not unfavourably with that of the ordinary day schools, in spite of the fact that compulsion is completely absent from the former, may be taken as an indication that the London child does not know what to do during the long vacation, and is anxious and ready to take advantage of any opportunity that may be afforded for work and play under conditions more healthy and congenial than the street or his home can offer." In another school the teachers report: "We had been asked to do our best to keep up the numbers. Our difficulty was to keep them down." "The discipline of the boys specially surprised the staff; a hint of possible expulsion was quite sufficient in dealing with two or three boys reported during the month."

The children, by their attendance, give the best evidence that the Vacation School is in their opinion a good way of spending a holiday and the report gives greater detail as to the reason. The teachers tell how "listless manners give place to animation and energy, and how the tendency prevalent among the boys to loaf or aimlessly to idle away their holidays was checked by the introduction of an objective, the absence of which is chiefly responsible for the loafing tendency. . . . The absence of restraint appears to lead to more honourable and more thoughtful conduct, and little acts of courtesy and politeness increased in frequency as the holidays drew to an end. . . . Educationally the children benefit in increased manual dexterity, by the creation of motive, the training of the powers of observation, and the development of memory and imagination. . . . In many cases . . . new capabilities were discovered, and talents awakened by the more congenial surroundings. Some children, who at first appeared dull and inattentive, brightened up and became most interested in one or more of their varied occupations. . . . Little chats on the Excursions revealed a marked widening of outlook."

In such testimony as this it is quite easy to find the reason why the children so greatly enjoyed themselves. They had a variety of new interests and they had the sense of "life" which comes in the exercise of new capacities. They were never bored and they felt well. The parents, whose burden during holidays is often forgotten, seem to have expressed great appreciation at the provision for the children's care, and as for the teachers, one goes so far as to say that "the kind of experience gained is a teacher's liberal education and training".

The Report as a result of such testimony, naturally recommends an extension of the plan of Vacation Schools, so that this summer a greater number may be provided. I would, however, submit that the testimony justifies something more thorough.

The proposals of the Report assume that holidays must fall in the month of August. Now there are many parents whose occupation keeps them in town during that month, and who cannot therefore take their children to the country. August too, is the period when all health resorts are most crowded and expensive. And lastly, if holidays are taken only in this autumn season the country of the spring and summer, with its haymaking, its flowers and its birds, remains unknown to the children. The obvious change—so obvious that one wonders why it has not long ago been adopted—is to let some schools take their holidays in the months of June and July. But I would myself suggest the best plan would be to keep all, or most, of the school in session during the whole summer, establishing for the three months a summer curriculum on the lines of those adopted in the Vacation Schools. The children would then be able to go with their friends, or through the Children's Country Holiday Fund for their Country Holiday without any interference with the regular school regime; and all, while they were at home, would have those resources in the school hours which have proved to be powerful to attract them from the streets. The teachers, free at last to take some of their holidays in June or July, would be able to benefit by the lower charges, to get, perhaps, a recreative holiday in the Alps instead of one at the English seaside in the somewhat stale companionship of a party of fellow-teachers.

This more thorough plan would do for all London children everything which Vacation Schools attempt, and it has the further advantage that it would put refreshing country visits within the reach of more children and teachers.

Middle-class families recognize the necessity of an annual visit to the sea or country, as a consequence of which great towns exist almost wholly as holiday resorts. The necessity of the middle class is much more the necessity of the working class, whose children have less room in their houses and fewer interests for their leisure. A pressure which cannot be resisted will insist that for their health's sake and for the child's sake, who is the father of the man, the children shall have each year the opportunity of breathing for at least a fortnight country air, and of learning to be Nature's playmates. The only practicable way in which such holidays may be provided is by the extension of the holiday period to include other than the month of August.

The plan I have suggested would make such extension practicable with the least possible interference with school work, while it would secure for all children some guidance in the use and enjoyment of the leisure, which the experiment of Vacation Schools has proved to be so acceptable. That guidance, by widening children's minds and awakening their powers of taking notice, would make the country visits more full of interests, and develop a love of Nature, to be a valuable resource in later life. If the Council's Report succeeds in moving London opinion it may mark a new departure in the use and enjoyment of holidays.

It almost seems as if the education given at such cost ran to waste during the holidays. There is a call for another Charles Booth, to make an inquiry into "the life and leisure of the people" which might be as epoch-making as that into "the life and labour of the people". Such an inquiry would show, I believe, the need of energetic effort if leisure is to be a source of strength and not of weakness to national life, a way to recreation and not to demoralization.

SAMUEL A. BARNETT.

RECREATION IN TOWN AND COUNTRY.[1]

RECREATION AND CHARACTER.

BY MRS. S. A. BARNETT.

October, 1906.

[1] A paper written for the Church Congress, and read at its meeting at Barrow-in-Furness by the Right Reverend the Lord Bishop of Truro, the late C. W. Stubbs.

A PEOPLE'S play is a fair test of a people's character. Men and women in their hours of leisure show their real admiration and their inner faith. Their "idle words," in more than one sense, are those by which they are judged.

No one who has reached an age from which he can overlook fifteen or twenty years can doubt but that pleasure-seeking has greatly increased. The railway statistics show that during the last year more people have been taken to seaside and pleasure resorts than ever before. On Bank Holidays a larger number travel, and more and more facilities are annually offered for day trips and evening entertainments.

The newspapers give many pages to recording games, pages which are eagerly scanned even when, as in the case of the "Daily News," the betting on their results is omitted.

Face to face with these facts we need some principles to enable us to advise this pleasure-seeking generation what to seek and what to avoid. To arrive at principles one has to probe below the surface, to seek the cause of the pleasure given by various amusements. Briefly, what persons of all ages seek in pleasure is (1) excitement, (2) interest, (3) memories. These are natural desires; no amount of preaching or scolding, or hiding them away will abolish them. It is the part of wisdom to recognize facts and use them for the uplifting of human nature.

May I offer two principles for your consideration?

1. Pleasure, while offering excitement, should not depend on excitement; it should not involve a fellow-creature's loss or pain, nor lay its foundation on greed or gain.

2. Pleasure should not only give enjoyment, it should also increase capacities for enjoyment. It should strengthen a man's whole being, enrich memory and call forth effort.

THE QUALITY OF ENGLISH PLAYING.

If these principles have a basis of truth, the questions arise, "Are the common recreations of the people such as to encourage our hope of English progress? Do they make us proud of the growth of national character, and give us a ground of security for the high place we all long that England shall hold in the future?" The country may be lost as well as won on her playing fields.

Recreation means the refreshment of the sources of life. Routine wears life, and "It is life of which our nerves are scant". The excitement which stirs the worn or sleeping centres of a man's body, mind or spirit, is the first step in such refreshment, but followed by nothing else it defeats its own ends. It uses strength and creates nothing, and if unmixed with what endures it can but leave the partaker the poorer. The fire must be stirred, but unless fuel be supplied the flames will soon sink in ashes.

It behoves us then to accept excitement as a necessary part of recreation, and to seek to add to it those things which lead to increased resources and leave purer memories. Such an addition is skill. A wise manager of a boys' refuge once said to me that it was the first step upwards to induce a lad to play a game of skill instead of a game of chance. Another such addition is co-operation, that is a call on the receiver to give something. It is better for instance to play a game than to watch a game. It may, perhaps, be helpful to recall the principle, and let it test some of the popular pleasures.

POPULAR PLEASURES.

Pleasure, while offering excitement, should not depend on excitement; it should not involve a fellow-creature's loss or pain, nor lay its foundation on greed or gain.

This principle excludes the recreations which, like drink or gambling, stir without feeding, or the pleasures which are blended with the sorrows of the meanest thing that feels. It excludes also the dull Museum which feeds without stirring, and makes no provision for excitement. Tried by this standard, what is to be said of Margate, Blackpool, and such popular resorts, with their ribald gaiety and inane beach shows? Of music halls, where the entertainment was described by Mr. Stead as the "most insufferable banality and imbecility that ever fell upon human ears," disgusting him not so much for its immorality as by the vulgar stupidity of it all. Of racing, the acknowledged interest of which is in the betting, a method of self-enrichment by another's impoverishment, which tends to sap the very foundations of honesty and integrity; of football matches, which thousands watch, often ignorant of the science of the game, but captivated by the hope of winning a bet or by the spectacle of brutal conflict; of monster school-treats or excursions, when numbers engender such monopolizing excitement that all else which the energetic curate or the good ladies have provided is ruthlessly swallowed up; shooting battues, where skill and effort give place to organization and cruelty; of plays, where the interest centres round the breaking of the commandments and "fools make a mock of sin".

Such pleasures may amuse for the time, but they fail to be recreative in so far as they do not make life fuller, do not increase the powers of admiration, hope and love; do not store the memory to be "the bliss of solitude". Of most of them it can be easily foretold that the "crime of sense will be avenged by sense which wears with time". Such pleasures cannot lay the foundation for a glad old age.

Does this sound as if all popular pleasures are to be condemned? No! brought to the test of our second principle, there are whole realms of pleasure-lands which the Christian can explore and introduce to others, to the gladdening, deepening, and strengthening of their lives. May I read the principle again?

Pleasure should not only give enjoyment, it should also increase the capacity for enjoyment. It should strengthen a man's whole being, enrich memory and call forth effort and co-operation.

Music, games of skill, books, athletics, foreign travel, cycling, walking tours, sailing, photography, picture galleries, botanical rambles, antiquarian researches, and many other recreations too numerous to mention call out the growth of the powers, as well as feed what exists; they excite active as well as passive emotions; they enlist the receiver as a co-operator; they allow the pleasure-seekers to feel the joy of being the creating children of a creating God.

As we consider the subject, the chasm between right and wrong pleasures, worthy and unworthy recreations, seems to become deeper and broader, often though crossed by bridges of human effort, triumphs of dexterity, evidences of skill wrought by patient practice, which, though calling for no thought in the spectator, yet rouses his admiration and provides standards of executive excellence, albeit directed in regrettable channels.

Still, broadly, recreations may be divided between those which call for effort, and therefore make towards progress, and those which breed idleness and its litter of evils; but (and this is the inherent difficulty for reformers) the mass of the people, rich and poor alike, will not make efforts, and as the "Times" once so admirably put it—"They preach to each other the gospel of idleness and call it the gospel of recreation".

The mass, however, is our concern. Those idle rich, who seek their stimulus in competitive expenditure; those ignorant poor, who turn to the examples of brute force for their pleasure; those destructive classes, whose delight is in slaying or eliminating space; they are all alike in being content to be "Vacant of our glorious gains, like a beast with lower pleasures, like a beast with lower pains".

OUR CHURCH AND RECREATION.

What can the clergymen and the clergy women do? It is not easy to reply, but there are some things they need not do. They need not promote monster treats, they need not mistake excitement for pleasure, and call their day's outing a "huge success," because it was accompanied by much noise and the running hither and thither of excited children; they need not use their Institutes and Schoolrooms to compete with the professional entertainer, and feel a glow of satisfaction because a low programme and a low price resulted in a full room; they need not accept the people's standard for songs and recitations, and think they have "had a capital evening," when the third-rate song is clapped, or the comic reading or dramatic scene appreciated by vulgar minds. Oh! the waste of curates' time and brain in such "parish work". How often it has left me mourning.

What the clergymen and women can do is to show the people that they have other powers within them for enjoyment, that effort promotes pleasure, and that the use of limbs, with (not instead of) brains, and of imagination, can be made sources of joy for themselves and refreshment for others. Too often, toys, playthings, or appliances of one sort or another are considered necessary for pleasure both of the young and the mature. Might we not concentrate efforts to provide recreation on those methods which show how people can enjoy *themselves*, their own powers and capacities? Such powers need cultivation as much as the powers of bread-winning, and they include observation and criticism. "What did you think of it?" should be asked more frequently than "How did you like it?" The curiosity of children (so often wearying to their elders) is a natural quality which might be directed to observation of the wonders of Nature, and to the conclusion of a story other than its author conceived.

"From change to change unceasingly, the soul's wings never furled," wrote Browning; and change brings food and growth to the soul; but the limits of interest must be extended to allow of the flight of the soul, and interests are often, in all classes, woefully restricted. It is no change for a blind man to be taken to a new view. Christ had to open the eyes of the blind before they could see God's fair world, and in a lesser degree we may open the eyes of the born blind to see the hidden glories lying unimagined in man and Nature. In friendship also there are sources of recreation which the clergy could do much to foster and strengthen, and the introduction and opportunities which allow of the cultivation of friendship between persons of all classes with a common interest, is peculiarly one which parsons have opportunities to develop.

And last but not least, there are the joys which come from the cultivation of a garden—joys which continue all the year round, and which can be shared by every member of the family of every age. These might be more widely spread in town as well as country. Municipalities, Boards of Guardians, School Managers, and private owners often have both the control of people and land. If the Church would influence them, more children and more grown-ups might get health and pleasure on the land. I must not entrench on the subject of Garden Cities and Garden Suburbs—but the two subjects can be linked together, inasmuch as the purest, deepest, and most recreative of pleasures can be found in the gardens which are the distinctive feature of the new cities and suburbs.

THE CLERGY AND THE PRESS.

If the clergy knew more of the people's pleasures they would yearn more over their erring flocks and talk more on present-day subjects. Take horse-racing for instance, who can defend it? Who can find one good result of it, and its incalculable evils of betting, lying, cheating, drinking? Yet the clergy are strangely loth to condemn it! Is it because King Edward VII (God bless him for his love of peace) encourages the Turf? The King has again and again shown his care for his people's good, and maybe he would modify his actions—and the world would follow his lead—if the Church would speak out and condemn this baneful national pleasure.

It is not for me to preach to the clergy, but they have so often preached to me to my edification, that I would in gratitude give them in return an exhortation; and so I beg you good men to give more thought to the people's pleasures; and then give guidance from the Pulpit and the Press concerning them.

HENRIETTA O. BARNETT.

SECTION III.

SETTLEMENTS.

Settlements of University Men in Great Towns—Twenty-one Years of University Settlements—The Beginning of Toynbee Hall.

SETTLEMENTS OF UNIVERSITY MEN IN GREAT TOWNS.[1]

BY CANON BARNETT.

1 A paper read at a meeting in the rooms of Mr. Sidney Ball at St. John's College, Oxford, November, 1883.

"SOMETHING must be done" is the comment which follows the tale of how the poor live. Those who make the comment have, however, their business—their pieces of ground to see, their oxen to prove, their wives to consider, and so there is among them a general agreement that the "Something" must be done by Law or by Societies. "What can I do?" is a more healthy comment, and it is a sign of the times that this question is being widely asked, and by none more eagerly than by members of the Universities. Undergraduates and graduates, long before the late outcry, had become conscious that social conditions were not right, and that they themselves were called to do something. It is nine years since four or five Oxford undergraduates chose to spend part of their vacation in East London, working as Charity Organization Agents, becoming members of clubs, and teaching in classes or schools. It is long since a well-known Oxford man said, "The great work of our time is to connect centres of learning with centres of industry". Freshmen have become fellows, since the Master of Balliol recommended his hearers, at a small meeting in the College Hall, to "find their friends among the poor".

Thus slowly has men's attention been drawn to consider the social condition of our great towns. The revelations of recent pamphlets have fallen on ears prepared to hear. The fact that the wealth *of* England means only wealth *in* England, and that the mass of the people live without knowledge, without hope, and often without health has come home to open minds and consciences. If inquiry has shown that statements have been exaggerated, and the blame badly directed, it is nevertheless evident that the best is the privilege of the few, and that the Gospel—God's message to this age—does not reach the poor. A workman's wages cannot procure for him the knowledge which means fullness of life, or the leisure in which he might "possess his soul". Hardly by saving can he lay up for old age, and only by charity can he get the care of a skilled physician. If it be thus with the first-class workman, the case of the casual labourer, whose strength of mind and body is consumed by anxiety, must be almost intolerable. Statistics, which show the number in receipt of poor relief, the families which occupy single rooms, the death rate in poor quarters, make a "cry" which it needs no words to express.

The thought of the condition of the people has made a strange stirring in the calm life of the Universities, and many men feel themselves driven by a new spirit, possessed by a master idea. They are eager in their talk and in their inquiries, and they ask "What can we do to help the poor?"

A College Mission naturally suggests itself as a form in which the idea should take shape. It seems as if all the members of a college might unite in helping the poor, by adopting a district in a great town, finding for it a clergyman and associating themselves in his work.

A Mission, however, has necessarily its limitations.

The clergyman begins with a hall into which he gathers a congregation, and which he uses as a centre for "Mission" work. He himself is the only link between the college and the poor. He gives frequent reports of his progress, and enlists such personal help as he can, always keeping it in mind that the "district" is destined to become a "parish". Many districts thus created in East London now take their places among the regular parishes, and the income of the clergyman is paid by the Ecclesiastical Commissioners, the patronage of the living is probably with the Bishop, and the old connexion has become simply a matter of history. Apart from the doubt whether this multiplication of parochial organizations, with its consequent division of interests, represents a wise policy, it is obvious that a college mission does not wholly cover the idea which possessed the college. The social spirit fulfils itself in many ways, and no one form is adequate to its total expression.

The idea was that all members of the college should unite in good work. A college mission excludes Nonconformists. "Can we do nothing," complained one, "as we cannot join in building a church?"

The idea was to bring to bear the life of the University on the life of the poor. The tendency of a mission is to limit efforts within the recognized parochial machinery. "Can I help," I am often asked, "in social work, which is not necessarily connected with your church or creed?" A college mission may—as many missions have done—result in bringing devoted workers to the service of the poor—where a good man leads, good must follow—but it is not, I think, the form best fitted to receive the spirit which is at present moving the Universities.

As a form more adequate, I would suggest a Settlement of University men in the midst of some great industrial centre.

In East London large houses are often to be found; they were formerly the residences of the wealthy, but are now let out in tenements or as warehouses. Such a house, affording sufficient sleeping rooms and large reception rooms, might be taken by a college, fitted with furniture, and (it may be) associated with its name. As director or head, some graduate might be appointed, a man of the right spirit, trusted by all parties; qualified by character to guide men, and by education to teach. He would be maintained by the college just as the clergyman of the mission district. Around such a man graduates and undergraduates would gather. Some working in London as curates, barristers, government clerks, medical students, or business men would be glad to make their home in the house for long periods. They would find there less distraction and more interest than in a West-End lodging. Others engaged elsewhere would come to spend some weeks or months of the vacation, taking up such work as was possible, touching with their lives the lives of the poor, and learning for themselves facts which would revolutionize their minds. There would be, of course, a graduated scale of payment so as to suit the means of the various settlers, but the scale would have to be so fixed as to cover the expense of board and lodging.

Let it, however, be assumed that the details have been arranged, and that, under a wise director, a party of University men have settled in East London. The director—welcomed here, as University men are always welcomed—will have opened relations with the neighbouring clergy, and with the various charitable agencies; he will have found out the clubs and centres of social life, and he will have got some knowledge of the bodies engaged in local government. His large rooms will have been offered for classes, directed by the University Extension or Popular Concert Societies, and for meetings of instruction or entertainment. He will have thus won the reputation of a man with something to give, who is willing to be friendly with his neighbours. At once he will be able to introduce the settlers to duties, which will mean introductions to friendships. Those to whom it is given to know the high things of God, he will introduce to the clergy, who will guide them to find friends among those who, in trouble and sickness, will listen to a life-giving message. Honour men have confessed that they have found a key to life in teaching the Bible to children, and not once nor twice has it happened that old truths have seemed to take new meaning when spoken by a man brought fresh from Oxford to face the poor. Those with the passion for righteousness the director will bring face to face with the victims of sin. In the degraded quarters of the town, in the wards of the workhouses, they will find those to whom the friendship of the pure is strange, and who are to be saved only by the mercy which can be angry as well as pitiful. As I write, I recall one who was brought to us by an undergraduate out of a wretched court, overwhelmed by the look and words of his young enthusiasm. I recall another who was taken from the police court by a Cambridge man, put to an Industrial School, and is now touchingly grateful, not to him, but to God for the service. Some, whose spare time is in the day, will become visitors for the Charity Organization Society, Managers of Industrial and Public Elementary Schools, Members of the Committees which direct Sanitary, Shoe Black, and other Societies, and in these positions form friendships, which to officials, weary of the dull routine, will let in light, and to the poor, fearful of law, will give strength. Others who can spare time only in the evening will teach classes, join clubs, and assist in Co-operative and Friendly Societies, and they will, perhaps, be surprised to find that they know so much that is useful when they see the interest their talk arouses. In one club, I know, whist ceases to be attractive when the gentleman is not there to talk. There are friendly societies worked by artisans, which owe their success to the inspiration of University men, and there is one branch of the Charity Organization Society which still keeps the mark impressed on it, when a man of culture did the lowest work.

The elder settlers will, perhaps, take up official positions. If they could be qualified, they might be Vestry-men and Guardians, or they might qualify themselves to become Schoolmasters. What University men can do in local government is written on the face of parishes redeemed from the demoralizing influence of out-relief, and cleansed by well-administered law. Further reforms are already seen to be near, but it has not entered into men's imaginations to conceive the change for good which might be wrought if men of culture would undertake the education of the people. The younger settlers will always find occupation day or night in playing with the boys, taking them in the daytime to open spaces, or to visit London sights, amusing them in the evening with games and songs. Unconsciously, they will set up a higher standard of man's life, and through friendship will commend to these boys respect for manhood, honour for womanhood, reverence for God. Work of such kind will be abundant, and, as it must result in the settlers forming many acquaintances, the large rooms of the house will be much used for receptions. Parties will be frequent, and whatever be the form of entertainment provided, be it books or pictures, lectures or reading, dancing or music, the guests will find that their pleasure lies in intercourse. Social pleasure is unknown to those who have no large rooms and no place for common meeting. The parties of the Settlement will thus be attractive just in so far as they are useful. The more means of intercourse they offer, the more will they be appreciated. The pleasure which binds all together will give force to every method of good-doing, be it the words of the preacher, spoken to the crowd, hushed, perhaps, by the presence of death, or be it the laughter-making tale told during the Saturday ramble in the country.

If something like this is to be the work of a College Settlement, "How far," it may be asked, "is it adequate to the hope of the college to do something for the poor?" Obviously, it *affords an outlet for every form of earnestness*. No man—call himself what he may—need be excluded from the service of the poor on account of his views. No talent, be it called spiritual or secular, need be lost on account of its unfitness to existing machinery. If there be any virtue, if there be any good in man, whatsoever is beautiful, whatsoever is pure in things will find a place in the Settlement.

There is yet a fuller answer to the question. A Settlement enables men to *live within sight of the poor*. Many a young man would be saved from selfishness if he were allowed at once to translate feeling into action. It is the facility for talk, and the ready suggestion that a money gift is the best relief, which makes some dread lest, after this awakening of interest, there may follow a deeper sleep. He who has, even for a month, shared the life of the poor can never again rest in his old thoughts. If with these obvious advantages, a Settlement seems to want that something which association with religious forms gives to the mission, I can only say that such association does not make work religious, if the workers have not its spirit. If the director be such a man as I can imagine, and if there be any truth in the saying that "Every one that loveth knoweth God," then it must be that the work of settlers, inspired and guided by love, will be religious. The man in East London, who is the simplest worker for God I know, has added members to many churches, and has no sect or church of his own. The true religious teacher is he who makes known God to man. God is manifest to every age by that which is the Best of the age. The modern representatives of those who healed diseases, taught the ignorant, and preached the Gospel to the poor, are those who make common the Best which can be known or imagined. Christ the Son of God is still the "Christ which is to be"—and even through our Best He will be but darkly seen.

That such work as I have described would be useful in East London, I myself have no doubt. The needs of East London are often urged, but they are little understood. Its inhabitants are at one moment assumed to be well paid workmen, who will get on if they are left to themselves; at another, they are assumed to be outcasts, starving for the necessaries of living. It is impossible but that misunderstanding should follow ignorance, and at the present moment the West-End is ignorant of the East-End. The want of that knowledge which comes only from the sight of others' daily life, and from sympathy with "the joys and sorrows in widest commonalty spread," is the source of the mistaken charity which has done much to increase the hardness of the life of the poor.

The much-talked of East London is made up of miles of mean streets, whose inhabitants are in no want of bread or even of better houses; here and there are the courts now made familiar by descriptions. They are few in number, and West-End visitors who have come to visit their "neighbours" confess themselves—with a strange irony on their motives—"disappointed that the people don't look worse".

The settlers will find themselves related to two distinct classes of "the poor," and it will be well if they keep in mind the fact that they must serve both those who, like the artisans, need the necessaries for *life*, and also those who, like casual labourers, need the necessaries for *livelihood*. They will not of course come believing that their Settlement will make the wicked good, the dull glad, and the poor rich, but they may be assured that results will follow the sympathy born of close neighbourhood. It will be something, if they are able to give to a few the higher thoughts in which men's minds can move, to suggest other forms of recreation, and to open a view over the course of the river of life as it flows to the Infinite Sea. It will be something if they create among a few a distaste for dirt and disorder, if they make some discontented with their degrading conditions, if they leaven public opinion with the belief that the law which provides cleanliness, light and order should be applied equally in all quarters of the town. It will be something, if thus they give to the one class the ideal of life, and stir up in the other those feelings of self-respect, without which increased means of livelihood will be useless. It will be more if to both classes they can show that selfishness or sin is the only really bad thing, and that the best is not "too good for human nature's daily food". Nothing that is divine is alien to man, and nothing which can be learnt at the University is too good for East London.

Many have been the schemes of reform I have known, but, out of eleven years' experience, I would say that none touches the root of the evil which does not *bring helper and helped into friendly relations*. Vain will be higher education, music, art, or even the Gospel, unless they come clothed in the life of brother men—"it took the Life to make God known". Vain, too, will be sanitary legislation and model dwellings, unless the outcast are by friendly hands brought in one by one to habits of cleanliness and order, to thoughts of righteousness and peace. "What will save East London?" asked one of our University visitors of his master. "The destruction of West London" was the answer, and, in so far as he meant the abolition of the influences which divide rich and poor, the answer was right. Not until the habits of the rich are changed, and they are again content to breathe the same air and walk the same streets as the poor, will East London be "saved". Meantime a Settlement of University men will do a little to remove the inequalities of life, as the settlers share their best with the poor and learn through feeling how they live. It was by residence among the poor that Edward Denison learned the lessons which have taken shape in the new philanthropy of our days. It was by visiting in East London that Arnold Toynbee fed the interest which in later years became such a force at Oxford. It was around a University man, who chose to live as our neighbour, that a group of East Londoners gathered, attracted by the hope of learning something and held together after five years by the joy which learning gives. Men like Mr. Goschen and Professor Huxley have lately spoken out their belief that the intercourse of the highest with the lowest is the only solution of the social problem.

Settlers may thus join the Settlement, looking back to the example of others and to the opinions of the wise—looking forward to the grandest future which has risen on the horizon of hope. It may not be theirs to see the future realized, but it is theirs to cheer themselves with the thought of the time when the disinherited sons of God shall be received into their Father's house, when the poor will know the Higher Life as it is being revealed to those who watch by the never silent spirit, when daily drudgery will be irradiated with eternal thought, when neither wealth nor poverty will hinder men in their pursuit of the Perfect life, because everything which is Best will be made in love common to all.

SAMUEL A. BARNETT.

This paper was reprinted in February, 1884, when the following words and names were added.

The following members of the University have undertaken to receive the names of any graduates or undergraduates who feel disposed to join a "Settlement" shortly or at any future time:—

    The Rev. the Master of University.
The Hon. and Rev. W. H. Fremantle, Balliol.
A. Robinson, Esq., New College.
A. H. D. Acland, Esq., Christ Church.
A. Sidgwick, Esq., C.C.C.
W. H. Forbes, Esq., Balliol.
A. L. Smith, Esq., Balliol.
T. H. Warren, Esq., Magdalen.
S. Ball, Esq., St. John's.
C. E. Dawkins, Esq., Balliol.
B. King, Esq., Balliol.
M. E. Sadler, Esq., Trinity.
H. D. Leigh, Esq., New College.
G. C. Lang, Esq., Balliol.

Names should be sent in as soon as possible.

OXFORD, Feb., 1884.

THE BEGINNINGS OF TOYNBEE HALL.[1]

BY MRS. S. A. BARNETT.

1903.

[1] From "Towards Social Reform". By kind permission of Messrs. Fisher Unwin.

"HOW did the idea of a University Settlement arise?" "What was the beginning?" are questions so often asked by Americans, Frenchmen, Belgians, or the younger generations of earnest English people, that it seems worth while to reply in print, and to trundle one's mind back to those early days of effort and loneliness before so many bore the burden and shared the anxiety. The fear is that in putting pen to paper on matters which are so closely bound up with our own lives, the sin of egotism will be committed, or that a special plant, which is still growing, may be damaged, as even weeds are if their roots are looked at. And yet in the tale which has to be told there is so much that is gladdening and strengthening to those who are fighting apparently forlorn causes that I venture to tell it in the belief that to some our experiences will give hope.

In the year 1869, Mr. Edward Denison took up his abode in East London. He did not stay long nor accomplish much, but as he breathed the air of the people he absorbed something of their sufferings, saw things from their standpoint, and, as his letters in his memoirs show, made frequent suggestions for social remedies. He was the first settler, and was followed by the late Mr. Edmund Hollond, to whom my husband and I owe our life in Whitechapel. He was ever on the outlook for men and women who cared for the people, and hearing that we wished to come Eastward, wrote to Dr. Jackson, then Bishop of London, when the living of St. Jude's fell vacant in the autumn of 1872, and asked that it might be offered to Mr. Barnett, who was at that time working as Curate at St. Mary's, Bryanston Square, with Mr. Fremantle, now the Dean of Ripon. I have the Bishop's letter, wise, kind and fatherly, the letter of a general sending a young captain to a difficult outpost. "Do not hurry in your decision," he wrote, "it is the worst parish in my diocese, inhabited mainly by a criminal population, and one which has I fear been much corrupted by doles".

How well I remember the day Mr. Barnett and I first came to see it!—a sulky sort of drizzle filled the atmosphere; the streets, dirty and ill kept, were crowded with vicious and bedraggled people, neglected children, and overdriven cattle. The whole parish was a network of courts and alleys, many houses being let out in furnished rooms at 8d. a night—a bad system, which lent itself to every form of evil, to thriftless habits, to untidiness, to loss of self-respect, to unruly living, to vicious courses.

We did not "hurry in our decision," but just before Christmas, 1872, Mr. Barnett became vicar. A month later we were married, and took up our life-work on 6 March, 1873, accompanied by our friend Edward Leonard, who joined us, "to do what he could"; his "could" being ultimately the establishment of the Whitechapel Committee of the Charity Organization Society, and a change in the lives and ideals of a large number of young people, whom he gathered round him to hear of the Christ he worshipped.

It would sound like exaggeration if I told my memories of those times. The previous vicar had had a long and disabling illness, and all was out of order. The church, unserved by either curate, choir, or officials, was empty, dirty, unwarmed. Once the platform of popular preachers, Mr. Hugh Allen, and Mr. (now Bishop) Thornton, it had had huge galleries built to accommodate the crowds who came from all parts of London to hear them—galleries which blocked the light, and made the subsequent emptiness additionally oppressive. The schools were closed, the schoolrooms all but devoid of furniture, the parish organization nil; no Mothers' meeting, no Sunday School, no communicants' class, no library, no guilds, no music, no classes, nothing alive. Around this barren empty shell surged the people, here to-day, gone to-morrow. Thieves and worse, receivers of stolen goods, hawkers, casual dock labourers, every sort of unskilled low-class cadger congregated in the parish. There was an Irish quarter and a Jews' quarter, while whole streets were given over to the hangers-on of a vicious population, people whose conduct was brutal, whose ideal was idleness, whose habits were disgusting, and among whom goodness was laughed at, the honest man and the right-living woman being scorned as impracticable. Robberies, assaults, and fights in the street were frequent; and to me, a born coward, it grew into a matter of distress when we became sufficiently well known in the parish for our presence to stop, or at least to moderate, a fight; for then it seemed a duty to join the crowd, and not to follow one's nervous instincts and pass by on the other side. I recall one breakfast being disturbed by three fights outside the Vicarage. We each went to one, and the third was hindered by a hawker friend who had turned verger, and who fetched the distant policeman, though he evidently remained doubtful as to the value of interference.

We began our work very quietly and simply: opened the church (the first congregation was made up of six or seven old women, all expecting doles for coming), restarted the schools, established relief committees, organized parish machinery, and tried to cauterise, if not to cure, the deep cancer of dependence which was embedded in all our parishioners alike, lowering the best among them and degrading the worst. At all hours, and on all days, and with every possible pretext, the people came and begged. To them we were nothing but the source from which to obtain tickets, money, or food; and so confident were they that help would be forthcoming that they would allow themselves to get into circumstances of suffering or distress easily foreseen, and then send round and demand assistance.

I can still recall my emotions when summoned to a sick woman in Castle Alley, an alley long since pulled down, where the houses, three stories high, were hardly six feet apart; the sanitary accommodation—pits in the cellars; and the whole place only fit for the condemnation it got directly Cross's Act was passed. This alley, by the way, was in part the cause of Cross's Act, so great an impression did it make on Lord Cross (then Mr. Cross) when Mr. Barnett induced him to come down and see it.

In this stinking alley, in a tiny dirty room, all the windows broken and stuffed up, lay the woman who had sent for me. There were no bedclothes; she lay on a sacking covered with rags.

"I do not know you," said I, "but I hear you want to see me."

"No, ma'am!" replied a fat beer-sodden woman by the side of the bed, producing a wee, new-born baby; "we don't know yer, but 'ere's the babby, and in course she wants clothes, and the mother comforts like. So we jist sent round to the church."

This was a compliment to the organization which represented Christ, but one which showed how sunken was the character which could not make even the simplest provision for an event which must have been expected for months, and which even the poorest among the respectable counts sacred.

The refusal of the demanded doles made the people very angry. Once the Vicarage windows were broken, once we were stoned by an angry crowd, who also hurled curses at us as we walked down a criminal-haunted street, and howled out as a climax to their wrongs "And it's us as pays 'em". But we lived all this down, and as the years went by reaped a harvest of love and gratitude which is one of the gladdest possessions of our lives, and is quite disproportionate to the service we have rendered. But this is the end of the story, and I must go back to the beginning.

In a parish which occupies only a few acres, and was inhabited by 8,000 persons, we were confronted by some of the hardest problems of city life. The housing of the people, the superfluity of unskilled labour, the enforcement of resented education, the liberty of the criminal classes to congregate and create a low public opinion, the administration of the Poor Law, the amusement of the ignorant, the hindrances to local government (in a neighbourhood devoid of the leisured and cultured), the difficulty of uniting the unskilled men and women, in trade unions, the necessity for stricter Factory Acts, the joylessness of the masses, the hopefulness of the young—all represented difficult problems, each waiting for a solution and made more complicated by the apathy of the poor, who were content with an unrighteous contentment and patient with an ungodly patience. These were not the questions to be replied to by doles, nor could the problem be solved by kind acts to individuals nor by the healing of the suffering, which was but the symptom of the disease.

In those days these difficulties were being dealt with mainly by good kind women, generally elderly; few men, with the exception of the clergy and noted philanthropists, as Lord Shaftesbury, were interested in the welfare of the poor, and economists rarely joined close experience with their theories.

"If men, cultivated, young, thinking men, could only know of these things they would be altered," I used to say, with girlish faith in human goodwill—a faith which years has not shaken; and in the spring of 1875 we went to Oxford, partly to tell about the poor, partly to enjoy "eights week" with a group of young friends. Our party was planned by Miss Toynbee, whom I had met when at school, and whose brother Arnold was then an undergraduate at Pembroke. Our days were filled with the hospitality with which Oxford still rejoices its guests; but in the evenings we used to drop quietly down the river with two or three earnest men, or sit long and late in our lodgings in the Turl, and discuss the mighty problems of poverty and the people.

How vividly Canon Barnett and I can recall each and all of the first group of "thinking men," so ready to take up enthusiasms in their boyish strength—Arnold Toynbee, Sidney Ball, W. H. Forbes, Arthur Hoare, Leonard Montefiore, Alfred Milner, Philip Gell, John Falk, G. E. Underhill, Ralph Whitehead, Lewis Nettleship! Some of these are still here, and caring for our people, but others have passed behind the veil, where perhaps earth's sufferings are explicable.

We used to ask each undergraduate as he developed interest to come and stay in Whitechapel, and see for himself. And they came, some to spend a few weeks, some for the Long Vacation, while others, as they left the University and began their life's work, took lodgings in East London, and felt all the fascination of its strong pulse of life, hearing, as those who listen always may, the hushed, unceasing moans underlying the cry which ever and anon makes itself heard by an unheeding public.

From that first visit to Oxford in the "eights week" of 1875, date many visits to both the Universities. Rarely a term passed without our going to

Oxford, where the men who had been down to East London introduced us to others who might do as they had done. Sometimes we stayed with Dr. Jowett, the immortal Master of Balliol, sometimes we were the guests of the undergraduates, who would get up meetings in their rooms, and organize innumerable breakfasts, teas, river excursions, and other opportunities for introducing the subject of the duty of the cultured to the poor and degraded.

No organization was started, no committee, no society, no club formed. We met men, told them of the needs of the out-of-sight poor; and many came to see Whitechapel and stayed to help it. And so eight years went by—our Oxford friends laughingly calling my husband the "unpaid professor of social philosophy".

In June, 1883, we were told by Mr. Moore Smith that some men at St. John's College at Cambridge were wishful to do something for the poor, but that they were not quite prepared to start an ordinary College Mission. Mr. Barnett was asked to suggest some other possible and more excellent way. The letter came as we were leaving for Oxford, and was slipped with others in my husband's pocket. Soon something went wrong with the engine and delayed the train so long that the passengers were allowed to get out. We seated ourselves on the railway bank, just then glorified by masses of large ox-eyed daisies, and there he wrote a letter suggesting that men might hire a house, where they could come for short or long periods, and, living in an industrial quarter, learn to "sup sorrow with the poor". The letter pointed out that close personal knowledge of individuals among the poor must precede wise legislation for remedying their needs, and that as English local government was based on the assumption of a leisured cultivated class, it was necessary to provide it artificially in those regions where the line of leisure was drawn just above sleeping hours, and where the education ended at thirteen years of age and with the three R's.

That letter founded Toynbee Hall. Insomnia had sapped my health for a long time, and later, in the autumn of that year, we were sent to Eaux Bonnes to try a water-cure. During that period the Cambridge letter was expanded into a paper, which was read at a college meeting at St. John's College, Oxford, in November of the same year. Mr. Arthur Sidgwick was present, and it is largely due to his practical vigour that the idea of University Settlements in the industrial working-class quarters of large towns fell not only on sympathetic ears, but was guided until it came to fruition. The first meeting of undergraduates met in the room of Mr. Cosmo Lang now (1908), about to become Archbishop of York. Soon after the meeting a small but earnest committee was formed; later on the committee grew in size and importance, money was obtained on debenture bonds, and a Head sought who would turn the idea into a fact. Here was the difficulty. Such men as had been pictured in the paper which Mr. Knowles had published in the "Nineteenth Century Review" of February, 1884, are not met with every-day; and no inquiries seemed to discover the wanted man who would be called upon to give all and expect nothing.

Mr. Barnett and I had spent eleven years of life and work in Whitechapel. We were weary. My health stores were limited and often exhausted, and family circumstances had given us larger means and opportunities for travel. We were therefore desirous to turn our backs on the strain, the pain, the passion and the poverty of East London, at least for a year or two, and take repose after work which had aged and weakened us. But no other man was to be found who would and could do the work; and, if this child-thought was not to die, it looked as if we must undertake to try and rear it.

We went to the Mediterranean to consider the matter, and solemnly, on a Sunday morning, made our decision. How well I recall the scene as we sat at the end of the quaint harbour-pier at Mentone, the blue waves dancing at our feet, everything around scintillating with light and movement in contrast to the dull and dulling squalor of the neighbourhood which had been our home for eleven years, and which our new decision would make our home for another indefinite spell of labour and effort. "God help us," we said to each other; and then we wired home to obtain the refusal of the big Industrial School next to St. Jude's Vicarage, which had recently been vacated, and which we thought to be a good site for the first Settlement, and returned to try and live up to the standard which we had unwittingly set for ourselves in describing in the article the unknown man who was wanted for Warden.

The rest of the story is soon told. The Committee did the work, bought the land, engaged the architect (Mr. Elijah Hoole), raised the money, and interested more and more men, who came for varying periods, either to live, to visit, or to see what was being done.

On 10 March, 1883, Arnold Toynbee had died. He had been our beloved and faithful friend, ever since, as a lad of eighteen, his own mind then being chiefly concerned with military interests and ideals, he had heard, with the close interest of one treading untrodden paths, facts about the toiling, ignorant multitude whose lives were stunted by labour, clouded by poverty, and degraded by ignorance. He had frequently been to see us at St. Jude's, staying sometimes a few nights, oftener tempting us to go a day or two with him into the country; and ever wooing us with persistent hospitality to Oxford. Once in 1879 he had taken rooms over the Charity Organization Office in Commercial Road, hoping to spend part of the

Long Vacation, learning of the people; but his health, often weakly, could not stand the noise of the traffic, the sullenness of the aspect, nor the pain which stands waiting at every corner; and at the end of some two or three weeks he gave up the plan and left East London, never to return except as our welcome guest. His share of the movement was at Oxford, where with a subtle force of personality he attracted original or earnest minds of all degrees, and turned their thoughts or faces towards the East End and its problems. Through him many men came to work with us, while others were stirred by the meetings held in Oxford, or by the pamphlet called the "Bitter Cry," which, in spite of its exaggerations, aroused many to think of the poor; or by the stimulating teaching of Professor T. H. Green, and by the constant, kindly sympathy of the late Master of Balliol, who startled some of his hearers, who had not plumbed the depths of his wide, wise sympathy, by advising all young men, whatever their career, "to make some of their friends among the poor".

The 10th of March, 1884, was a Sunday, and on the afternoon of that day Balliol Chapel was filled with a splendid body of men who had come together from all parts of England in loving memory of Arnold Toynbee, on the anniversary of his death. Dr. Jowett had asked my husband to preach to them, and they listened, separating almost silently at the chapel porch, filled, one could almost feel, by the aspiration to copy him in caring much, if not doing much, for those who had fallen by the way or were "vacant of our glorious gains".

We had often chatted, those of us who were busy planning the new Settlement, as to what to call it. We did not mean the name to be descriptive; it should, we thought, be free from every possible savour of a Mission, and yet it should in itself be suggestive of a noble aim. As I sat on that Sunday afternoon in the chapel, one of the few women among the crowd of strong-brained, clean-living men assembled in reverent affection for one man, the thought flashed to me, "Let us call the Settlement Toynbee Hall". To Mr. Bolton King, the honorary secretary of the committee, had come the same idea, and it, finding favour with the committee, was so decided, and our new Settlement received its name before a brick was laid or the plans concluded.

On the first day of July, 1884, the workmen began to pull down the old Industrial School, and to adapt such of it as was possible for the new uses; and on Christmas Eve, 1884, the first settlers, Mr. H. D. Leigh, of Corpus, and Mr. C. H. Grinling, of Hertford, slept in Toynbee Hall, quickly followed by thirteen residents, some of whom had been living in the neighbourhood of Whitechapel, some for a considerable length of time, either singly or in groups, one party inhabiting a small disused public-house, others in model dwellings or in lodgings, none of them being altogether suitable for their own good or the needs of those whom they would serve. Those men had become settlers before the Settlement scheme was conceived, and as such were conversant with the questions in the air. It was an advantage also, that they were of different ages, friends of more than one University generation, and linked together by a common friendship to us.

The present Dean of Ripon had for many years lent his house at No. 3, Ship Street, for our use, and so had enabled us to spend some consecutive weeks of each summer at Oxford; and during those years we had learnt to know the flower of the University, counting, as boy friends, some men who have since become world-widely known; some who have done the finest work and "scorned to blot it with a name"; and others who, as civil servants, lawyers, doctors, country gentlemen, business men, have in the more humdrum walks of life carried into practice the same spirit of thoughtful sympathy which first brought them to inquire concerning those less endowed and deprived of life's joys, or those who, handicapped by birth, training, and environment, had fallen by the way.

As to what Toynbee Hall has done and now is doing, it is difficult for any one, and impossible for me, to speak. Perhaps I cannot be expected to see the wood for the trees. Those who have cared to come and see for themselves what is being done, to stay in the house and join in its work, know that Toynbee Hall, Whitechapel, is a place where twenty University men live in order to work for, to teach, to learn of the poor. Since 1884 the succession of residents has never failed. Men of varied opinions and many views, both political and religious, have lived harmoniously together, some staying as long as fifteen years, others remaining shorter periods. All have left behind them marks of their residence; sometimes in the policy of the local Boards, of which they have become members; or in relation to the Student Residences; or the Antiquarian, Natural History, or Travelling Clubs which individuals among them have founded; or by busying themselves with classes, debates, conferences, discussions. Their activities have been unceasing and manifold, but looking over many years and many men it seems to my inferior womanly mind that the best work has been done by those men who have cared most deeply for individuals among the poor. Out of such deep care has grown intimate knowledge of their lives and industrial position, and from knowledge has come improvement in laws, conditions, or administration. It is such care that has awakened in the people the desire to seek what is best. It is the care of those, who, loving God, have taught others to know Him. It is the care of those who, pursuing knowledge and rejoicing in learning, have spread it among the ignorant more effectively than books, classes or lectures could have done. It is the care for the degraded which alone rouses them to care for themselves. It is the care for the sickly, the weak, the oppressed, the rich, the powerful, the happy, the teacher and taught, the employed and the employer, which enables introduction to be made and interpretation of each other to be offered and accepted. From this seed of deep individual care has grown a large crop of friendship, and many flowers of graceful acts.

It is the duty of Toynbee Hall, situated as it is at the gate of East London, to play the part of a skilful host and introduce the East to the West; but all the guests must be intimate friends, or there will be social blunders. To quote some words out of a report, Toynbee Hall is "an association of persons, with different opinions and different tastes; its unity is that of variety; its methods are spiritual rather than material; it aims at permeation rather than conversion; and its trust is in friends linked to friends rather than in organization". . . .

It was a crowded meeting of the Universities Settlements Association that was held in Balliol Hall in March, 1892, it being known that Dr. Jowett, who had recently been dangerously ill, would take the chair. He spoke falteringly (for he was still weakly), and once there came an awful pause that paled the hearers who loved him, in fear for his well-being. He told something of his own connexion with the movement; of how he had twice stayed with us in Whitechapel, and had seen men's efforts to lift this dead weight of ignorance and pain. He referred to Arnold Toynbee, one of the "purest-minded of men," and one who "troubled himself greatly over the unequal position of mankind". He told of the force of friendship which was to him sacred, and "some of which should be offered to the poor". He dwelt on his own hopes for Toynbee Hall, and of its uses to Oxford, as well as to Whitechapel; and he spoke also of us and our work, but those words were conceived by his friendship for and his faith in us, and hardly represented the facts. They left out of sight what the Master of Balliol could only imperfectly know—the countless acts of kindness, the silent gifts of patient service, and the unobtrusive lives of many men; their reverence before weakness and poverty, their patience with misunderstanding, their faith in the power of the best, their tenderness to children and their boldness against vice. These are the foundations on which Toynbee Hall has been built, and on which it aims to raise the ideals of human life, and strengthen faith in God.

HENRIETTA O. BARNETT.

TWENTY-ONE YEARS OF UNIVERSITY SETTLEMENTS.[1]

By Canon Barnett.

June, 1905.

[1] From "The University Review". By permission of the Editor.

TWENTY-FIVE years ago many social reformers were set on bringing about a co-operation between the Universities of Oxford and Cambridge and the industrial classes. Arnold Toynbee thought he could study at Oxford during term time and lecture in great cities during the vacation. Professor Stuart thought that University teaching might be extended among working people by means of centres locally established. There were others to whom it seemed that no way could be so effective as the way of residence, and they advocated a plan by which members of the University should during some years live their lives among the poor.

Present social reformers have, however, other business on hand. They think that something practical is of first importance, some alteration in the land laws, which would make good houses more possible—some modification of the relation between labour and capital, which would spread the national wealth over a larger number of people. They see something which Parliament or the municipal bodies could do, which seems to be very good, and they are not disposed to spend time on democratizing the old Universities or on humanizing the working-man.

The present generation of reformers claim to be practical, but one who belongs to the past generation and is not without sympathy with the present, may also claim that much depends on the methods by which good objects are secured. There is truth in the saying that means are more important than ends. Many present evils are due to the means—the force, the flattery, the haste—by which good men of old time achieved their ends. "God forgive all good men" was the prayer of Charles Kingsley.

Reformers may to-day pass laws which would exalt the poor and bring down the rich, but if in the passing of such laws bitterness, anger, and uncharitableness were increased, and if, as the result, the exalted poor proved incapable of using or of enjoying their power—another giant behaving like a giant—where would be the world's gain? The important thing surely is not that the poor shall be exalted, but that rich and poor shall equally feel the joy of their being and, living together in peace and goodwill, make a society to be a blessing to all nations.

Co-operation between the Universities and working men, between knowledge and industry, might—it seemed to the reformers of old days—

make a force which would secure a reform not to be reformed, a repentance not to be repented of, a sort of progress whose means would justify its end.

The Universities have the knowledge of human things. Their professors and teachers have, in some measure, the secret of living, they know that life consists not in possessions, and that society has other bonds than force or selfishness, and they offer in their homes the best example of simple and refined living. They have studied the art of expression, and can put into words the thoughts of many hearts. They look with the eye of science over the fields of history, they appreciate tradition at its proper value, and are familiar with the mistakes which, in old times, broke up great hopes. Their minds are trained to leap from point to point in thought. They have followed the struggles of humanity towards its ideals, they know something of what is in man, and something of what he can possibly achieve.

If these national Universities, with their wealth of knowledge, felt at the same time the pressure of those problems which mean suffering to the workmen, they would be watch-towers from which watchmen would discern the signs of the times, those movements on the horizon now as small as a man's hand but soon to cover the sky. If by sympathy they felt the unrest, which all over the world is giving cause for disquietude to those in authority, they would give a form to the wants, and show to those who cry, and those who listen, the meaning of the unrest. If they were in touch with the industrial classes, they would adapt their teaching to the needs and understandings of men, struggling to secure their position in a changing industrial system, and better acquainted with facts than with theories about facts. A democratized University would be constrained to give forth the principles which underlie social progress, to show the nation what is alterable and unalterable in the structure of society—what there is for pride or for shame in its past history, what is the expenditure which makes or destroys wealth—it would be driven to help to solve the mystery of the unemployed, why there should be so much unemployment when there must be so great a demand for employment if people are to be fitly clothed and fed and housed. It would, at any rate, guide the nation to remedies which would not be worse than the disease.

"How," it was once asked of an Oxford professor, "can the University be adapted to take its place in modern progress." His answer was "By establishing in its neighbourhood a great industrial centre." The presence, that is to say, of workmen would bring the Universities to face the realities of the day, raise their policy to something more important than that of compulsory Greek, and direct their teaching to other needs than those felt by the limited class, whose children become undergraduates or listeners to an "extension lecturer". A committee of the University dons has been described as a meeting where each member is only a critic, where nothing simple or practical has a chance of adoption, and only a paradox gets attention. If labour were heard knocking at its doors, and demanding that the national knowledge, of which the Universities are the trustees, should be put at its service, the same committee would cease criticizing and begin to be practical. Knowledge without industry is often selfishness.

If Oxford and Cambridge need what workmen can give, the workmen have no less need of the Universities. Workmen have the strength of character which comes of daily contact with necessity, the discipline of labour, sympathy with the sorrow and sufferings of neighbours with whose infirmities they themselves are touched. The working classes have on their side the force of sacrifice and the power of numbers. They have the future in their hands. If they had their share of the knowledge stored in the National Universities they would know better at what to aim, what to do, and how to do it. They, as it is, are often blind and unreasoning. Blind to the things which really satisfy human nature while they eagerly follow after their husks, unable to pursue a chain of thought while they readily act on some gaudy dogma, inclined to think food the chief good, selfishness the one motive of action, and force the only remedy. The speeches of candidates for workmen's constituencies—their promises—their jokes—their appeals are the measure of the industrial mind. How would a Parliament of workmen deal with those elements which make so large a part of the nation's strength—its traditions—its literature—its natural scenery—its art? What sort of education would it foster? Would it recognize that the imagination is the joy of life and a commercial asset, that unity depends on variety, that respect and not only toleration is due to honest opponents? How would it understand the people of India or deal reverently with the intricate motives, the fears and hopes of other nations? How would workmen themselves fulfil their place in the future if well-fed, well-clothed, and well-housed, they had no other recreation than the spectacle of a football match? Industry without knowledge is often brutality.

Workmen have the energy, the honesty, the fellow feeling, the habit of sacrifice which are probably the best part of the national inheritance, but as a class they have not knowledge of human things, the delicate sense which sees what is in man—the judgment which knows the value of evidence—the feeling which would guide them to distinguish idols from ideals and set them on making a Society in which every human being shall enjoy the fullness of his being. They have not insight nor far-sight and their frequent attitude is that of suspicion. If sometimes I am asked what I desire for East London I think of all the goodness, the struggles, the suffering I have seen—the sorrows of the poor and the many fruitless remedies—and I say "more education," "higher education". People cannot really be raised by gifts or food or houses. A healthy body may be used for low as for high objects. People must raise themselves—that which raises a man like that which defiles a man comes from within a man. People therefore must have the education which will reveal to them the powers within themselves and within other men, their capacities for thinking and feeling, for admiration, hope and love. They must be made something more than instruments of production, they must be made capable of enjoying the highest things. They need therefore something more than technical teaching, it is not enough for England to be the workshop of the world, it must export thoughts and hopes as well as machines. The Tower of London would be a better defence for the nation if it were a centre of teaching, than as a barracks for soldiers. The working class movement which is so full of promise for the nation seems to me likely to fail unless it be inspired by the human knowledge which the Universities represent. Working-men without such knowledge will—to say nothing else—be always suspicious as to one another and as to the objects which they seek.

The old Universities and industry must, if this analysis be near the truth, co-operate for social reform. There are many ways to bring them together. The University extension movement might be worked by the hands of the great labour organizations—legislation might adapt the constitution of the Universities to the coming days of labour ascendancy—workmen might be brought up to graduate in colleges, and they might, as an experiment, be allowed to use existing colleges during vacations.

But the subject of this paper is the "way of Settlements". Members of the Universities, it is claimed, may for a few years settle in industrial centres, and in natural intercourse come into contact with their neighbours. There is nothing like contact for giving or getting understanding. There is no lecture and no book so effective as life. Culture spreads by contact. University men who are known as neighbours, who are met in the streets, in the clubs, and on committees, who can be visited in their own rooms, amid their own books and pictures, commend what the University stands for as it cannot otherwise be commended. On the other hand workmen who are casually and frequently met, whose idle words become familiar, whose homes are known, reveal the workman mind as it is not revealed by clever essayists or by orators of their own class. The friendship of one man of knowledge and one man of industry may go but a small way to bring together the Universities and the working classes, but it is such friendship which prepares the way for the understanding which underlies co-operation. If misunderstanding is war, understanding is peace. The men who settle may either take rooms by themselves, or they may associate themselves in a

Settlement. There is something to be said for each plan. The advantage of Settlement is that a body of University men living together keep up the distinctive characteristics of their training, they better resist the tendency to put on the universal drab, and they bring a variety into their neighbourhood. They are helped, too, by the companionship of their fellows, to take larger views of what is wanted, their enthusiasm for progress is kept alive and at the same time well pruned by friendly and severe criticism.

But whether men live in lodgings or in Settlements, there is one necessary condition besides that of social interest if they are to be successful in uniting knowledge and industry in social reform. They must live their own life. There must be no affectation of asceticism, and no consciousness of superiority. They must show forth the taste, the mind and the faith that is in them. They have not come as "missioners," they have come to settle, that is, to learn as much as to teach, to receive as much as to give.

Settlements which have been started during the last twenty years have not always fulfilled this condition. Many have become centres of missionary effort. They have often been powerful for good, and their works done by active and devoted men or women have so disturbed the water, that many unknown sick folk have been healed. They, however, are primarily missions. A Settlement in the original idea was not a mission, but a means by which University men and workmen might by natural intercourse get to understand one another, and co-operate in social reform.

There are many instances of such understanding and co-operation.

Twenty years ago primary education was much as it had been left by Mr. Lowe. Some University men living in a Settlement soon became conscious of the loss involved in the system, they talked with neighbours who by themselves were unconscious of the loss till inspired, and inspiring they formed an Education Reform League. There were committees, meetings, and public addresses. The league was a small affair, and seems to be little among the forces of the time. But every one of its proposals have been carried out. Some of its members in high official positions have wielded with effect the principles which were elaborated in the forge at which they and working men sweated together. Others of its members on local authorities or as citizens have never forgotten the inner meaning of education as they learnt it from their University friends.

Another instance may be offered. The relief of the poor is a subject on which the employing and the employed classes naturally incline to take different views. They suspect one another's remedies. The working men hate both the charity of the rich and the strict administration of the economist, while they themselves talk a somewhat impracticable socialism. University men who assist in such relief, are naturally suspected as members of the employing class. A few men, however, who as residents had become known in other relations, and were recognized as human, induced some workmen to take part in administering relief. Together they faced actual problems, together they made mistakes, together they felt sympathy with sorrow, and saw the break-down of their carefully designed action. The process went on for years, the personnel of the body of fellow-workers has changed, but there has been a gradual approach from the different points of view. The University men have more acutely realized some of the causes of distress, the need of preserving and holding up self-respect, the pressure of the industrial system, and the claim of sufferers from this system to some compensation. They have learnt through their hearts. The workmen, on the other hand, have realized the failure of mere relief to do permanent good, the importance of thought in every case, and the kindness of severity. The result of this co-operation may be traced in the fact that workmen, economists and socialists have been found advocating the same principle of relief, and now more lately in the establishment of Mr. Long's committee which is carrying those principles into effect. Far be it from me to claim that this committee is the direct outcome of the association of University and working-men, or to assert that this committee has discovered the secret of poverty, but it is certain that this committee represents the approach of two different views of relief, and that among some of its active members are workmen and University men who as neighbours in frequent intercourse learnt to respect and trust one another.

There is one other instance which is also of interest. Local Government is the corner-stone in the English Constitution. The people in their own neighbourhoods learn what self-government means, as their own Councils and Boards make them happy or unhappy. The government in industrial neighbourhoods is often bad, sometimes because the members are self-seekers, more often because they are ignorant or vainglorious. How can it be otherwise? If the industrial neighbourhood is self-contained, as for example in East London, it has few inhabitants with the necessary leisure for study or for frequent attendance at the meetings. If it is part of a larger government—as in county boroughs—it is unknown to the majority of the community. The consequence is that the neighbourhoods wanting most light and most water and most space have the least, and that bodies whose chief concern should be health and education waste their time and their rates arranging their contracts so as to support local labour. In a word, industrial neighbourhoods suffer for want of a voice to express their needs and for the want of the knowledge which can distinguish man from man, recognize the relative importance of spending and saving, and encourage mutual self-respect.

University men may and in some measure have met this want. They, by residence, have learnt the wants, and their voice has helped to bring about the more equal treatment which industrial districts are now receiving. They have often, for instance, been instrumental in getting the Libraries' Act adopted. They have as members of local bodies learnt much and taught something. They have always won the respect of their fellow-members, and if not always successful in preventing the neighbourly kindnesses which seem to them to be "jobs," or in forwarding expenditure which seems to them the best economy, they have kept up the lights along the course of public honour.

There are other examples in which results cannot be so easily traced. There have been friendships formed at clubs which have for ever changed the respective points of view affecting both taste and opinion. There have been new ideas born in discussion classes, which, beginning in special talk about some one subject, have ended in fireside confidences over the deepest subjects of life and faith. There have been common pleasures, travels, and visits in which every one has felt new interest, seeing things with other eyes, and learning that the best and most lasting amusement comes from mind activity. The University man who has a friend among the poor henceforth sees the whole class differently through that medium, and so it is with the workman who has a University man as his friend. The glory of a Settlement is not that it has spread opinions, or increased temperance, or relieved distress, but that it has promoted peace and goodwill.

But enough has been said to illustrate the point that by the way of residence the forces of knowledge and industry are brought into co-operation. The way, if long, is practicable. More men might live among the poor. The effort to do so involves the sacrifice of much which habits of luxury have marked as necessary. It involves the daring to be peculiar, which is often especially hard for the man who in the public school has learnt to support himself on school tradition.

Nothing has been said as to the effect of Settlements on Oxford and Cambridge. There does not seem to be much change in the attitude of these Universities to social reform, and they are not apparently moved by any impulse which comes from workmen. But judgment in this matter must be cautious as changes may be going on unnoticed. It is certain, at any rate, that the individual members who have lived among the poor are changed. If a greater number would live in the same way that experience could not fail ultimately to influence University life.

Social reform will soon be the all-absorbing interest as the modern realization of the claims of human nature and the growing power of the people, will not tolerate many of the present conditions of industrial life. The well-being of the future depends on the methods by which reform proceeds. Reforms in the past have often been disappointing. They have been made in the name of the rights of one class, and have ended in the assertion of rights over another class. They have been made by force and produced reaction. They have been done for the people not by the people, and have never been assimilated. The method by which knowledge and industry may co-operate has yet to be tried, and one way in which to bring about such co-operation is the way of University Settlements.

SAMUEL A. BARNETT.

SECTION IV.

POVERTY AND LABOUR.

The Ethics of the Poor Law—Poverty, its Cause and Cure—Babies of the State—Poor Law Reform—The Unemployed—The Poor Law Report—Widows under the Poor Law—The Press and Charitable Funds—What is Possible in Poor Law Reform—Charity Up To Date—What Labour wants—Our Present Discontents.

THE ETHICS OF THE POOR LAW.[1]

By Mrs. S. A. Barnett.

October, 1907.

[1] A Paper read at the Church Congress at Yarmouth.

FOR the purpose of this paper, I propose to divide the history of the Poor Laws into five divisions, and briefly to trace for 500 years the growth of thought which inspired their inception and directed their administration.

During the first period, from the reign of Richard II (1388) to that of Henry VII, such laws as were framed were mainly directed against vagrancy. There was no pretence that these enactments, which controlled the actions of the "valiant rogue" or "sturdy vagabond," were instituted for the good of the individual. It was for the protection of the community that they were framed, the recognition that a man's poverty was the result of his own fault being the root of many statutes.

Against begging severe penalties were enforced: men were forbidden to leave their own dwelling-places, and the workless wanderer met with no pity and scant justice. Later, as begging seemed but little nearer to extinction, the justices were instructed to determine definite areas in which beggars could solicit alms.

Thus was inaugurated the first effort to make each district responsible for its own poor. Persons who were caught begging outside such areas were dealt with with a severity which now seems almost incredible. For the first offence they were beaten, for the second they had their ears mutilated (so that all men could see they had thus transgressed), and for the third they were condemned to suffer "the execution of death as an enemy of the commonwealth". Later, the further sting was added, "without benefit of clergy".

Put briefly, these laws said, "Poverty demands punishment".

But men could not deny that all the dependent poor were not so by choice. In the reign of Henry VIII (1536), discrimination was made between "the poor impotent sick and diseased persons not being able to work, who may be provided for, holpen, and relieved," and "such as be lusty and able to get their living with their own hands". For the assistance of the former, the clergy were bidden to exhort their people to give offerings into their hands so that the needy should be succoured. This began what I may call the second period, when pity scattered its ideas among the leaves of the statute book. In the reign of Edward VI (the child King), the first recognition of the duty of rescuing children appears to be the subject of an Act whereby persons were "authorized to take neglected children between five and fourteen away from their parents to be brought up in honest labour". This was followed by the declaration that the neglect of parental duties was illegal, and punishments were specified for those who "do run away from their parishes and leave their families".

Put briefly, these laws said, "Poverty demands pity".

During the fifty years (1558-1603) when Elizabeth held the sceptre, important changes took place. Her realm, we read, was "exceedingly pestered" by "disorderly persons, incorrigible rogues, and sturdy beggars," while the lamentable condition of "the poor, the lame, the sick, the impotent and decayed persons" was augmented by the suppression of the monasteries and other religious organizations which had hitherto done much to assuage their sufferings. The noble band of men, whom that great woman attracted and stimulated, faced the subject as statesmen, and the epoch-making enactment of 1601 still bears fruit in our midst. Broadly, the position of the supporters in relation to the supported was considered, and for the advantage of both it was enacted that "a stock of wool, hemp, flax, iron, and other stuff" should be bought "to be wrought by those of the needy able to labour," so that they might maintain themselves. "Houses of correction" were established, to which any person refusing to labour was to be committed, where they were to be clothed "in convenient apparel meet for such a body to weare," and "to be kept straitly in diet and punished from time to time". In this Act the duty of supporting persons in "unfeigned misery" was made compulsory, power being given to tax the "froward persons" who "resisted the gentle persuasions of the justices" and "withheld of their largesse".

Thus the system of poor rating was established, and the maintenance of the needy drifted out of the hands of the Church into the hands of the State.

Neither of the motives which had ruled action in the previous centuries was disclaimed. That the idle poor deserve punishment, and that the suffering poor demand pity, were still held to be true, but to these principles was added the new one that the State was responsible for both. In order to ease the burdens of the charitable, the idle must be compelled to support themselves, and in the almost incredible event of any one who, having this world's goods, yet refused to be charitable, provision was made to compel him to contribute, so as to hinder injustice being done to the man who gave willingly.

Put briefly, these laws said, "Poverty demands scientific treatment".

During the next two centuries great strides were made in the directions indicated by each of these three principles. The right to punish persons who would not work "for the ordinary wages" was extended from that legalized in Elizabeth's time of being "openly whipped till his body was bloody," to the drastic statute of the reign of Charles II, when it became lawful to transport the beggars and rogues "to any of the English plantations beyond the seas," while the effort to create the shame of pauperism was made by the legislators of William III, who commanded that every recipient of public charity should wear "a large 'P' on the shoulder of the right sleeve of his habilement". Pity was shown to the old, for whom refuges were provided and work such as they could perform arranged; the lame were apprenticed; the lives of the illegitimate protected; the blind relieved; the children whose parents could not or would not keep them were set to work or supported; lunatics were protected; and infectious diseases recognized.

The whole gamut of the woes of civilization as they gradually came into being were brought into relation with the State, whose sphere of duty to relieve suffering or assuage the consequences of sin was ever enlarging, until, in the reign of George III, we find it including penitentiaries, and the apprenticing of lads to the King's ships. The organization to meet these needs grew apace; guardians were appointed, unions were formed, workhouses were built (the first erected at Bristol in 1697), a system of inspection was instituted, relieving officers were established, areas definitely laid down, and the function of officials prescribed. But abuses crept in, and in 1691 we find that an Act recites "that overseers, upon frivolous pretences, but chiefly for their own private ends, do give relief to what persons and number they think fit". And yet another Act was passed to enable parish authorities to be punished for paying the poor their pittances in bad coin.

Still, it is probable that out of the two principles (roughly consistent with the unwritten laws of God in nature) there would have been evolved some practicable method of State-administered relief, had it not happened that the high cost of provisions (following the war with France) and the consequent sufferings of the "industrious indigent" so moved the magistrates at the end of the eighteenth century, that in 1795 they decided to give out-relief to every labourer in proportion to the number of his family and the price of wheat, without reference to the fact of his being in or out of employment. The effect was disastrous. The rich found no call to give their charity, and the poor no call to work. The rates ate up the value of the land, and farms were left without tenants, because it became impossible to pay the rates, which often reached £1 per acre. But an even worse effect was the demoralization of society. The stimulus towards personal effort and self-control was removed, for the idle and incompetent received from the rates what their labour or character failed to provide for them; and wages were reduced because employers realized that their workmen would get relief. Drink and dissipation, deception and dependence, cheating and chicanery, became common.

Society threatened in those years to break up. It is a curious comment that a humane poor law stands out as chief amid the dissolving forces, so blind is pity if it be not instructed.

This condition of things pressed for reform, and in 1832 a Poor Law Commission was appointed, which has left an indelible mark on English life.

The Commissioners, like able physicians, diagnosed the disease, and dealt directly with its cause, prescribing for its cure remedies which may be classed under two heads:—

I.—The Principle of National Uniformity.

II.—The Principle of Less Eligibility.

The principle of national uniformity—that is, identity of treatment of each class of destitute persons from one end of the kingdom to the other—had for its purpose the reduction of the "perpetual shifting" from parish to parish, and the prevention of discontent in persons who saw the paupers of a neighbouring parish treated more leniently than themselves.

The principle of less eligibility, or, to put it in the words of the report, that "the situation of the individual relieved" shall not "be made really or apparently so eligible as the situation of the independent labourer of the lowest class," had for its purpose the restoration of the dignity of work and the steadying of the labour market.

Put briefly, the Commission said, "Poverty demands principles."

The workhouse system, with all its ramifications, has grown out of these two principles, and in its development it has, if not wholly dropped the principles, at least considerably confused them. National uniformity no longer exists, even as an ideal. Less eligibility is forgotten, as boards vie with each other to produce more costly and up-to-date institutions. Out-relief is still given, after investigation and to certain classes of applicants and under particular conditions; but the creation of the spirit of institutionalism is the main result of the 1834 commission.

And now, to-day, what do we see? An army of 602,094 paupers, some 221,531 of whom are hidden away in monster institutions. Let us face the facts, calmly realize that one person in every thirty-eight is dependent on the rates, either wholly or partially.

Where are the old, the honoured old? In their homes, teaching their grand-children reverence for age and sympathy for weakness? No; sitting in rows in the workhouse wards waiting for death, their enfeebled lives empty of interest, their uncultivated minds feeding on discontent, often made querulous or spiteful by close contact.

Where are the able-bodied who are too ignorant and undisciplined to earn their own livelihood? Are they under training, stimulated to labour by the gift of hope? No; for the most part they are in the workhouses. Have you ever seen them there? Resentment on their faces, slackness in their limbs, individuality merged in routine, kept there, often fed and housed in undue comfort, but sinking, ever sinking, below the height of their calling as human beings and Christ's brothers and sisters?

Where are the 69,080 children who at the date of the last return were wholly dependent on the State? In somebody's home? Sharing somebody's hearth? Finding their way into somebody's heart? No; 8,659 are boarded out, but 21,366 are still in workhouses and workhouse infirmaries, and 20,229 in large institutions; disciplined, taught, drilled, controlled, it is true, often with kindliness and conscientious supervision, but for the most part lacking in the music of their lives that one note of love, which alone can turn all from discord to harmony.

Where are the sick, the imbecile, the decayed, worn out with their lifelong fight with poverty? Are they adequately classified? Are the consumptive in open-air sanitoria? the imbeciles tenderly protected, while encouraged to use their feeble brains? No; they are in infirmaries, often admirably conducted, but divorced from normal life and its refreshment or stimulus, deprived of freedom, put out of sight in vast mansions; all sorts of distress often so intermingled as to aggravate disorders and embitter the sufferer's dreary days.

And yet we all know that the rates are very heavy, and that the struggling poor are cruelly handicapped to keep the idle, the old, the young, the sick. We have all read of the culpable extravagance and dishonest waste which goes on behind the high walls of the palatial institutions governed by the "guardians," who should be the guardians of the public purse as well as of the helpless poor.

The village built for the children of the Bermondsey Union has cost over £320 per bed, and last year each child kept there cost £1 0s. 6½d. per week. It is said that the porcelain baths provided for the children of the Mile End Union were priced at from £18 to £20 each, while it is stated that the cost of erecting and equipping the pauper village for the children chargeable to the Liverpool Select Vestry worked out at £330 per inmate. For England and Wales the pauper bill was in 1905 £13,851,981, or £15 13s. 3¼d. for each pauper.

And are we satisfied with what we are purchasing with the money? Is even the Socialist content with the giant workhouses—"'Omes of rest for them as is tired of working," as a tourist tram-conductor described the Brighton Workhouse? With the children's pauper villages composed of electrically-lit villa residences? With the huge barrack schools, oppressively clean and orderly, where many apparatus for domestic labour-saving are considered suitable for training girls to be workmen's wives?

Are we, as Londoners, proud to reply to the intelligent foreigner that the magnificent building occupying one of the best and most expensive sites on a main thoroughfare of West London is the "rubbish heap of humanity," where, cast among enervating surroundings, a full stop is put to any effortful progress for character building?

No; and I know I shall find an echo of that emphatic "No" in the heart of each of my hearers. We, as Christians, are *not* satisfied with the treatment of our dependent poor. The spirit of repression which was paramount before Elizabeth's time is with us still; the spirit of humanitarianism which arose in her great reign is with us still; but both have taken the form of institutionalism, and with that no one who believes in the value of the individual can be rightfully satisfied; for while the body is pampered no demands are made on the soul, no calls for achievement, for conquest of bad tendencies or idle habits.

Broadly speaking, the repression policy failed because it was not humanitarian; the humanitarian policy failed because it was not scientific; the scientific policy is failing because by institutionalism individualism is crushed out.

What is it we want? There is discontent among the thoughtful who observe; discontent among the workers who pay; discontent among the paupers who receive. But discontent is barren unless married to ideals, and they must be founded on principles. May I suggest one?

"All State relief should be educational, aiming by the strengthening of character to make the recipient independent."

If the applicant be idle, the State must develop in him an interest in work. It must, therefore, detain him perhaps for years in a workhouse or on a farm; but not to do dull and dreary labour at stone-breaking or oakum-picking. It must give him work which satisfies the human longing to make something, and opens to him the door of hope. If the applicant be ignorant and workless, it must teach him, establishing something like day industrial schools, in which the man would learn and earn, but in which he would feel no desire to stay when other work offers.

We must revive the spirit of the principle of 1834, and see that the position of the pauper be not as eligible as that of the independent workman; there must always be a centrifugal force from the centre of relief, driving the relieved to seek work; but this force need not be terror or repression. A system of training, a process of development, would be equally effective in deterring imposition. Scientific treatment of the poor need not, therefore, be inconsistent with that which is most humane.

The same principle as to the primary importance of developing character must be kept in view, though with somewhat different application, when the people to be helped are the sick, the old, and the children.

Thus the sick, by convalescent homes, by the best nursing and the most skilled attention, should be as quickly as possible made fit for work.[2]

[2] How does this harmonize with the practice of turning the lying-in mother out after fourteen days?

The children should be absorbed into the normal life of the population, and helped to forget they are paupers.[3]

[3] How does this harmonize with the practice of keeping them in barrack schools, in pauper villages?

The aged should be left in their own homes, supported by some system of State pensions, unconsciously teaching lessons of patience to those who tend them, and giving of their painfully obtained experience lessons of hope or warning.[4]

<u>4</u> How does this harmonize with the fact that there are thousands of people over sixty years of age in our State institutions? Has it ever occurred to the statistical inquirers to ascertain the death-rate of babies in relation to the absence of their grand-parents?

The revelation to this age is the law of development, and it can be seen in the laws which govern Society as well as those which govern Nature. Slowly has been evolved the knowledge of the duty of the State to its members. Repression of evil, pity for suffering, systematizing of relief; each has given place to the other, and all have left the Christian conscience ill at ease. Development of character is before us, and it is for the Church to "see visions" and to open the eyes of the blind to its ideals. What shall they be? As teachers of the reality of the spiritual life I would ask you, as clergy, first, to serve on poor-law boards, and, secondly, to consider each individual as an individual capable of development; each drunken man, each lawless woman, each feeble-minded creature, each unruly child, each plastic baby, each old crone, each desecrated body: let us place each side by side with Christ and their own possibilities, and then vote and work to give each an upward push, remembering that to allow freedom for choice and to withhold aid are often duties, for on all individual souls is laid the command to "work out their *own* salvation in fear and trembling".

Put briefly, Christians must say, "Poverty demands prayer".

HENRIETTA O. BARNETT.

POVERTY, ITS CAUSE AND ITS CURE.[1]

By Canon Barnett.

[1] A Paper read at the Summer School for the Study of Social Questions held at Hayfield, June 22nd to 29th, 1907.

POVERTY is a relative term. The citizen whose cottage home, with its bright housewife and happy children, is as light in our land, is poor in comparison with the occupant of some stately mansion. But his poverty is not an evil to be cured. It is a sign that life does not depend on possessions, and the existence of poor men alongside of rich men, each of whom lives a full human life in different circumstances, make up the society of the earthly paradise. The poverty which has to be cured is the poverty which degrades human nature, and makes impossible for the ordinary man his enjoyment of the powers and the tastes with which he was endowed at his birth. This is the poverty familiar in our streets, more familiar, we are told, than in the streets of any foreign town. This is the poverty by which men and women and children are kept from nourishment and sent out to work weak in body and open to every temptation to drink. This is the poverty which makes men slaves to work and uninterested in the magnificent drama of nature or life. This is the poverty which lets thousands of our people sink into pauperism.

What is the cause and the cure of this poverty?

The cause may be said to be the sin or the selfishness of rich and poor, and its cure to be the raising of all men to the level of Christ. The world might be as pleasant and as fruitful as Eden, but so long as some men are idle and some men are greedy, poverty and other evils are sure to invade. Man is always stronger than his environment. He may be a prisoner in the midst of pleasures, and he may prove that walls cannot a prison make. Character may thus be truly said to be the one necessary equipment for climbing the hill of life, and every remedy which is suggested for those who stumble and fall must be judged by its effect on character. The dangers of the relief which weakens self-reliance have been recognized, the kindness which removes every hindrance from the way has been seen to relax effort; but even so there is no justification for law and custom to intrude obstacles to make the way harder or to bind on life's wayfarer extra burdens.

Our subject thus presents two questions: 1. How is character to be strengthened? 2. How are the obstacles imposed by law and custom to be removed?

1. Character largely depends on health and education. Children born of overworked parents; fed on food which does not nourish; brought up in close air and physicked over-much cannot have the physical strength which is the basis of courage. The importance of health is recognized, and every year more is done to spread knowledge and enforce sanitary law. But the neglect of past generations has to be made up, and few of us yet realize what is necessary. The rate of infant mortality is a safe index of unhealthy conditions, and until that is lowered we may be sure of a drift towards poverty.

There are two directions in which energy should push effort: (*a*) More space should be secured about houses so that in the fullest sense every inhabited house might be a "living" house, with a sufficiency of air and space and water to enable every inmate to feel in himself the spring of being. (*b*) The Medical Officer of Health should be responsible for the health of every one in his district. He should be at the head of the Poor Law Medical Officers, of the Dispensary, of the Hospitals, and of the Infirmary. He should be able not only to report on unhealthy areas but to order for every sick person the treatment which is necessary. Medical relief and direction should be a right, not a favour grudgingly given through Relieving Officers. He should be able to prevent mothers working under conditions prejudicial to the health of their children. He should be the authorized recognized centre of information and direct the spread of knowledge. Disraeli, years ago, set up as a Reform cry, *Sanitas sanitatum, omnia sanitas*. Much money has been spent in the name of health, and hospitals have been doubled in efficiency, but because of physical weakness recruits are unfit for the army, and family after family drop into poverty. The need is some authority to bring the many efforts into order, and that authority should be, I submit, a Medical Officer responsible for the health of every person in his district.

But when children are strong in body they do not necessarily become strong characters. They must be educated. Perhaps it might be said that it would be a fair division of labour if, while the school developed children's minds, the home developed their characters. But the fact must be faced that either through neglect or greed the home has largely failed in its part. The schools of the richer classes recognize this fact and set themselves to develop character. They produce, as a rule, self-reliant men and women, wanting, perhaps, in sympathy and moral thoughtfulness, careless, perhaps, of others' poverty, not always intelligent, but strong in qualities which keep them from poverty. The schools of the industrial classes are models of order, the teachers teach admirably and work hard, the children satisfy examiners and inspectors, their handwriting is good, their pronunciation— in school—is careful, they can answer questions on hygiene, on thrift, on history, on chemistry, and a half a dozen other subjects. But they have not resourcefulness, they are without interests which occupy their minds, they shun adventure and seek safe places, they have not the character which enjoys a struggle and resists the inroads of poverty, they have little hold on ideals which force them to sacrifice, they soon become untidy, they are an easy prey to excitement, and depend on others rather than on themselves. The problem how to educate character is full of difficulties. Happily there are workmen's homes where, by the example of the parents and by the order of the household, children enter the world well equipped, and become leaders in industry and politics, but how in the twenty-seven hours of school time each week to educate mind *and* character is a problem not to be solved in a few words.

Perhaps the first thing to be done is to extend the hours of school time; children might come to the school buildings on Saturdays, and daily between five and seven, to play ordered games, and learn to take a beating without crying; boys and girls might be compelled to attend continuation schools up to the age of eighteen, and experience the joy of new interests; the age of leaving might be raised; the classes in the day schools might be smaller; the subjects taught might be fewer; the teachers might be left more responsible; and the recreation of the children might be more considered. Persons, not subjects, make character. The teachers in our elementary schools must, therefore, be more in number, have more time to know their pupils, and feel more responsible for each individual.

Religion is, of course, the great character former, but our unhappy divisions put the subject outside friendly discussion. All that can be said is that the religious teacher who recognizes in all his ways that he is "under Authority" unconsciously moulds character, and all we can wish is that he may have more time and a smaller class. We, who set ourselves to root out poverty, will do well to look above the cries and claims of religious denominations, while we consider how our national schools may help to form the character, without which neither health nor wealth, nor even denominational equality, will avail much.

2. It is time, however, to consider the second question. Character may overcome every obstacle, and our memories tell of men like Adam Bede or Abraham Lincoln or some of the present labour members, who have triumphed in the hardest circumstances. Circumstances must always be hard. God has so ordered the world; but there is no justification for law and custom to make them harder. Many men might have strength to get over what may be called natural difficulties, but fail upon those which have been artificially made.

Our second question, therefore, in considering the cure of poverty is: How are the obstacles imposed by law and custom to be removed? I take as an example the laws which govern the use of land. The land laws were made by our forefathers, because in those days such laws seemed the best to force from the land its greatest use to the community. These laws made one man absolute owner, so that by his energy the land might become most productive. But times have changed, and now these laws, instead of making wealth, seem to help in making poverty. The country labourer may have strong arms; he may have some ambition to use his arms and his knowledge to make a home in which to enjoy his old age; but he sees land all around him which is serving the pleasures of the few, and not the needs of the many; he is shut out from applying his whole energy to its development, for he cannot hope to get secure tenure of a small plot. He leaves the country and goes to the town, where his strong arms are welcomed. But here, again, because the land is in the absolute control of its owner, house is crowded against house, so that health and enjoyment become almost impossible; and here, also, because so large a portion of profit must go to the owner who has done no share of his work, his wage must be reduced. He gives in, and his wife lets dirt and untidiness master his home, and he at last comes into poverty. Law, with good intention, created the obstacle which he could not surmount. Law could remove the obstacle. Law for the common good could interfere with that absolute ownership which for the common good it in the old days created. Country men might have the possibility of holding land, with security of tenure, which they could cultivate for their own and their children's enjoyment. Town municipalities might be given the right to take possession of the land in their environment, on which houses could be built with space for air and for gardens.

The subject is a large one, but the point I would make is that poverty is increased by the obstacles which our land laws have put in the man's way. The landlord prevents the application of energy to the soil, and so taxes industry that a large share of others' earnings automatically reach his pocket. The change of law may involve great cost to individuals, or to the State. But patriotism compels sacrifice, and a people which willingly gives its hundreds of millions to be for ever sunk in a war, may even more willingly surrender rights and pay taxes, so that its fellow-citizens may develop the common-wealth, and escape poverty.

Custom is perhaps as powerful as law in putting obstacles in the way of life's wayfarers. It is by custom that the poor are treated as belonging to a lower, and the rich to a higher class; that employers expect servility as well as work for the wages they pay; that property is more highly regarded than a man's life; that competition is held in a sort of way sacred. It is custom which exalts inequality, and makes every one desirous of securing others' service, and to be called Master. Many a man is, I believe, hindered in the race because he meets with treatment which marks him out as an inferior. He is discouraged by discourtesy, or he is tempted to cringe by assertions of inferiority. Charity to-day is often an insult to manhood. Many of our customs, which survive from feudalism, prevent the growth of a sense of self-respect and of human dignity. Men breathe air which relaxes their vigour, they complain of neglect, they seek favour, they follow after rewards, they give up, and thus sink into poverty.

It may not seem a great matter, but among the cures for poverty I may put greater courtesy; a wider recognition of the equality in human nature; a more set determination to regard all men as brothers. It is not only gifts which demoralize; it is the attitude of those who think that gifts are expected of them, and of those who expect gifts. Gifts are only safe between those who recognize one another as equals.

The subject is so vast that one paper can hardly scratch the surface, but I hope I have suggested some lines of thought. In conclusion, I would repeat that for the cure of poverty, nothing avails but personal influence. He does best who turns one sinner to righteousness, that is, who helps to make one poor man more earnest of purpose, and one rich man more thoughtfully unselfish. But circumstances also are important, and he does second best who helps to alter the laws and customs which put stumbleblocks in the ways of the simple.

SAMUEL A. BARNETT.

THE BABIES OF THE STATE.[1]

By Mrs. S. A. Barnett.

July, 1909.

[1] From "The Cornhill Magazine". By permission of the Editor.

WITHOUT organization and without combination a widespread and effective strike has been slowly taking place—the strike of the middle and upper-middle class women against motherhood.

Month by month short paragraphs can be seen in the newspapers chronicling in stern figures the stern facts of the decrease of the birth rate. At the same time the marriage rate increases, and the physical facts of human nature do not change. The conclusion is, therefore, inevitable that the wives have struck against what used to be considered the necessary corollary of wifehood—motherhood.

The "Cornhill Magazine" is not the place to discuss either the physics or the ethics of this subject, but it is the place to suggest thoughts on the national and patriotic aspects of this regrettable fact.

The nation demands that its population should be kept up to the standard of its requirements; the classes which, for want of a better term, might be called "educated" are refusing adequately to meet the need; the classes whose want of knowledge forbids them to strike, or whose lack of imagination prevents their realizing the pains, responsibilities, and penalties of family duties, still obey brute nature and fling their unwanted children on to the earth. "Horrible!" we either think or say, and inclination bids us turn from the subject and think of something pleasanter. But two considerations bring us sharply back to the point: first, that the nation, and all that it stands for, needs the young lives; and, secondly, that the babies, with their tiny clinging fingers, their soft, velvety skins, their cooey sounds and bewitching gestures, are guiltless of the mixed and often unholy motives of their creation. They are on this wonderful world without choice, bundles of potentialities awaiting adult human action to be developed or stunted.

How does the nation which wants the children treat them? The annals of the police courts, the experience of the attendance officers of the London County Council, the reports of the National Society for Prevention of Cruelty to Children, the stories of the vast young army in truant or industrial schools, the tales of the Waifs and Strays Society and Dr. Barnardo's organization are hideously eloquent of the cruelty, the neglect, and the criminality of thousands of parents. For their action the State can hardly be held directly responsible (a price has to be paid for liberty), but for the care of the children whose misfortunes have brought them to be supported by the State the nation is wholly responsible. Their weal or woe is the business of every man or woman who reads these pages. To ascertain the facts concerning their lives every tax-payer has dipped into his pocket to meet the many thousands of pounds which the Royal Commission on the Poor Laws has cost, and yet the complication of the problem and the weight of the Blue-books are to most people prohibitive, and few have read them. Even the thoughtful often say: "I have got the Reports, and hope to tackle them some day, but——," and then follow apologies for their neglect owing to their size, the magnitude of the subject, or the pressure of other duties or pleasures. Meanwhile the children! The children are growing up, or are dying. The children, already handicapped by their parentage, are further handicapped by the conditions under which the State is rearing them. The children, which the nation needs—the very life-blood of her existence, for which she is paying, are still left under conditions which for decades have been condemned by philanthropists and educationists, as well as by the Poor Law Inspectors themselves.

On 1 January, 1908, according to the Local Government Board return: 234,792 children were dependent on the State, either wholly or partially. Of these:—

22,483 were in workhouses and workhouse infirmaries;

11,602 in district and separate, often called "barrack," schools;

17,090 in village communities, scattered, receiving, and other Guardians' homes;

11,251 in institutions other than those mentioned above;

8,565 boarded out in families of the industrial classes; and

163,801 receiving relief while still remaining with their parents. It is a portentous array, of nearly a quarter of a million of children, and each has an individual character.

Pageants are now the fashion. Let us stand on one side of the stage (as did Stow, the historian, in the Whitechapel children's pageant) and pass the verdict of the onlooker, as, primed with the figures and facts vouched for by the Royal Commissioners, we see the children of the State exhibit themselves in evidence of the care of their guardians.

First the babies. Here they come, thousands of them, some born in the workhouse, tiny, pink crumpled-skinned mites of a few days old; others toddlers of under three, who have never known another home.

"What a nice woman in the nurse's cap and apron! I would trust her with any child. The head official, I suppose. But her under staff! What a terrible set! Those old women look idiotic and the young ones wicked. The inmates told off to serve in the nurseries you say they are! Surely no one with common humanity or sense would put a baby who requires wise observation under such women!"

"Alas! but the Guardians do."

The Report states:—

"The whole nursery has often been found under the charge of a person actually certified as of unsound mind, the bottles sour, the babies wet, cold, and dirty. The Commission on the Care and Control of the Feeble-minded draws attention to an episode in connexion with one feeble-minded woman who was set to wash a baby; she did so in boiling water, and it died."

But this is no new discovery made by the recent Royal Commission. In 1897 Dr. Fuller, the Medical Inspector, reported to the Local Government Board that

"in sixty-four workhouses imbeciles or weak-minded women are entrusted with the care of infants, as helps to the able-bodied or inferior women who are placed in charge by the matron, without the constant supervision of a responsible officer".

"We recognise," acknowledges the Report of the Royal Commissioners, "that some improvement has since taken place; but, as we have ourselves seen, pauper inmates, many of them feeble-minded, are still almost everywhere utilized for handling the babies. . . . As things are, the visitor to a workhouse nursery finds it too often a place of intolerable stench, under quite insufficient supervision, in which it would be a miracle if the babies continued in health."

"How thin and pale and undersized many of them are! Surely they are properly fed and clothed and exercised!"

"In one large workhouse," writes the Commissioners, "it was noticed that from perhaps about eighteen months to two and a half years of age the children had a sickly appearance. They were having their dinner, which consisted of large platefuls of potatoes and minced beef—a somewhat improper diet for children of that age." "Even so elementary a requirement as suitable clothing is neglected." "The infants," states a lady Guardian, "have not always a proper supply of flannel, and their shirts are sometimes made of rough unbleached calico." "Babies of twelve months or thereabouts have their feet compressed into tight laced-up boots over thick socks doubled under their feet to make them fit into the boots." "In some workhouses the children have no toys, in others the toys remain tidily on a shelf out of reach, so that there may be no litter on the floor."

"In another extensive workhouse it was found that the babies of one or two years of age were preparing for their afternoon sleep. They were seated in rows on wooden benches in front of a wooden table. On the table was a long narrow cushion, and when the babies were sufficiently exhausted they fell forward upon this to sleep! The position seemed most uncomfortable and likely to be injurious."

In another place it was stated:—

"That the infants weaned, but unable to feed themselves, are sometimes placed in a row and the whole row fed with one spoon . . . from one plate of rice pudding. The spoon went in and out of the mouths all along the row."

"We were shocked," continues the Report, "to discover that the infants in the nursery of the great palatial establishments in London and other large towns *seldom or never got into the open air.*"

"We found the nursery frequently on the third or fourth story of a gigantic block, often without balconies, whence the only means of access even to the workhouse yard was a flight of stone steps down which it was impossible to wheel a baby carriage of any kind. There was no staff of nurses adequate to carrying fifty or sixty infants out for an airing. In some of these workhouses it was frankly admitted that these babies never left their own quarters (and the stench that we have described), and never got into the open air during the whole period of their residence in the workhouse nursery."

In short, "we regret to report," say the Commissioners, "that these workhouse nurseries are, in a large number of cases, alike in structural arrangements, equipment, organization, and staffing, wholly unsuited to the healthy rearing of infants".

"See, here come the coffins!"

Coffins—tiny wooden boxes—of just cheap deal; some with a wreath of flowers, and followed by a weeping woman; others just conveyed by officials—unwanted, unregretted babies.

As far as one's eye can reach they come. Coffins and coffins, and still more coffins; almost as many coffins as there were babies?

Not quite. The Report repeats the evidence of the Medical Inspector of the Local Government Board for Poor-Law purposes, who some years ago made a careful inquiry and found that one baby out of every three died annually. "A long time ago," did I hear you murmur, "and things are better now"?

Would that it were so, but a more recent inquiry made by the Commissioners shows that "out of every thousand children born in the Poor-Law institutions forty to forty-five die within a week, and out of 8483 infants who were born during 1907, in the workhouses of the 450 Unions inquired into, no fewer than 1050 (or 13 per cent) actually died on the premises before attaining one year." "The infantile mortality in the population as a whole," writes the authors of the Minority Report, "exposed to all dangers of inadequate medical attendance and nursing, lack of sufficient food, warmth, and care, and parental ignorance and neglect, is admittedly excessive. The corresponding mortality among the infants in the Poor-Law institutions, where all these dangers may be supposed to be absent, is between two and three times as great."

"It must be the fault of the system, it is often said, that children, like chickens, cannot for long be safely aggregated together."

"It is difficult to say whether it is the system or the administration which is most to blame, but the facts are incontrovertible. In some workhouses 40 per cent of the babies die within the year. In ten others 493 babies were born, and only fourteen, or 3 per cent, perished before they had lived through four seasons. In ten other workhouses 333 infants saw the light, and through the gates 114 coffins were borne, or 33 per cent of the whole."

This variation would appear to point to faults of administration. On the other hand, the system is contrary to nature; for the natural law limits families to a few children, and usually provides that King Baby should rule as sole monarch for eighteen months or two years. On this the Report says:—

"It has been suggested to us by persons experienced in the peculiar dangers of institutions for infants of tender years, that the high death rate, especially the excessive death rates after the first few weeks of life, right up to the age of three or four, may be due to some adverse influence steadily increasing in its deleterious effect the longer the child is exposed to it. In the scarlet fever wards of isolation hospitals it has been suggested that the mere aggregation of cases may possibly produce, unless there are the most elaborate measures for disinfection, a dangerous 'intensification' of the disease. In the workhouse nursery there is practically no disinfection. The walls, the floors, the furniture, must all become, year after year, more impregnated with whatever mephitic atmosphere prevails. The very cots in which the infants lie have been previously tenanted by an incalculable succession of infants in all states of health and morbidity."

"Is the long undertaker's bill to be deplored, considering the parentage of this class of children and the way the Guardians rear them?"

The nation wants the babies; indeed, to maintain its position it must have them, and "the tendency of nature is to return to the normal"—a scientific fact of profound civic importance. Besides, the Report says:—

"We find that it is generally assumed that the women admitted to the workhouse for lying-in are either feeble-minded girls, persistently immoral women, or wives deserted by their husbands. Whatever may have been the case in past years, this is no longer a correct description of the patients in what have become, in effect, maternity hospitals. Out of all the women who gave birth to children in the Poor-Law institutions of England and Wales during 1907, it appears that about 30 per cent were married women. In the Poor-Law institutions of London and some other towns the proportion of married women rises to 40 and even to 50 per cent."

As to how the Guardians rear the babies that is another matter. But let us leave Institutions with the high walls, the monotony which stifles, the organization which paralyses energy, the control which alike saps freedom and initiation, and the unfailing provision of food no one visibly earns, so that we may go and visit some of the homes which the Guardians subsidize, and where they keep, or partially keep, out of the ratepayers' pockets 163,801 children.

I.—A clean home this, mother out at work, earning 4s. 6d. by charing; the Guardians giving 7s. 6d. Four children (thirteen, nine, six, four), left to themselves while she is out, but evidently fond of home and each other. A small kitchen garden which would abundantly pay for care, but fatigue compels its neglect. No meat is included in her budget, and but 3d. a week for milk; but 12s. a week, and 4s. 6d. of it depending on her never ailing and her employers always requiring her, is hardly adequate on which to pay rent and to keep five people, providing the children with their sole items of life's capital—health, height, and strength.

II.—A dirty home this, in a filthy court. The mother is out; the children playing among the street garbage. Their clothes are ragged, their heads verminous, their poor faces sharp with that expression which always wanting and never being satisfied stamps indelibly on the human countenance. One bed and a mattress pulled on to the floor is all that is provided for the restful sleep of six people; and 3s. a week is what a pitiful public subscribes via the rates to show its appreciation of such a home life. Waste and worse. The Majority Report quotes with approval the words of

Dr. McVail: "In many cases the amount allowed by the Guardians for the maintenance of out-door pauper children cannot possibly suffice to keep them even moderately well". This could be applied to Case I. "Many mothers having to earn their living . . . cannot attend to their children at home, so that there is no proper cooking, the house is untidy and uncomfortable, and the living rooms and bedrooms unventilated and dirty." This could be applied to Case II.

III. A disgraceful home this, best perhaps described in the words of the Majority Report:—

"A widow with three children, a well-known drunken character, was relieved with 3s., one of her children earning 7s. making a total of 10s. It was urged by the relieving officer that it was no case for out relief, as it was encouraging drunkenness and immorality. . . . It was held that the relief having been suspended for a month, she had suffered sufficient punishment. The officer said: 'She still drinks,' and that 4s. relief was given on 13 December, 'to tide her over the holidays'. She had been before the police for drunkenness. It was considered (by the Guardians) to meet the disqualification of the case by reducing the relief to 3s. instead of 4s."

IV. An immoral home this, again best described in official words:—

"I saw in one instance out-relief children habitually sent out to pilfer in a small way, others to beg, some whose mothers were drunkards or living immoral lives. . . . These definitely bad mothers were but a small minority of the mothers whom we visited, but there were many of a negatively bad type, people without standard, whining, colourless people, often with poor health. If out relief is given at all . . . those who give it must take the responsibility for its right use."

In 1898, when Lord Peel was the Chairman of the State Children's Association, its Executive Committee brought out a chart which showed that there were children nationally supported under the Local Government Board, under the Home Office, under the Education Department, under the Metropolitan Asylums Board, under the Lunacy Commissioners, each using its own administrative organization. At that time the same children were being dealt with by what may be called rival authorities, without any machinery for co-operation or opportunities of interchange of knowledge or experience. Since then there has been but little change, the Reports point out forcibly the existence of the same conditions only worse, inasmuch as more parents now seek free food and other assistance for their children from official hands.

Face to face with such a serious confusion of evils, affecting as they do the character of the people—the very foundation of our national greatness; confronted with the complicated problem how to simplify machinery which has been growing for years, and is further entangled with the undergrowth of vast numbers of officials and their vested interests; distressed on the one hand by the clamour of that section of society who think that everything should be done by the State, and on the other by the insistent demand of those who see the incalculable good which springs from volunteer effort or agencies, the bewildered statesman might be sympathized with, if not excused, if he did feel inclined to agree with Mr. John Burns's suggestion, and leave it all to him.

"I care for the people," in effect he said, "I know their needs. I have the officials to do the work. I am the President of the Local Government Board. Be easy, leave it all to me, I will report to the House once in three months. All will be well."

It sounds a simple plan, but, before it can be even seriously advocated, it would be as well to survey the recent history of the Local Government Board, and see if, even under this President, its past record gives hope for future effective achievement. Once more let us begin with—

(a) *The Babies.*—Sir John Simon, Chief Medical Officer of the Local Government Board, wrote forcibly on the subject more than a generation past. Dr. Fuller's Report was made years ago. Again and again reform has been urged by Poor Law Inspectors and workhouse officials, who have asked for additional powers to obtain information or classification or detention. What has the Local Government Board done? The following extract from the Minority Report can be the reply:—

"Alike in the prevention of the continued procreation of the feeble-minded, in the rescue of girl-mothers from a life of sexual immorality, and in the reduction of infantile mortality in respectable but necessitous families, the destitution authorities, in spite of their great expenditure, are to-day effecting no useful results. With regard to the two first of these problems, at any rate, the activities of the Boards of Guardians are, in our judgment, actually intensifying the evil. If the State had desired to maximize both feeble-minded procreation, and birth out of wedlock, there could not have been suggested a more apt device than the provision, throughout the country, of general mixed workhouses, organized as they are now to serve as unconditional maternity hospitals. . . . While thus encouraging . . . these evils they are doing little to arrest the appalling preventible mortality that prevails among the infants of the poor."

(b) *The Children in the Workhouses.*—"So long ago as 1841 the Poor-Law Commissioners pointed out forcibly the evils connected with the maintenance of children in workhouses." In 1896 the Departmental Committee, of which Mr. Mundella was chairman, and on which I had the honour of sitting, brought before the public the opinion of inspectors, guardians, officials, educationists and child-lovers, all unanimous in condemning this system. "In the workhouse the children meet with crime and pauperism from day to day." "They are in the hands of adult paupers for their cleanliness, and the whole thing is extremely bad." "The able-bodied paupers with whom they associate are a very bad class, almost verging on criminal, if not quite," is some of the evidence quoted in the Report, and the Committee unanimously signed the recommendation "that no children be allowed to enter the workhouse," and now, thirteen years afterwards, the same conditions prevail. The Majority Report thus describes cases of children in workhouses:—

"The three-year-old children were in a bare and desolate room, sitting about on the floor and on wooden benches, and in dismal workhouse dress. The older ones had all gone out to school . . . except a cripple, and a dreary little girl who sat in a cold room with bare legs and her feet in a pail of water as a 'cure' for broken chilblains. . . . The children's wards left on our minds a marked impression of confusion and defective administration. . . . In appearance the children were dirty, untidy, ill-kept, and almost neglected. Their clothes might be described with little exaggeration as ragged. . . . The boys' day-room is absolutely dreary and bare, and they share a yard and lavatories with the young men. . . . An old man sleeps with the boys. It is a serious drawback (says the inspector) that every Saturday and Sunday, to say nothing of summer and winter holidays, have for the most part to be spent in the workhouse, where they either live amid rigid discipline and get no freedom, or else if left to themselves are likely to come under the evil influence of adult inmates. The Local Government Board inspectors point out that, even if the children go to the elementary schools for teaching, the practice of rearing them in the workhouse exposes them to the contamination of communication with the adult inmates whose influence is often hideously depraving."

"Terrible!" my reader will say; "but surely the reform requires legislation, and the Poor Law is too large a subject to tinker on, it must be dealt with after time has been given for due thought." To this I would reply that even if it did require legislation there has been time enough to obtain it during all these years that the evils have existed; but to quote the Majority Report: "So far as the 'in-and-out' children are concerned it is probable that no further power would be needed, since the Guardians already have power under the Poor Law Act, 1899, to adopt children until the age of eighteen." This Act, I may say in passing, was initiated, drafted, and finally secured, not by the responsible authorities but by the efforts of the State Children's Association.

Why, then, has not the Local Government Board removed the children from the workhouses? Why, indeed?

(*c*) *The Ins and Outs.*—In 1896 the Departmental Committee quoted the evidence of Mr. Lockwood, the Local Government Board Inspector, who referred to "cases of children who are constantly in and out of the workhouse, dragged about the streets by their parents, and who practically get no education at all," and he puts in a table of "particulars of eleven families representing the more prominent 'ins and outs'" of one Metropolitan West-end workhouse of whom "one family of three children had been admitted and discharged sixty-two times in thirteen months." Other cases were given, for instance:—

"D——, a general labourer, who has three boys and a girl, who come in and out on an average once a week.

"A family named W——. The husband drunken, and has been in an asylum; the wife unable to live with him. He would take his boys out in the early morning, leave them somewhere, meet them again at night, and bring them back to the workhouse; they had had nothing to eat, and had wandered about in the cold all day."

"This state of things is cruel and disastrous in every respect," writes the Committee in 1896, appointed, be it remembered, by the Department to elicit facts and "to advise as to any changes that may be desirable". Yet we find that in 1909 the same conditions exist. To quote the Report:—

"Out of twenty special cases of which details have been obtained, twelve families have been in and out ten or more times; one child had been admitted thirty-nine times in eleven years; another twenty-three times in six years. The Wandsworth Union has a large number of dissolute persons in the workhouse with children in the intermediate schools. The parents never go out without taking the children, and seem to hold the threat of doing so as a rod over the heads of the Guardians. One mother frequently had her child brought out of his bed to go out into the cold winter night. One boy who had been admitted twenty-five times in ten years had been sent more than once to Banstead Schools, but had never stayed there long. Whenever he knew he was to go there he used to write to his mother in the workhouse, when she would apply for her discharge and go out with him."

In the thirteen years which have passed since the issue of the two Reports, what has the Local Government Board done? It has induced some of the Boards to establish receiving or intermediary houses at the cost, in the Metropolis, of about £200,000, but that is but attacking the symptom and leaving the disease untouched. Without an ideal for child-life or appreciation of child-nature, it has been content to let this hideous state of things go on. Again to quote the Report:—

"It has done nothing to prevent the children from being dragged in and out of the workhouse as it suits their parents' whim or convenience. The man or woman may take the children to a succession of casual wards or the lowest common lodging-houses. They may go out with the intention of using the children, half-clad and blue with cold, as a means of begging from the soft-hearted, or they may go out simply to enjoy a day's liberty, and find the children only encumbrances, to be neglected and half-starved. . . . The unfortunate boys and girls who are dragged backwards and forwards by parents of the 'in-and-out' class practically escape supervision. They pass the whole period of school age alternately being cleansed and 'fed up' in this or that Poor Law institution, or starving on scraps and blows amid filth and vice in their periodical excursions in the outer world, exactly as it suits the caprice or convenience of their reckless and irresponsible parents."

And the Local Government Board has stood it for years and stands by still and lets the evils go on. Meanwhile it is the children who suffer and die; it is the children who are being robbed of their birthright of joy as they pass a miserable childhood in poverty in workhouses or in huge institutions; it is the children whose potentialities for good, and strength, and usefulness are being allowed to wither and waste and turn into evil and pain. It is the children who are needed for the nation; it is the nation who supports them; and it is the nation who must decide their future.

Speaking for myself (not in any official capacity), twenty-two years' experience as manager of a barrack school, two years' membership of the Departmental Committee, twelve years' work as the honorary secretary of the State Children's Association have brought me to the well-grounded opinion that the children should be removed altogether from the care of the Local Government Board and placed under the Board of Education. This Board's one concern is children. Its inspectors have to consider nothing beyond the children's welfare, and its organization admits the latest development in the art of training, both in day and boarding schools.

However much courtesy demanded moderation, the fact remains that both the Reports are a strong condemnation of the whole of the Poor-Law work of the Local Government Board, both in principle and administration. The condition of the aged, the sick, the unemployed, the mentally defective, the vagrant, the out-relief cases, as well as the children, alike come in for strong expressions of disapproval or for proposals for reform so drastic as to carry condemnation. If such a report had been issued on the work of the Admiralty or the War Office, the whole country would have demanded immediate change. "They have tried and failed," it would be said; "let some one else try"; and a similar demand is made by those of us who have seen many generations of children exposed to these evils, and waited, and hoped, and despaired, and waited and hoped again. But once more some of the best brains in the country have faced the problem of the poor, and demanded reforms, and so far as the children are concerned almost the identical reforms demanded thirteen years ago; once more the nation has been compelled to turn its mind to this painful subject, and there is again ground for hope that the lives of the wanted babies will be saved, and their education be such as to fit them to contribute to the strength and honour of the nation.

HENRIETTA O. BARNETT.

POOR LAW REFORM.[1]

By Canon Barnett.

November, 1909.

[1] From "The Contemporary Review". By permission of the Editor.

A COMPROMISE between kindliness and cruelty often stands—according to Mr. Galsworthy—for social reform. The Poor Law is an example of such compromise. In kindliness it offers doles of out-relief to the destitute and builds institutions at extravagant cost. In cruelty it disregards human feelings, breaks up family life, suspects poverty as a crime, and degrades labour into punishment.

The Poor Law, however, receives almost universal condemnation. Its cost is enormous, amounting to over fourteen millions a year. The incidence is so unfair that its call on the rich districts is comparatively light, and in poor districts inordinately heavy. Its administration is both confused and loose. Its relief follows no principle—out-relief is given in one district and refused in others;—its institutions sometimes attract and sometimes deter applications, and its expenditure is often at the mercy of self-seeking Guardians, whose minds are set on securing cheap labour or even on secret commissions.

The poor, whom at such vast cost and with such parade of machinery it relieves, are often demoralized. There is neither worth nor joy to be got out of the pauper, who has learned to measure success in life by skill in evading inquiry. And, what is most striking of all, the Poor Law has allowed a mass of poverty to accumulate which has led to the erection of charity upon charity, and is still, by its squalor, its misery and hopelessness, a disgrace and a danger to the nation. The public, recognizing the failure of the Poor Law, has become indifferent to its existence, and now only a small percentage of the electors record their votes at an election of the guardians of the poor.

The case for reform is clear.

What that reform should be is a question not to be answered in the compass of a short article. The best I can do is to offer for the consideration of my readers some principles which I believe to underlie reform. Those principles once accepted, it will be for every one to consider with what modifications or extensions they may be applied to the different circumstances of town and country, young and old, weak and strong.

The last great reform of the Poor Law was in 1834. The Reformers of those days took as their main principle *that the position of the person relieved should be less attractive than that of the workman.* They were driven to adopt this principle by the condition to which the Elizabethan Poor Law had brought the nation. When, under that Poor Law, the State assumed the whole responsibility "for the relief of the impotent and the getting to work of those able to work," and when by Gilbert's Act in 1782 it was further enacted that "out-relief should be made obligatory for all except the sick and impotent," it followed that larger and larger numbers threw themselves on the rates. Relief offered a better living than work. The number of workers decreased, the number receiving relief increased. Ruin threatened the nation, and so the Reformers came in to enforce the principle that relief should offer a less attractive living than work.

The principle is good; it is, indeed, eternally true, because it is not by what comes from without, but by what comes from within that a human being is raised. It is not by what a man receives, but by that he is enabled to do for himself that he is helped. This principle was applied in 1834 by requiring from every applicant evidence of destitution, by refusing relief to able-bodied persons, except on admission to workhouses, and by making the relief as unpleasant or as "deterrent" as possible.

This harsh application of the principle may have been the best for the moment. The nation required a sharp spur, and no doubt under its pressure there was a marvellous recovery. Men who had been idle sought work, and men who had saved realized that their savings would no longer be swallowed up in rates. The spur and the whip had their effect, but such effect, whether on a beast or a man, is always short-lived.

The tragedy of 1834 is that the reforming spirit, which so boldly undertook the immediate need, did not continue to take in other needs as they arose. It is, indeed, the tragedy of the history of the State, of the Church, and of the individual, that moments of reform are followed by periods of lethargy. People will not recognize that reform must be a continuous act, and that the only condition of progress is eternal vigilance. Indolence, especially mental indolence, is Satan's handiest instrument, and so after some great effort a pause is easily accepted as a right.

After the reform of 1834 there was such a pause. New needs soon came to the front, and the face of society was gradually changed. The strain of industrial competition threw more and more men on to the scrap heap, too young to die, too worn to work, too poor to live. The crowding of house against house in the towns reduced the vitality of the people so that children grew up unfit for labour, and young people found less and less room for healthy activities of mind or body. Education, made common and free, set up a higher standard of respectability and called for more expenditure. A growing sense of humanity among all classes made poverty a greater burden on social life, provoking sometimes charity and sometimes indignation.

These, and such as these, were the changes going on in the latter part of the nineteenth century, but the spirit of the reformers of 1834 was dead, and in their lethargy the people were content that the old principle should be applied without any change to meet new needs. Institutions were increased, officials were multiplied, and inspectors were appointed to look after inspectors. Any outcry was met by expedients. Mr. Chamberlain authorised municipal bodies to give work. Mr. Chaplain relaxed the out-relief order. New luxuries were allowed in the workhouse, the infirmaries were vastly improved, and the children were, to some extent, removed from the workhouses and put, often at great cost, in village communities or like establishments. But reliance was always placed on making relief disagreeable and deterrent. One of the latest reforms has been the introduction of the cellular system in casual wards, so that men are kept in solitary confinement, while as task work they break a pile of stones and throw them through a narrow grating. Poverty, indeed, is met by a compromise between kindliness and cruelty.

The reformers of 1834 looked out on a society weakened by idleness. They faced a condition of things in which the chief thing wanted was energy and effort, so they applied the spur. The reformers of to-day look out on a very different society, and they look with other eyes. They see that the people who are weak and poor are not altogether suffering the penalty of their own faults. It is by others' neglect that uninhabitable houses have robbed them of strength, that wages do not provide the means of living, and that education has not fitted them either to earn a livelihood or enjoy life. The reformers of to-day, under the subtle influence of the Christian spirit, have learnt that self-respect, even more than a strong body, is a man's best asset, and that willing work rather than forced work makes national wealth.

Sir Harry Johnson, who speaks with rare authority, has told us how negroes with a reputation for idleness respond to treatment which, showing them respect, calls out their hope and their manhood. Treat them, he implies, as children, drive them as cattle, and you are justified in your belief in their idleness. Treat them as men, give them their wages in money, open to them the hope of better things, and they work as men.

The relief given in the casual ward may be sufficient for the body of the casual, but the penal treatment, the prison-like task and the solitary confinement make him set his teeth against work, and he becomes the enemy of the society which has given him such treatment.

The Reformers of to-day, with their greater knowledge of human nature, and in face of a society the fault of which is not just idleness, will do well then to take another principle as the basis of their action. Such a principle is *that relief must develop self-respect*. They will have, indeed, to remember that the form of relief must still be less attractive than that offered by work, but less attractiveness must be attained not by an insolent inquisition of relief officers into the character of applicants, not by treating inmates as prisoners, and not by making work as distasteful as possible. It might possibly be sufficient if relief, so far as regarded the able-bodied, took the form of training for work. There is no degradation in requiring men and women to fit themselves to earn,—no loss of self-respect is brought on anyone by being called to be a learner;—but, at the same time, opportunities for learning are not attractive to idlers, nor are they likely to encourage the reliance on relief which brought disaster on the nation before 1834.

The Whitechapel Guardians, many years ago, determined that the workhouse should more and more approximate to an adult industrial school. They did away with stone breaking and oakum picking, they abolished cranks turned by human labour, they instituted trade work and appointed a mental instructor to teach the inmates in the evening. They had no power of detention, so the training was not of much use, but as a deterrent the system was most effective, and fewer able-bodied men came to Whitechapel Union than to neighbouring workhouses. Regard for the principle that relief must develop self-respect is not, therefore, inconsistent with the principle that relief must offer a position which is less attractive than that offered by work.

But let me suggest some further application of the principle.

1. It implies, I think, the abolition of Boards of Guardians and of all the special machinery for relief. It implies, perhaps, the abolition of the Poor Law itself. There is no class of "the poor" as there is a class of criminals. Poverty is not a crime, and there are poor among the most honourable of the people. Poverty is a loose and wide term, involving the greater number of the people. There must, therefore, be some loss of self-respect in those of the poor who feel themselves set apart for special treatment. One poor man goes to the hospital, his neighbour—his brother, it may be—goes to the Poor Law infirmary. Both are in the same position, but the latter, because he comes under the Guardians, loses his self-respect, and has acquired a special term—he is "a pauper".

Those men and women who through weakness, through ignorance or through character are unable to do their work and earn a living are, as much as the rich and the strong, members of the nation. All form one body and depend on one another. Some for health's sake need one treatment and some another. There is no reason in putting a few of them under a special law and calling them "paupers," the use of hard names is as inexpedient for the Statute Book as it is for Christians. Reason says that all should be so treated that they may, as rapidly as possible, be restored to economic health by the use of all the resources of the State, educational and social. There is no place for a special law, a specially elected body of administrators and a special rate.

A further objection to Boards of Guardians is that an election does not involve interests which are sufficiently wide or sufficiently familiar. Side issues have to be exalted so as to attract the electors' attention. Such a side issue was found in the religious question, which gave interest to the old School Board elections; no such side issue has been found in Guardian elections, and so only a small minority of ratepayers record their votes. Experience, therefore, justifies the proposal that with a view to encouraging the growth of self-respect in the economically unhealthy members of the nation, the present system of Poor Law machinery should be abolished.

2. The principle further implies that the same municipal body which is responsible for the health, for the education, and for the industrial fitness of some members of the community should be responsible in like manner for all the members, whatever their position.

(*a*) *The Sick.*—The County Council appoints a medical officer of health and itself administers many asylums. It establishes a sort of privileged class which receives its benefits and, unless it extends its operations so that all who are sick may be reached, must lower the self-respect of those who are excluded and driven to beg for relief.

The medical officer might be in fact what he is in name, responsible for the health of the district, and as the superior officer of the visiting doctors see that ill-health was prevented and cured. The interest of the community is universal good health; how unreasoning is the system which deters the sick man from trying to get well by making it necessary for him to endure the inquisition of the relieving officer before getting a doctor's visit! The strength of the community is in the self-respect of its members; how extravagant is the system which offers relief only on condition of some degradation.

(*b*) *The Children.*—The County Council is responsible for the education of the children; it must—unless one set of children is to be kept in a less honourable position—extend its care over all the children. There must be no such creature as a "pauper child," and no distinction between schools in which children are taught or boarded. The child who has lost its parents, the child who has been deserted, the child who has no home, must be started in life equipped with equal knowledge and on an equal footing with other children. Every child must be within reach of the best which the State can offer. The inclusion of the care of all children under the same municipal authority would help to develop in all a sense of self-respect, and at the same time enable the authority to make better use of the existing buildings in the classification of their uses, apportioning some, *e.g.*, as technical schools, some as infirmaries, and some for industrial training. Dr. Barnardo, who has taught the nation how to care better for its children, adopted some such method.

(*c*) *The Able-Bodied.*—A greater difficulty occurs in applying the principle to the care of the able-bodied. How, it may be asked, is the County Council to deal with the unemployed and with the loafer so as to relieve them and at the same time develop their sense of respect? The County Council has lately been made responsible for dealing with the unemployed, and experience has shown that at the bottom of the problem lies the custom of casual labour, the use of boys in dissipating work, and the ignorance of the people. The Council has in its hands the power of dealing with these causes. It can establish labour registers, it can prevent much child labour, and it can provide education. It may be necessary to increase its powers, but already it can do something to prevent unemployment in the future.

The need, however, of the present unemployed is training. The Council might be empowered to open for them houses or farms of discipline, in which such training could be given. The man with a settled home could be admitted for a short period, the loafer could be detained for three or four years. The work in every case, while less attractive than other work, could be such as to interest the worker; the discipline, such as to involve no degradation; and the door of hope could be studiously kept open. The farms or houses could indeed be adult industrial schools offering a livelihood, not indeed as attractive as that offered by work, but such as any man might take with gain to his sense of self-respect.

The County Council might thus take over the duties performed by Guardians. The same body which now looks after the housing and the cleanliness of the streets, would possibly realize the cost of neglect in doing those duties, if they also had the care of the broken in body and in heart. In other words, a more scientific expenditure of the rates might be expected to ensue if the body responsible for the relief of poverty were the same body as is now responsible for its prevention. The claims of education would perhaps become more popular.

Enough, perhaps, has now been said to suggest a line of reform, and hours might be spent in discussing a thousand details, each of which has its importance. But not even a slight article could be complete without some reference to the mass of charity—£10,000,000 is said to be spent in London alone—which is annually poured out on the poor. Charity, unless it be personal—from a friend to a friend—is often as degrading as Poor Law relief. Attempts have been made at organization, and much has been done to bring about personal relationships between the Haves and the Have-nots. Years ago it was suggested that the Charity Organization Society might take as a motto, "Not relief, but a friend".

Much has been done, but with a view to putting a further limit on the competition of charities and on the fostering of cringing habits, some reformers suggest that a statutory body of representatives of charities should be formed in each district. Over these a County Council official might preside. At weekly meetings cases of distress which have been noticed by the doctors, the school officers or any private person could be considered. These cases would then be handed over to individuals or charities, who would report progress at the next meeting, or they would be undertaken by the presiding officer and dealt with efficiently by one of the committees of the County Council.

"The strength of a nation," according to a saying of Napoleon quoted by Mr. Fisher, "depends on its history." No reform is likely to endure which does not fit in with the traditions of the past. It might be possible to elaborate on paper a perfect scheme for the care of the weak and the sickly, but it would not avail if it disregarded history. Here in England the State has, during many centuries, recognized its obligation for the well-being of all its members, and it has performed its obligations by the service of individuals. The State, in more senses than one, is identified with the Church. In the new times, in the face of new needs and with the command of new knowledge, it is still the State which must organize the means to restore the fallen and it must still use as its instruments the willing service of individual men and women. The sketch of Poor Law reform which I have presumed to offer in this article fulfils, I believe, these requirements.

SAMUEL A. BARNETT.

THE UNEMPLOYED.[1]

By Mrs. S. A. Barnett.

November, 1904.

<u>1</u> A Paper read at a meeting in a West-End drawing room and afterwards printed by request.

I AM often asked to speak publicly, and when I express wonder as I open my letters at my breakfast-table, my family (with that delightful candour which is so good for one's character) say, "Oh, they ask you because you always make them hear and sometimes make them laugh". Ladies, to-day I shall, I hope, make you hear, but I cannot make you laugh.

Those of us who have lived among the poor, as my dear old friend Emma Cons and I have done, in Lambeth and Whitechapel for over thirty years, know that there is no joke connected with the unemployed. Those of us who went through the awful winter of 1886, and saw the sad suffering which caused the still more sad sin, as the people lied and cringed and begged and bullied to get a share—(what they considered a lawful share, some called it "The ransom of the rich") of the Mansion House Fund, know that this condition of want of employment is not only an economic question, but one involving deep and far-reaching moral issues, and it is this problem that is before us now.

The number of unemployed in London is variously estimated, some say 30,000 some 100,000, no one can tell, for it so much depends on what is meant by unemployed. Do we mean those workers in seasonal trades, such as the painters whose labour ceases in the winter? and the bricklayers' labourers who are stopped by a frost? Do we mean those thousands which Mr. Charles Booth calculates never have an income sufficient to keep the family in health, who are always partially unemployed because their labour is of so inefficient a kind that they are not worth a "living wage". "Why," one may ask the frequenters of the Relief Office, "have you come to this?" the answer in a hundred different forms will be the same. "I fell out of work owing to bad trade—I struggled for a year, but things got worse and worse—I am no longer fit for continuous work and I couldn't do it if I got it". They have, that is, lost their power, which makes efficient labour.

On this matter there is need of clear thinking, but leaving for a moment or two the task of defining and classifying the unemployed, let us realize the large army of men, with the still larger army of women and children dependent on them, who, on this cold, cheerless day are out of work—what do they want? Food, fire, shelter,—on this we all agree, and the plan of some kind persons is to supply their needs. Thus Soup Kitchens, Free Breakfasts, Shelters for the Homeless, Meals for the Children, Blankets for the Old, Coals for the Cold, Clothing for the Destitute, Doles of all kinds for all kinds of people are begged for, and we are told, often with regrettable exaggeration, that to support this charity or that organization will relieve the suffering which (whatever our politics) we all combine to deplore.

But those of us who have thought with our brains, as well as with our hearts, know that to ease the symptoms is not to cure the disease, and that this social ulcer needs first an exhaustive diagnosis by the most experienced social physicians, and then infinite patience and great firmness as we build up again the constitution of the unfit, which, through long years has become physically weakened and morally deteriorated.

I seem to hear my listeners say: "But at least it cannot do harm to feed the children," and there I confess my economics break down! I have lived long enough in Whitechapel to see three generations, and I have watched the underfed boy grow into the undersized man, pushed aside by stronger arms in the labour market. I have seen the underfed girl grown into the enfeebled woman, producing in motherhood puny children. But, and it is a big but, if you feed the children, you must feed them adequately, and feed them as individuals by individuals. The practice of giving children two or three dinner tickets a week is bad economy, bad for the children's digestion, bad for the mother's housekeeping, and bad for the father's sense of responsibility. We should not like our own children to be fed thus, and indeed if we would consider each child of the poor as we consider our own, the problem of feeding the children would soon be solved. I know you will think me Utopian, but if every one of us here were to have two or three children as kitchen guests daily! Well! It perhaps would not do much, but once we were told ten righteous men might have saved the city.

This is a long digression, but the individual treatment of children is a subject that occupies much of my thought, and one which I would ask you to consider carefully as throwing light on many loudly voiced schemes of reform, which, lacking the personal touch, are apt to miss the deeper and spiritual forces by which character must be nourished if it is to grow.

Now to return to the unemployed. Briefly they can be put into four classes:—

1. The skilled mechanic.

2. The unskilled labourer.

3. The casual worker.

4. The loafer.

Concerning the first, the Chart published in the "Labour Gazette" shows that the number approaches 7 per cent as against nearly 5 per cent last year. This is the only class about which we have accurate figures, but the returns of pauperism, and the experience of charitable agencies combine in agreeing that there is more want of employment in the other three classes than is usual at this time of the year, and that there are fewer "bits of things" to go to the pawnshop than usual, because, owing to the war, and some think to the fiscal agitation, the summer trade has been slack, and wages low and uncertain.

No one can read the daily papers without seeing how many schemes are now being put forward to aid the unemployed, and in the space of time given to me it is impossible to name all these, let alone to discriminate between them, but certain principles can be laid down. (1) The form of help should be work. (2) The work should be such as will uplift and not degrade character. (3) The work should be paid sufficiently to keep up the home and adequately feed the family. (4) The work, if it be relief work—i.e., that not required in the ordinary channels by ordinary employers—should not be more attractive than the worker's normal labour.

It should never be forgotten that provision of work may become as dangerous to character as doles of money have proved to be. Work is of so many sorts; that which is effortful to some men may be child's play to others, or it might be so carelessly supervised as to encourage the casual ways and self-indulgent habits which lie at the root of much poverty. Human nature in every walk of life has a tendency to take the easiest courses, and many men are tempted to relax the efforts which the higher classes of employment demand.

"Why," I said to a butler who had taken £80 a year in service, "did you become a cabman?" "Well, madam," he said, "in service one has always to be spruce." In other words he had resented the control of order, and so he had sunk from a skilled trade to a grade lower.

"Why," I asked an old friend, a Carter Paterson driver, "did you leave your regular work?" "'Tis like this," he said, "it means being out in all weathers, now I can go home if things is too nasty outside." He had yielded to the temptation of comfort and gone down a grade lower to casual work.

"Why did you go on the tramp?" was asked of a man in the casual ward. "If yer takes to the road," he said with perfect candour, "yer never knows what's before yer. Yer may be in luck or yer mayn't but it's all on the chance." The spirit of gambling had got the better of him and he had gone down a grade lower.

These examples illustrate the importance of the principles laid down. The help must be work and the work must be steady and continuous, and capable, by drawing forth each man's best powers, to uplift him in character and maintain his own self-esteem. The work must be of many kinds. It is folly to expect the tailor, the cigarette-maker, the working jeweller, to do only road sweeping and that badly, and lastly the work, while always strengthening character, must be given only under such conditions as will not attract men to leave their regular calling, which makes demands on their powers of self-discipline, and throw themselves on what is charity, even though offered in the form of labour.

Last year the Mansion House Committee carried out on a small scale an experiment in relief, which in many ways followed these principles. It sent the men to Labour Colonies, where they had good food and honest work, away from the attractions of the streets, and while they were away it provided the women and children with sufficient money for the upkeep of health and home. It brought to individuals the care of individuals, as week by week superintendents reported on the workers' work, and visitors carried the money to the families. It offered facilities for training men for emigration to the colonies, or for migration to the country. It provided employment which was not so attractive as to draw men from their regular work, nor the loafer from the streets, and it offered to every one hope and a way out in the future. The experiment has shown what is possible, and encourages those who worked it to believe that some year, if not this year, there will be humane and scientific dealing with the problem of unemployment.

"Oh, yes," I was told by a young married woman the other day, "people talk so much of the unemployed now. It is all the fashion, but I think quite half of them could get work if they wanted to."

"Really," I said, recalling the hopeless eyes, gaunt figures, and worn boots of many an out-of-work friend, the pathetic patience of their women and white faces of the children, "Is that your experience?"

"Oh, no!" she replied, "but I am sure I have heard it said—and I expect it is true."

I could have shaken her—but I did not—only that sort of thing is what discounts women's opinion so often with the men (the governing sex), and as it is, I fear, not uncommon, it behoves us, the thinking, caring women, to think more clearly, and to care more deeply. If we bore more continuously this sad suffering in mind, if we studied, and read, and thought in the effort to probe its cause to its roots, if we resolved by personal effort to find or provide labour for at least one family during the winter, the problem would be nearer solution, but we must see to it that reforms go on lines which recognize that character is more important than comfort, and that a man is more wronged if Society steals his responsibility than if it steals his coat.

HENRIETTA O. BARNETT.

THE POOR LAW REPORT.[1]

By Canon Barnett.

April, 1909.

[1] From "The Contemporary Review". By permission of the Editor.

THE Poor Law has too long blocked the way of social progress, and its ending or its mending has become a matter of urgent necessity. The Report just issued may thus mark the beginning of a new age. The "condition of the people" is, from some points of view, even more serious than it was in 1834, when the first Commissioners brought out the Report which called "check" to many processes of corruption. In those days a lax system of relief had so tempted many strong men to idleness and so reduced incentives to investment, that the nation was threatened with bankruptcy. In these days, when a confusion of methods alternates between kindliness and cruelty in their treatment of the poor; when begging is encouraged by gifts, public and private, said to reach the amount of £80,000,000 a year; when giving provokes distrust and leaves such evidence of human starvation and degradation as may daily be seen amid the splendours of the Embankment, it sometimes seems as if the nation were within measurable distance of something like a bankruptcy of character.

The present Poor Law system, valuable as it was in checking "various injurious practices," has been applied to conditions and people who were not within its makers' range of vision, and is now responsible for more trouble than is at once apparent. It preaches by means of palatial institutions which every one sees, and of officials who are more ubiquitous and powerful than parsons. Its sermon is: "Look outside yourselves for the means of livelihood; grudge if you are not satisfied". It preaches selfishness and illwill; it encourages a scramble for relief; it discounts energy and trust. The present Poor Law does not really relieve the poor, and it does tend to weaken the national character.

The admirable statistical survey which introduces the Report represents the failure of the present system in striking figures. The number of paupers—markedly of males—is increasing. In London alone 15,800 more paupers are being maintained than there were twenty years ago, and the rate of pauperism through the country has reached 47 in the 1000. The cost has also increased, and the country is now spending more than double the amount on each individual which was spent in 1872, "making a total which is now equivalent to nearly one half of the present expenditure on the Army". The increase goes on, as the Commissioners remark, notwithstanding the millions of money now spent on education and sanitation, and notwithstanding the rise in wages, affording clear proof "that something in our social organization is seriously wrong".

The Commissioners are unanimous in their condemnation of the system which produces such results. They have gathered evidence upon evidence of its failure, and, while they praise the devoted service of many Guardians and officials, both the Majority and Minority Reports agree recommending radical changes.

The revelation of the abuse is itself a valuable contribution to the needs of the time. The public, unless they know the extent of the mischief, will never be moved to the necessary effort of reform; and teachers of the public, through the Pulpit and the Press, could hardly do better than publish extracts from the Report showing the waste of money, the demoralization, the ill-will, which gathers round workhouses, casual wards and out relief.

The ordinary reader of this evidence might naturally inquire, "What has the Local Government Board been doing to prevent the abuses which it must have known? Why, if conviction was not possible, was not Parliament asked for further powers or for some reform? What is the use of inspectors? Why should a controlling department exist if the nation is to stand convicted of such neglect, and to be brought into such danger?" The Report implies, indeed, some slight blame to the Local Government Board, because it did not at all times afford sufficient direction; and the Minority Report, in its more trenchant way, sometimes emphasizes the confusion it has caused by its varying decisions; but the thought naturally occurs that if the Board had not been so strongly represented on the Commission, or if a body representative of the best guardians were called on to render a report, the supreme authority which has so long known the evil and done so little for its reform would have been roundly condemned.

The Commissioners, however, pass their judgment on the system, and proceed to make their recommendations. There are two sets, those of the Majority and those of the Minority. They extend over 1238 large pages, and deal with thousands of details. A close examination is therefore impossible in a short article, but there are certain tests by which the principal recommendations may be tried. I would try just two such tests: (1) Do they make it possible to relieve needs without demoralizing character? (2) Do they stimulate energy without raising the devil in human nature?

The people who need relief are roughly divided into two great classes, "the unable" and "the able". The recommendations of the Report—Majority and Minority—as they affect these two classes may be tried by the suggested test.

The Unable.

I. "The unable" include the sick, the old, the children and infirm, and—although on this matter the Local Government Board gave uncertain guidance—widows with children. The present system, starting from the principle laid down in 1834, aims at deterring people from application by a barbed-wire fence of regulations. The sick can only have a doctor after inquiry by the relieving officer. The old and infirm are herded in a general workhouse together with people whose contact often wounds their self-respect. The children are isolated from other children, and treated as a class apart. Widows with children can only get means of maintenance by applying at the relief table in company with the degraded, by enduring the close inquisition of the relieving officer, and then by attendance at the Board of Guardians, where, standing in the middle of the room, they have to face their gaze, answer their questions, and at the end be grateful for a pittance of relief.

This system does not, in the first place, relieve the necessities of the poor. Many of the sick defer their application till their condition becomes serious, or they set themselves to beg for hospital letters. Many of the old and infirm, rather than submit to the iniquities of the workhouse, live a life of semi-starvation. Few of the widows who receive a few shillings a week for the maintenance of their families, are able unaided to look after their children and give them the necessary care and food.

"A few Boards," says the Minority Report, "restrict to the uttermost the grant of out relief to widows with children; many refuse it to the widow with only one child or with only two children, however young these may be; others grant only the quite inadequate sum of 1s. or 1s. 6d. a week per child, and nothing for the mother. Very few Guardians face the problem of how the widow's children . . . can under these circumstances be properly reared. . . . In at least 100,000 cases their children are growing up stunted, under-nourished, and to a large extent neglected, because the mother is so hard driven that she cannot properly attend to them. The irony of the situation appears in the fact that if the mother thereupon dies the children will probably be 'boarded out' with a payment of 4s. or 5s. per week each, or three or four times as much as the Guardians paid for them before, or else be taken into the Poor Law school or cottage homes at a cost of 12s. to 21s. per week each."

The vast sum of money—this £20,000,000 a year—which is spent misses to a large extent its object to give relief, and, further than this, causes widespread demoralization. The sick who have overcome their shrinking to face the relieving officer to ask for a medical officer, are found readily treading the same path to ask for other relief. The workhouses—one of which, lately built, has cost £126,612, or £286 a bed—"are," we read, "largely responsible for the considerable increase of indoor pauperism," and evidence is given "that life in a workhouse deteriorates mentally, morally, and physically the habitual inmates". It must be so, indeed, when young girls are put "to sleep with women admitted by the master to be frequently of bad character".

Out relief has been the battlefield of rival schools of administrators, and the Commissioners find in the system "of trying to compensate for inadequacy of knowledge by inadequacy of relief" two obvious points: "First, that when the applicants are honest in their statements they must often suffer great privations; and, second, that when they are dishonest, relief must often be given quite unnecessarily". Evidence, too, is given of instances where out relief is being applied to subsidize dirt, disease and immorality, justifying the conclusion that it is "a very potent influence in perpetuating pauperism and propagating disease".

When the Commissioners have admitted that much has been done by wise Boards of Guardians in providing infirmaries for the sick which are as good as hospitals, and in administering out relief with sympathy and discrimination, the conclusion must still remain that the present system does not relieve the necessities of the poor, while it tends to spread demoralization. It fails under the suggested test.

The Commissioners' proposed reforms must be tried by the same tests. Their proposals include (1) the constitution of a new authority, and (2) the principles on which that authority is to act. The principles—keeping in mind for the moment the class of "the unable"—recommended by the Majority and Minority are practically identical. In the words of the Majority:—

1. The treatment of the poor who apply for public assistance should be adapted to the needs of the individual, and if constitutional should be governed by classification.

2. The system of public assistance thus established should include processes of help which would be preventive, curative and restorative.

3. Every effort should be made to foster the instincts of independence and self-maintenance amongst those assisted.

The same principles appear when the Minority Report urges the (1) "paramount importance of subordinating mere relief to the specialized treatment of each separate class, with the object of preventing or curing its distress".

(2) "The expediency of ultimately associating this specialized treatment of each class with the standing machinery for enforcing both before and after the period of distress the fulfilment of personal and family obligations."

The differences between the Reports are manifest in that the Minority is more anxious to secure a co-ordination of public authorities, but both alike agree that relief must be thorough and regard primarily the necessities of the individual. The general workhouse is therefore to be broken up, and separate institutions set apart for children, the old, the sick, mothers, and feeble-minded. Out relief is to be given on uniform principles and under strict supervision, whether by skilled officials or by a registrar. (The majority make the interesting—if it be practicable—suggestion that there shall be proscribed districts in which no out relief shall be given, on account of their slum character.) The sick are to have the means of treatment brought within their reach, whether it be by the officer of the Health Committee or by means of provident dispensaries. The two Reports often differ as to the means by which the ends are to be reached, and the consideration of the means they propose would make matter for many articles. But their main difference is as to the constitution of the authority which will apply their principles to practice.

They both agree in making the County Council the source of the authority and in taking the county as the area. The Majority would create, by a somewhat intricate system of co-optation and nomination, a "Public Assistance Authority," with local "assistance committees," to deal with all cases of need. The Minority would authorize the existing committees of the Council—the Education, the Health, the Asylums, and the Parks Committees—to deal with such cases of need as may meet them in their ordinary work. The Majority would create an *ad hoc* authority, for the purpose of giving such relief; the Minority would leave relief to the direction of committees whose primary concern is education or health, the feeble-minded or the old. The Majority is, further, at great pains to establish a Voluntary Aid Council, which shall be representative of the charitable funds and charitable bodies of the area. This council is to have a recognized position, and to work in close co-operation with the Public Assistance authority. The Minority, though willing to use voluntary charity, suggests no plan for its control or organization. This omission in a scheme otherwise so complete is somewhat remarkable. The administration of the Poor Law may account for most of the mischief in the condition of the people, but the administration of charity is also to a large extent responsible. This extent of charity is unknown. In London alone it is said to amount to more than £7,000,000 a year, and much money is given of which no record is possible. Hitherto all attempts at organization have failed, and it is quite clear that no organization can be enforced. The Majority Report suggests a scheme by which charitable bodies and persons may be partly tempted and partly constrained to co-operate with official bodies. Mr. Nunn, in an interesting note, suggests a further development of a plan by which they might be given a more definite place in the organization of the future. The establishment of Public Welfare Societies in so many localities is a proof that charitable forces are drawing together, and gives hope that if a place is found for them in the established system they may become powerful for good and not for mischief.

The recommendations, however, which we are now considering are not dependent on the establishment of a Voluntary Aid Council; they depend on the principles, as to which both Reports agree. Those principles satisfy the suggested test. If relief in every case be subordinate to treatment, if it be given with care and with full consideration for each individual, there must be good hope that the relief will help and not demoralize, stimulate and not antagonize the recipient. Everything, however, depends on securing an authority and administrators who are willing and able to apply the principles to action. The Majority aim, by the substitution of nomination and co-optation for direct election, to get an authority which will do with new wisdom the old duties of Boards of Guardians. The Minority evidently fear that, if any body of people is established as a relief agency, no change in the method of appointment will prevent the intrusion of the old abuses. The Majority believe that it is the persons on the present Boards which have caused the breakdown, and that if all Boards were as good as the best Boards there would have been no need for the Commission. The Minority, on the other hand, believe that it is the system which is at fault, and that a single authority created to deal with destitution only must fail when it is called on to deal with many-sided human nature in its various struggles and trials.

The difference is one on which much may be said on both sides. It may be argued that a committee and officials whose special and daily duty it is to deal with cases of distress will become experts in such dealing; and it may be equally argued that experts tend to think more of the perfection of their system than of the peculiar needs of individuals, so that their action becomes rigid and incapable of growth. The Charity Organization Committees are such experts, and although they have done service not always recognized, they have become unpopular because they have seemed to be more careful as to their methods than as to the needs of the poor. It may be argued that the Education and Health and other committees have neither the time nor the experience to administer relief to the cases of distress with which their duties bring them into contact; and it may equally be argued that it is because they have in view education or health that their ways of relief will be elastic and human, and therefore guided to the best ends. It may be argued that, as the important matter is to check the use of public funds by necessitous persons, therefore it is the better plan to have in each county one authority skilled in dealing with such persons. It may, on the other hand, be argued that as the more important matter is to prevent any one becoming a necessitous person, therefore it is the better plan to let those authorities which have dealings with people as to education, or health, or any other object, deal with them also when they are threatened or overtaken by distress. Knowledge is more necessary than skill, and the people who need their neighbour's guidance do not form a special class in the community. Society is better regarded as a body of cooperators than as a community divided into "an assistance body" and "the assisted".

The Majority Report in its recommendation is discounted by the fact that the Boards of Guardians—an *ad hoc* body—have failed; and the Minority Report is discounted by the fact that there is a science of relief for which long training is necessary. Both alike seem conscious that success must really depend on the character of the administrators; the Majority therefore recommend many precautions as to the appointment of clerks and relieving officers; the Minority frankly leave the control of relief in the hands of a registrar, whose duty it will be to register every case of relief recommended by any committee, to assess the amount which ought to be repaid, and to proceed to the recovery of the amount. The registrar would therefore, by means of his own officials, make inquiries into the circumstances of every case, and would put his administration of out relief or of, as it is called, "home aliment" on a basis of uniform and judicial impartiality.

The Minority Report has the advantage of scientific precision, but it is somewhat hard on the spirit of compromise so long characteristic of English procedure, and it takes small account of the disturbance which may be caused by the vagaries of weak human nature, and it leaves charity without any control. The Majority has the advantage of securing some continuity with present practices, but in the ingenious attempt to conciliate diverse opinions and to put new pieces on to the old garment, some rents seem to have been made which it will be hard to fill.

The public will, during the next few months, be called upon to decide as to the authority to direct the relief of the poor. The decision cannot be easily made, and ought not to be attempted without much time and thought. One of the tests by which the two systems may be tried during the necessary delay is, I submit, whether (1) an *ad hoc* committee with its subject expert officials or (2) committees appointed for special objects with an independent expert official, are the more likely to administer relief without spreading demoralization, and to stimulate energy without rousing animosity.

THE ABLE.

II. The failure of the present system with the able, the vagrant, the loafer, and the unemployed, who are physically and mentally strong, is the most marked; and reform is an immediate necessity. The Government can hardly go through another Session without doing something to prevent the growth of pauperism among comparatively young men, to check the habit of vagrancy which threatens to become violent, and to meet the demands of the honest unemployed.

The present system deals with the able-bodied by means of the workhouse—the labour yard, the casual ward, the test workhouse—and also by means of out relief and the Unemployed Workmen's Act. The Commission—Majority and Minority—condemn each of these means.

The workhouse, we are told, creates the loafer. "The moment this class of man"—i.e., the easy-going, healthy fellow who feels no call to work—"becomes an inmate so surely does he deteriorate into a worse character still"; and we read also that "the features in the present workhouse system make it not only repellent (as is perhaps necessary), but also, as is unnecessary, degrading. Of all the spectacles of human demoralization now existing in these islands, there can scarcely be anything worse than the scene presented by the men's day ward of a large urban workhouse during the long hours of leisure on week-days or the whole of Sundays. Through the clouds of tobacco-smoke that fill the long low room, the visitor gradually becomes aware of the presence of one or two hundred wholly unoccupied males, of every age between fifteen and ninety—strong and vicious men, men in all stages of recovery from debauch, weedy youths of weak intellect, old men dirty and disreputable . . . worthy old men, men subject to fits, occasional monstrosities or dwarfs, the feeble-minded of every kind, the respectable labourer prematurely invalided, the hardened, sodden loafer, and the temporarily unemployed man who has found no better refuge. In such places there are congregated this winter certainly more than 10,000 healthy, able-bodied men."

The labour yard, we learn, tends to become the habitual resort of the incapables, and "a stay there will demoralize even the best workmen". "In short," says the Minority Report, "whether as regards those whom it includes or those whom it excludes for relief, the labour yard is a hopeless failure, and positively encourages the worst kind of under-employment." The expense of this failure is so great that in one yard the stone broken cost the Guardians £7 a ton.

Casual wards have long been known as the nurseries of a certain class of vagrant—men and women who become familiar with their methods and settle down to their use. They fail as resting-places for honest seekers after work as they travel from town to town, and they fail also—even when made harsher than prisons—to stimulate energy. Poor Law reformers, like Mr. Vallance, have through many years called for their abolition.

Test workhouses represent the supreme effort of the ingenuity of Poor Law officials, and are still recommended to Guardians. In these establishments everything which could possibly attract is excluded. The house is organized after the fashion of a prison, although the officials have neither the training nor the knowledge considered to be necessary for men who hold their fellow-men in restraint; hard and uncongenial work is enforced; the diet is of the plainest, and no association during leisure hours is permitted. The test is so severe that the house is apt to remain empty till the Guardians, overborne by the expense, admit inmates too weak to bear the strain, who therefore break down the system. The inspectors claim credit for success, because applications are prevented, but the Minority Report deals with this claim in an admirably written examination of the whole position. It is no success, for on account of the severity more men are driven on to the streets to provoke the charity of the unthinking; and it is a failure if such treatment adds to the sum of envy, hatred and malice.

The Commissioners of 1834 aimed at abolishing *out-door relief* for the able-bodied, and to this end the central authority and its inspectorate has worked, but exceptions have been allowed "on account of sudden or urgent necessity," and now it is reported that 10,000 different men, mostly between the ages of twenty-five and fifty-five, receive such relief in the course of the year, while at least 10,000 or 20,000 more able-bodied men are allowed out relief by the special authority of the Local Government Board. These numbers tend to increase, and will go on increasing, because nothing is done to give them "such physical or mental restorative treatment as will fit them for employment".

The means, therefore, by which the Poor Law has attempted to deal with the able-bodied may be said to have disastrously failed. Distress has grown, and the people have been demoralized. Ill-will threatens to become violent. The nation, in a hurry to do something, passed the Unemployed Act of 1905, and the Commissioners deal faithfully with the work of the Distress Committees created under that Act. There is much in the work which is suggestive, and many recommendations, such as those which affect the use of labour and farm colonies, are founded on their experience. But the Commissioners are unanimous in the conclusion that relief works are economically useless. "Either," they say, "ordinary work is undertaken, in which case it is merely forestalled . . . or else it is sham work, which we believe to be even more demoralizing than direct relief." "Municipal relief works" (to which the work given by district councils has approximated) "have not assisted, but rather prejudiced, the better class of workman . . . they have encouraged the casual labourers by giving them a further supply of the casual work which is so dear to their hearts and so demoralizing to their character. They have encouraged and not helped the incapables; they have discouraged and not helped the capables."

The present system of dealing with the able-bodied, whether by the means adopted by the Poor Law or by those introduced under the Unemployed Act, fails under our test. It does not relieve those who need relief, it spreads wide demoralization, and it stirs ill-will.

The Commissioners recognize the failure, and recommend a new system. The two Reports agree in their main recommendations. There is need for a check to be placed on the employment of boys "in uneducative and blind-alley occupations," and for the better education of children, both in elementary and continuation schools. There should be a national system of labour exchanges working automatically all over the country, so that workers permanently displaced might easily pass to new occupations, travelling expenses, if necessary, being paid or advanced out of the common purse, and so that the need of work might be tested by the offer of a situation. The Minority Report would enforce on certain employers the use of the register. Both Reports agree that the work given out by Government departments and by local authorities might be regularized, so that most public work would be done when there was least demand for labour by private employers. If at any time afforestation was undertaken, this also might be put on the market as the labour barometer showed labour to be in excess of the demand. Both agree also that there should be some scheme of unemployment insurance, and that with this object subsidies might be given to the unemployment funds of trade unions.

These recommendations, if adopted, might be expected to do much to prevent many of the evils of casual labour and unemployment from falling on future generations; but to meet existing needs the Commissioners recommend emigration and industrial training in institutions, some close to the homes of the workers, some in the country, some farm colonies from which workers would be free to come and go, some detention colonies in which they would be detained for more or less long periods.

There would thus be established, says the Majority Report, in every county four organizations with the common object of maintaining or restoring the workmen's independence: (*a*) An organization for insurance against unemployment, (*b*) a labour exchange, (*c*) a voluntary aid committee, (*d*) an authority which will deal with individuals, according to their needs, by emigration, by migration, or by means of day training institutions, farm colonies and detention colonies. The Minority would secure the same provision by means of one organization in each county.

The workman who, being out of work or unfit for any work on the labour register, or for whom no work is possible, would be referred to the official who, by inquiry, would decide whether he should be trained, mentally or physically, in some near institution, or whether he should be sent to some special and more distant labour colony, his family receiving sufficient money for their daily support. If, having had a fair opportunity, he refused to work, or if he resumed the practice of mendicity or vagrancy, he would, by a magistrate's order, be committed to a detention colony, where, again, he would be given the opportunity during three or four years of gaining the power of self-support.

This in a few words represents the dealing practically recommended by both Reports. It meets the test which the present system fails to meet. The relief is in every case provided which need demands, and, as it is accompanied by training, demoralization is prevented. At the same time, as no relief is given without training, every one is stimulated, while no one can have a sense of injustice. Even those committed to detention colonies are so committed that they may have a chance of restoration. The scheme, it will be observed, deals only with those mentally and physically fit to earn their own living. Those not so fit must be classed among the "unable," and receive treatment which may be compared with that recommended for the feeble-minded.

The two Reports thus agree in their main recommendations, though there are important differences which demand subsequent consideration. The principal difference is that, whereas the Majority Report would make the authority controlling the use of training institutions subject to the county council, the Minority would make it subject only to a central department, such as the Board of Trade or a Labour Minister, who would appoint an official in every county who would superintend the labour registry, the organization for insurance against unemployment, and also the use of the training institutions.

The weight of argument would seem to lie with the Minority's recommendation. One authority—with whom might easily be associated an advisory board from the employers and workmen of the district, and a council representing local charities—having the control of the labour registry, would be best fitted to deal with individuals wanting work; and a national authority, having knowledge of training institutions all over the country, would have the best opportunity for putting a man in the institution most likely to meet his needs.

It might, indeed, be said in conclusion of the whole matter that the recommendations of the Majority Report as to the able-bodied might be adopted, with the substitution of a national for a local authority in the control of the use and management of the training institutions; or that those of the Minority might be adopted, with certain modifications and additions suggested in the Majority Report.

THE FIRST THING TO BE DONE.

When there is such a body of agreement, when that body of agreement applies to the treatment of the able-bodied whose needs are most pressing, and when the recommendations can be adopted with very little interference with existing machinery, the obvious course seems to be the immediate dealing with the unemployed.

There is always a danger lest public interest should be diverted to discuss principles, and it may be that the advocates of a "new Poor Law" and those advocating "no Poor Law" may fill the air with their cries while nothing is done for the poor, just as the advocates of different principles of religious education have prevented knowledge reaching the children. The first thing to do before this discussion begins, and before the Guardians and their friends, obtrusively or subtly, make their protest felt, is, I submit, to take the action which affects the able-bodied. There is no doubt that there should be some form of more continuous education enforced on boys and girls up to the age of eighteen. There is no doubt that there should be labour registries, some form of unemployment insurance, and some regularization of industry, which must be undertaken by a national authority. It would not be unreasonable to ask that the same national authority should organize training institutions, and through its own local official select individuals for training. The Guardians, inasmuch as they would be relieved of the care of casual wards and of provision in their workhouses for the physically and mentally strong, might fairly be called on to provide the necessary payment to keep the families during the period when the wage-earners were in training. This treatment of the able-bodied in a thorough way is suggested by the Report, and offers a compact scheme of reform, which may be carried through as a whole without dislocating existing machinery.

If this be successfully done, then another step might later be taken in dealing with the children or with the sick; and, last of all, when the public mind has become familiar with the respective needs of different classes, it might be decided whether, as the Majority recommend, there should be a special relieving body, or whether, as the Minority recommend, relief should be undertaken by other bodies in the course of their own particular work.

The public, or at any rate the political, mind is always most interested in machinery, and when the cry of "rights" is raised passion is likewise roused. If proposals are now made to abolish Guardians the interest excited will distract attention, and many forces will be moved for their protection.

The chief thing at present is, it seems to me, to draw the public mind to consider the condition of the people as it is laid bare in this Report, to make them feel ashamed that the Poor Law has allowed, and even encouraged, the condition, and to be persistent in insisting on reform. The way to reform is never the easy or short way; it always demands sacrifice, and the public will not make the hard sacrifice of thought till they feel the sufferings and wrongs of the people. The public will, I believe, be made both to feel and to think if the first thing proposed is a complete scheme for dealing with the able-bodied on lines recommended by both Reports.

SAMUEL A. BARNETT.

WIDOWS WITH CHILDREN UNDER THE POOR LAW.[1]

By Mrs. S. A. Barnett.

September, 1910.

[1] A Paper read at the Church Congress, Cambridge.

THE last time that I addressed this Congress of "discreet and learned persons" was three years ago at Yarmouth, when I read a paper on "The Ethics of the Poor Law". It was not a specially good nor interesting paper, but it brought me both letters and interviews, with the result that now the lives of many people, both children and old folk, are better and happier. God grant that this evening's discussion may be as fruitful.

First let us face the magnitude of the subject for discussion—"Widows with Children," not out-of-works, not illegitimate, not deserted wives, all these classes are excluded, and our subject narrowed down to married women, with their legitimate offspring, who have lost the family's breadwinner. Of these, to quote the Poor Law Commissioners' Report,[2] in January, 1907, there were 34,749 widows and 96,342 children in receipt of relief. The large majority of these persons were receiving assistance in their own homes, there being only 1240 widows and 2998 children in receipt of indoor relief in the workhouses.

[2] Majority Report, pp. 35, 36.

Let us, then, follow some of these 96,342 children into their homes, and see what the nation is paying for:—

The first case is quoted from the Majority Report:[3]—

(4) "Widow with seven children, none working. Received 10s. per week relief. Rent £5 10s. Said to be paid by friends. I visited the home, and found it in a very dirty, I might say filthy, condition. The woman is a sloven. She went about the house in a dazed manner. I tried to get particulars of the way she spent her money, but found it impossible. One of the children was at home from school ill, but had not been seen by a doctor. It is obvious . . . that a family of eight persons could not live on 10s. per week."

(5) "Mrs. W., a widow with five children, receives 10s. per week. She is a notorious drunkard, and has lately been turned out of a house in a street where drunkards abound, because her drunken habits disturbed the whole street. When we called she refused to open the door; the relieving officer concluded she was drunk."

[3] Majority Report, p. 150.

That the Local Government Board inspectors are and have been fully aware that such conditions exist is shown again and again by their own words.

Mr. Baldwyn Fleming said:[4]—

"There were many cases receiving outdoor relief where the circumstances . . . were very undesirable. . . . The relieving officers were well acquainted with the cases."

[4] *Ibid.*, p. 151.

Mr. Wethered reported:—

"Some were clean and tidy, but in very many instances the rooms were dirty, ill kept, and sometimes verminous".

Mr. Bagenal's experience speaks of the out-relief class as "Bankrupt in pocket and character," and describes their homes in these words:—

"Cleanliness and ventilation are not considered of any account. The furniture is always of the most dilapidated kind. The beds generally consist of dirty palliasses or mattresses with very scanty covering. The atmosphere is offensive, even fetid, and the clothing of the individuals—old and young—is ragged and filthy. The children are neglected, and furnish the complaints of the National Society for Prevention of Cruelty to Children."

Mr. Williams said:—

"I found far too much intemperance, and sometimes even drunkenness, in cases in which out-relief was being granted. . . . Closely allied to it were filth, both of persons and surroundings, and sadder even was the neglect and resultant cruelty to the children, who were ill-fed and ill-clad."

"Exceptional cases!" I hear you say; "why dwell on them?" So I will read you the words of the Majority Report, ever ready to take the lenient view of the work of the Guardians. Such cases, it reports, "occur with sufficient frequency to be a very potent influence in perpetuating pauperism and propagating disease".

Perhaps, however, figures will convey more startlingly the facts. In order to classify the investigators divided the mothers into four classes[5]— I., good; II., mediocre; III., very unsatisfactory, i.e., slovenly and slipshod; IV., bad, i.e., drunkards, immoral, wilfully neglecting their children.

[5] Minority Report, p. 753.

The percentages in the rural districts were 19 per cent in the third class, 6 per cent in the fourth. "In the towns conditions were, as a rule, much worse." In one urban union 18 per cent came under Class IV. In another great union the appalling percentage rose to 22 per cent. To sum up, the number of children on out relief on 1 January, 1908, in "very unsatisfactory" homes in England and Wales, was more than 30,000; while 20,000 were being paid for in homes "wholly unfit for children". "We can add nothing," say the Commissioners, "to the force of these terrible figures."

Neither are the evils only moral ones. "Investigation," write the authors of the Minority Report, "as to the physical condition of these outdoor relief children in London, Liverpool, and elsewhere brings to light innumerable cases of untreated sores and eczema, untreated erysipelas and swollen glands, untreated ringworm, heart disease, and phthisis," a seed crop the products of which are the unemployed and unemployable.

But now I would propose that we leave these haunts of evil and go to see the home of a respectable widow who is endeavouring to bring up her children to be God-fearing and industrious.

"Mother a seamstress, earning about 9s. a week, and the Board of Guardians granting another 6s. Four children (eleven, nine, six, and two) made happy by the motherly love of a steady, methodical and careful woman, who, however, cannot support them except by working unceasingly, as well as by getting charitable help towards their clothes from the Church, country holidays from the Children's Country Holiday Fund, official help in dinners from the Educational Authority, and medical help from the health visitor or nurse engaged by the Town Council."

What a confusion of sources, what want of inquiry, what danger of overlapping; five organizations to aid the same family, three of them State supplied, two supported by religious or philanthropic persons. On this confusion, which is not only extravagant to the ratepayers, but corrupting to the character of the recipients, the Minority Report lays great stress.

Time forbids me to give more examples, but with this vision of wholesome family affection let us read with attention the following words from the Minority Report:—[6]

"In the vast majority of cases the amount allowed by the Guardians is not adequate". "The children are under-nourished, many of them poorly dressed, and many barefooted. . . . The decent mother's one desire is to keep herself and her children out of the workhouse. She will, if allowed, try to do this on an impossibly inadequate sum, until both she and her children become mentally and physically deteriorated." . . . "It must be remembered," adds a medical expert, "that semi-starvation is not a painful process, and its victims do not recognize what is happening."

    6 Minority Report, p. 747.

Do not all of us who know our parishes know that woman? Her poverty, her strenuousness, her patience, her fatigue, her hopefulness, her periods of hopelessness, and above, below, around all her Mother-love and her faith in God—and what is the result of her efforts, her heroism? Children strong, healthy, skilled, able to support her in her old age and themselves rear a family worthy of such noble moral ancestry? No! her reward will be to see her children weakly men and undergrown girls, all alike in having no stamina, among the first to be pushed out of the labour market. All the love, all the industry, all the heroism ever showered by devoted mothers cannot take the place of milk and bread and air and warmth.

But, it may be asked, "Why does this careful mother so dread the workhouse; there, at least, although she herself would be deprived of her freedom, she would know that her children were well cared for!" To reply to this question it will be necessary once more to turn to the ponderous Blue Book and search the 1238 pages for descriptions of what goes on behind the great walls of those pauper palaces.

It is true that the widow has not read the reports nor even heard of the Poor Law Commission and its colossal labours, worthy of the gratitude and reverence of all who love their country. But these things filter out though not couched in official language. "I can't a-bear of them to go, ma'am," says some work-beaten mother. "There's Mrs. Jones, she lost her baby when they had to go in, as her husband was took with galloping consumption, and her Billy got bad eyes and Susie seemed to lose all her gaiety like." "No! I'd rather go hungry than see them that way and not be able to kiss 'em when they cries." But is it true? It is understandable that individual homes which the Guardians only subsidize may not always be all that they could wish, but when the children are entirely under their care surely what this poor woman alleges cannot be true. Alas! it is far less than the truth. Let us read again and see how the children, not being babies, fare when they are kept in the workhouses.

The following are extracts:[7]—

"The children are not kept separate from the adult inmates. The children's wards left on our minds a marked impression of confusion and defective administration. . . . The eyes of some of the children seemed suspiciously 'weak' and in two or three cases to be suffering from some serious inflammation."

"The chief defect here, as in so many workhouses, is in the accommodation for the children. The girls use the sewing-room as a day-room. The older children go to school one and a half miles distant, taking bread and butter or jam with them, and dining on their return when the other inmates have their tea. The dining-hall is used by all inmates at the same time. . . . Altogether, there is great need for reform in the treatment of the children."

[7] Majority Report, pp. 186, 187.

It is true that children of school age maintained in the workhouses attend the public elementary schools, save for 651 who are still educated within workhouse walls, but the school hours account only for about one-third of the children's waking existence, and during the other two-thirds, which include the long winter evenings, Saturdays and Sundays, and all school holidays, the workhouse is still their only home.

"We cannot," says the Minority Report,[8] "too emphatically express our disagreement with those who accept this [the attendance of children reared in workhouses at public elementary schools] as any excuse for retaining children in the workhouse at all. . . . We paid special attention to this point of the provision for children on our visits to workhouses, large and small, in town and country, in England, Wales, Scotland and Ireland. We saw hardly any workhouse or poorhouse in which the accommodation for children was at all satisfactory. We unhesitatingly agree with the Inspector of the Local Government Board, who gave it to us as his opinion that 'no serious argument in defence of the workhouse system is possible. The person who would urge that the atmosphere and associations of a workhouse are a fit up-bringing for a child merely proves his incapacity to express an intelligent opinion upon the matter.'"

[8] Minority Report, pp. 802, 803.

"We are strongly of opinion," says the Majority Report,[9] "that effective steps should be taken to secure that the maintenance of children in the workhouse be no longer recognized as a legitimate way of dealing with them."

[9] Majority Report, p. 187.

This evil is of long standing; for a dozen years the pressing necessity for the removal from such surroundings of these State-dependent children has been represented to successive Presidents of the Local Government Board, and to Boards of Guardians, and the saddest fact of all is that, at the date of the latest Local Government Board Return, 24,175 children (more than one-third of the total number who are entirely maintained out of the rates) are still being reared in this unsuitable environment, actually a larger number than in any preceding year since 1899.

To all those gentlemen who have read the Royal Commissioners' Report I must apologize for quoting it so largely. Those who have not read it will recognize something of the extreme interest of its contents and take it for their winter's reading.

But to return again to the Widows and Children on out relief. The Majority Report says:—

"The Guardians give relief without knowing whether the recipients can manage on it; they go on giving it without knowing how they are managing on it." "In short, there is a widespread system of trying to compensate for inadequacy of knowledge by inadequacy of relief."

This is a severe condemnation both of the Guardians and the Local Government Board, whose inspectors we know had been long aware of the facts. Moved by the outcry caused by the publication of these revelations, a circular on the "Administration of Outdoor Relief" was issued by the Central Authority last March to the Boards of Guardians, calling on them for greater discrimination in the selection of cases and the adoption of uniform principles.

That these demands were not unnecessary is shown by the following instances of unequal treatment given in the Reports:—

"In one case a widow with four dependent children, and one boy earning 15s. a week, with a total income to the family of 25s., received 7s. from the Guardians, bringing their total up to 32s. a week for six persons. One Board gives 6d. and 5 lb. of flour per week for each child; another family received 5s. a week, bringing their total to 51s. 6d. per week; another 6s. a week for the mother and three children (all little tots) with 'no other known income'."

The action of Boards on this circular has been varied. Some have declared themselves "satisfied with their proceedings," and that "no alteration is required". Others have set to work to settle a scale of payments for certain defined cases; but though every one must rejoice that a circular (though a belated one) has been issued from the Local Government Board, and that the Guardians are moving, yet the proposals do not seem to me to meet the case. The world cannot be divided into good or bad, white or black—infinite are the shades of grey. More, much more, than adequacy or uniformity of payment is required. Many classes of help are needed. I would suggest as possible solutions of this difficult problem (and my long experience of thirty-three years' life in Whitechapel does not allow me to minimize the difficulty) the following plans:—

I.—The children could be boarded out with their own mothers. We have to travel back to Egypt to see how well it succeeded when tried on Moses, and it succeeded because it obtains for the child the one essential basis of all education—i.e. Love. The plan is based on quite a simple principle.

Women have to be engaged by the State to rear children—it is done in workhouses, barrack schools, scattered homes, village communities, and in boarding-out. Why should not some of the women so engaged be the children's own mothers? The mother so employed must be of good character, and have thrifty, home-making virtues, the same sort of qualities, in short, as are sought for in the foster parents of boarded-out children. She would be moved into the country, or into a healthy suburb, and, if her own family is not large enough adequately to employ her, she could have one or two more children or babies sent to her. She would be under close inspection, and the Boarding-out Committee would make her feel that, though the children were her own, yet it was the duty of the State to see that she did her duty to them on a high plane.

For some families this seems to me the best of all possible solutions, but I have to recognize that it is not practicable except for self-respecting worthy women.

II.—To suit those affectionate mothers who are too untutored to do without set tasks of employment and daily supervision, there might be some sort of modification of the plan. Some twenty of these women could be placed in small cottages, or tenements in a quadrangle, and employed for part of the day at one of the giant official institutions for the infirm or imbecile which are scattered all over the country. The children could be kept at school for dinner, and care taken that the women's hours of labour were short enough to enable them to home-make morning and evening when the children return from school.

III.—For other women, who, as the Report says, are "too ignorant to be effective mothers," and yet whose only thought is their children, teaching colonies might be established, the mothers putting themselves into training, with the hope of being ultimately counted as worthy to rear their own children at the expense of the State—a goal to strive for when they have mastered the skilled trade of "mothering".

IV.—For women who are already employed at suitable work, special arrangements could be made as the condition of their receiving out-relief, either concerning their hours of labour or to secure the household assistance necessary to maintain their children as children of every class ought to be kept. I can imagine certain employers, such as the ever public-spirited Mr. Cadbury, being willing to arrange shifts of labour to suit these needs.

V.—From other mothers the children should be removed altogether, and for these children I should counsel emigration, for all workers can cite cases of the ruin of young people, when they reach wage-earning ages, by bad parents claiming their rights over them.

To turn these suggestions into facts would take much work, thought, patience, prayer. "Each case," as the Majority report says, "seems to call for special and individual attention." But is it not worth while? Can we as Christians allow the present condition of things to go on?

Gentlemen, there are 178,520 children in your parishes being more or less supported by the State. Do the clergy know them? What have the clergy done about them? Have many joined the Board of Guardians? Have they remonstrated at the inadequacy of the relief given? Have they made themselves even acquainted with the facts of Poor Law administration in their unions? The other day, I, by chance, met a clergyman—a nice man, vicar of a big church in a large watering-place. His conversation showed he was alert and up-to-date on all controversial matters, even to the place of a comma in the Lord's Prayer, but to my questions as to how the Poor Law children were dealt with in his parish he had to reply, and he did so unashamed, "I don't know". I remember as a child thinking that it was a cruel injustice to punish the man for breaking the Sabbath, when he did not know that there was a law to command him to keep it, and now, looking back down the vista of many years' experience, I understand that Moses but expressed in a detail the law of God which affects the whole of social life. The man was punished because he did not know. At least he bore the penalty of his own ignorance, but in this case it is the children who are punished because of our ignorance.

No! the clergy have not known hitherto; but now they can know. The facts are before them in that vast and fascinating storehouse of knowledge bound in blue, and, having learnt, they can speak; and speaking, what will they say?

Will they blame the Guardians? Will they scold the Local Government Board? Will they shrug their shoulders and talk about "the difficulties of social problems in a complex civilization," or will each say to himself, "Thou art the man" whose fault this is, and then speak and work to get things altered?

Gentlemen, you tell us often that children, child-bearing, child-teaching, child-rearing, child-loving is the vocation of my sex. I agree with you. I want no better calling myself than home-making and child protection, and therefore you will not take it amiss that I, a woman, speak boldly for the children's sake. You have joined in the neglect of these State-dependent children hitherto. You have allowed them by your ignorance to be injured. Are you now going to injure them further by sitting helplessly down before these terrible revelations? The whole world knows how England treats State-supported children, its national assets, the representatives of those the Master took up in His arms—the whole world waits to see what England will do. It is for you to lead. Are you going to accept the facts as irremediable, or by getting them altered thus pay your vows to the Lord?

HENRIETTA O. BARNETT.

THE PRESS AND CHARITABLE FUNDS.[1]

By Canon Barnett.

July, 1906.

[1] From "The Independent Review". By permission of Messrs. Fisher Unwin & Co.

THE Press had been the Church's ablest ally in its effort to fulfil the apostolic precept, and teach the nation to remember the poor. The social instinct may be native to humanity, but it requires an impulse and a direction. The Press has again and again stirred such an impulse and given such direction. Charity was never more abundant, and methods of relief were never more considered.

The Press has been the ally of the Church in creating the better world of the present. But the Press, caught in these later years (as so many persons and bodies have been caught) by the lust of doing and the praise thereof, has aspired to be an administrator of relief. It has not been content with the rôle of a prophet or of a teacher, it has taken a place alongside of Ladies Bountiful, Relief Committees, and Boards of Guardians. It has invaded another province, and rival newspapers have had their own funds, their own agents, and their own systems of relief.

The result is probably an increase in the volume of money given by the readers of the papers. A large fund may, however, be a fallacious test of sympathy. The money subscribed under the pressure of appeal may have been diverted from other objects; and gifts are sometimes made, not for the relief of the poor so much as for the relief of the givers. People have been known to give, that they may enjoy themselves more comfortably; and they may relieve their feelings by a gift, so as to be free to spend a family's weekly income on their own dinner. A large fund is not, therefore, a sufficient evidence of increased sympathy.

But let it be granted that the Press action has brought more money to the service of the poor. The question is: Has it been for good?

I.

The first characteristic of a Press fund is that, when a newspaper undertakes the administration of relief, it has to create its own machinery. It may begin by sending down to the distressed district a clever young man with a cab-load of tickets. Nothing seems easier than to give to those who ask, and so money is poured into the hands of applicants, or sent to the clergy for distribution. A rough experience soon enforces the necessity of inquiry and organization. In West Ham, in the winter of 1904-5, when the Borough Council was spending £28,000 on relief, when the Guardians had 20,000 persons on their out-relief lists and 1300 men in the stone yard, the Press funds were distributed without any inquiry or any attempt at co-operation. I gather a few notes from reports made at the time by a resident in the district.

"Mr. C—— received a large sum from the *D. T.* He relieved 400 regularly; and there was no interchange of names."

"I found one street in which nearly every one had relief."

"I was asked to visit a starving case on Sunday; and found a good dinner stowed away under the table."

"One man in receipt of 47s. a week in wages received twelve tickets from the *D. N.* on Christmas Eve, and did not turn up to his work for four days, though extra pay was offered for Boxing Day."

"A man," says a relieving officer, "came to me on Friday and had 3s. He went to the Town Hall and got 4s. His daughter got 3s. from the same source; his wife 5s. from a Councillor, and late the same night a goose."

Another relieving officer reported:—

"Outside my office a 4-lb. loaf could be bought for 1d., and a 2s. relief ticket for two pots of beer."

"The public-houses did far better when the relief funds were at work."

"My impression is, that more than 500 people who were in receipt of out relief in my district received relief from the funds; but we were never consulted."

"The relieving officers had to be under police protection for four months."

Such an experience naturally forced the newspapers to consider their ways. The system of doles was abandoned, and local organizations were established to give relief in some approved method. Let it be granted, without prejudice, that the administration was made so effective as to justify a report of good work to the subscribers to the fund. Let it be granted that a large number of the unemployed were given work, that families were emigrated, and that the hands of existing agencies were strengthened. There are still two criticisms which may be directed against the Press position as an administrator of relief. The first is, that the experience by which it learns wisdom is disastrous to the people. The waste of money is itself serious, but that is a small matter alongside of the bitter feeling, the suspicion, the loss of heart, the loss of self-respect, the lying, which are encouraged when gifts are obtained by clamour and deceit. Gifts may be poisons as well as food, and gifts badly given make an epidemic of moral disease.

The second criticism is, that the organization, when it is created, disturbs, displaces, and confuses other organizations, while it is not itself permanent. The Press action leaves, it may be said, a trail of demoralization, and does not remain sufficiently long in existence to clear up its own abuses.

II.

Another characteristic of a Press fund is, that a newspaper raises its money by word pictures of family poverty. Its interviewers break in on the sacredness of home. They come to the poor man's house without the sympathy of long experience, without any friendly introduction, with an eye only to the "copy" which may best provoke the gifts of their readers. They write about the secrets of sorrow and suffering. They make public the bitterness of heart which is precious to the soul, and thus intermeddle with the grief which no stranger can understand. Their tales lower the standard of human dignity; they make the poor who read the tales proud of conditions of which they should be ashamed, and they make the rich think of the distress rather than of the self-respect of their neighbours.

The effects of the Press method of raising money by uncovering the secrets of private sorrow may be summed up under three heads.

(*a*) It increases poverty. Poverty comes to be regarded as a sort of domestic asset. The family which can make the greatest show of suffering has the greatest chance of relief, and examples are found of people who have made themselves poor, or appear poor, for the sake of the fund.

(*b*) It degrades the poor. A subtle effect of this advertisement of private suffering is, that people so advertised lose their self-respect. They, as it were, like to expose themselves, and make a show of what ought to be hidden; they glory in their shame, and accept at others' hands what they themselves ought to earn. They beg, and are not ashamed; they are idle, and are not self-disgraced. They are content to be pitied.

(*c*) It hardens the common conscience. A far-reaching effect of these tales of suffering heaped on suffering is, that the public demands more and more sensation to move it to benevolence. The natural human instinct which makes a man care for a man is weakened; and he who yesterday shrank from the thought of a sorrowing neighbour, is to-day hardly moved by a tale of starvation, anguish, and death.

Feeling, we are taught, which is acted on and not actively used, becomes dulled; and the Press tales which work on the feeling of their readers at last dry up the fountain of real charity. The public in a way finds its interest, if not its enjoyment, in the news of others' suffering.

III.

A third characteristic of a Press fund is, the daily bold advertisement of the amount received. Rival funds boast themselves one against another; and rivalry is successful in drawing in thousands and tens of thousands of pounds. The magnitude of these sums is, however, always misleading; and people for whom the money is subscribed think there is no end to the resources for their relief. The demand is increased; people pour in from the country to share the benefit; workmen lay down their tools to put in their claims; energy is relaxed; greed is encouraged; and, when it is found that the relief obtained is small, there are suspicion and discontent. The failure of the funds which depend on advertisement suggests the wisdom of the Divine direction, that charity should be in secret.

Such are some of the criticisms which I would offer on the Press funds. I grant that they apply to all "funds"; and most of us who have tried to "remember the poor" have seen our work broken by the intrusion of some outside and benevolent agency. The truth is, that the only gift which deserves the credit of charity is the personal gift—what a man gives at his own cost, desiring nothing in return, neither thanks nor credit. What a man gives, directed by loving sympathy with a neighbour he knows and respects, this is the charity which is blessed; and its very mistakes are steps to better things. A "fund" cannot easily have these qualities of charity. Its agents do not give at their own cost; its gifts cannot be in secret; it cannot walk along the path of friendship; it is bound to investigate. When, therefore, any "fund" assumes the ways of charity, when it claims irresponsibility, when it expects gratitude, when it is unequal and irregular in its action, it justifies the strange cry we have lately heard: "Curse your charity".

A "fund," voluntary or legal—it seems to me—should represent an effort to do justice, and should follow the ways of justice. Its object should be, not to express pity, or even sympathy, and it should not ask for gratitude. Its object is to right wrong, to redress the unfairness which follows the triumph of success, and give to the weak and disherited a share in the prosperity they have done their part to create. A "fund" because its object is to do justice, ought to follow scientific lines; it ought to be guided by sound judgment; it ought to be administered by skilled officials; and it ought to do nothing which can lower any man's strength and dignity. On the contrary, it ought to do everything to open to the lowest the way of honourable living. Its action must be just, and seem to be just; it must represent the mind, not of one class only, but of all classes.

There have been "funds" which more or less approach this ideal. The Mansion House Fund of 1903-4 issued a Report which stands as a model of what is possible; and its ideal is that of the ablest Poor Law reformers. Press funds created by excitement, and directed in a hurry, will hardly reach such an ideal. They will neither by their genesis nor by their action represent the ways of justice.

The Press, I submit, deserts its high calling when it offers itself as a means by which its readers may easily do their duty to the poor. The relief of the poor can never be easy—the easiest way is almost always the wrong way. The Press, when it makes it possible for rich people to satisfy their consciences by a donation to its "funds" lets them escape their duty of effort, of sacrifice, and of personal sympathy. It spoils the public, as foolish parents spoil children by taking away the call to effort.

The Press has great possibilities in teaching people to remember the poor. It might educate the national conscience to make a national effort to remove the causes of want of employment, physical weakness, and drunkenness. It might rouse the rich to the patriotism which the Russian noble expressed, when he said that "the rights of property must give way to national needs". It might set the public mind to think of a heart of the Empire in which there should be no infant of days, no young man without hope, and no old man without the means of peace. The Press has done much. It seems to me a loss if, for the sake of the immediate earthly link, if for the sake of creating a "fund" to relieve present distress, it misses the eternal gain—the creation of a public mind which will prevent any distress.

SAMUEL A. BARNETT.

WHAT IS POSSIBLE IN POOR LAW REFORM.[1]

By Canon Barnett.

22 September, 1909.

[1] From "The Westminster Gazette". By permission of the Editor.

THE Archbishop of Canterbury did good service in the House of Lords in forcing upon public attention the condition of the people as has been revealed by the Poor Law Commission. There was only a small attendance of Peers to hear his statement, and the public mind has hardly been stirred. The imagination is not trained in England. For want of it, as Lord Goschen used to say, our fathers lost America, and for want of it we are likely to blunder into social trouble. The Lords, who are so keen in defence of property, do not realize that there are greater dangers to property in the presence of the unemployed than in the weapons forged by the Budget, and the public mind forgets in the summer the "bitter cries" which every winter rise from broken homes and shattered lives.

But the facts remain as they have been stated by the Archbishop. There is poverty; there is distress; the community suffers grievous loss while strong men lose their power to work and hearts are hardened by want. All the time "out relief is administered so as to foster and encourage dirt, disease, and immorality, and the workhouse accommodation for the aged is in some cases so dreary as to be absolutely appalling, while in others it is palatial". The Archbishop "absolutely challenged the statement that these difficulties could be met except by a new system under a new law". The whole evidence showed that things are radically wrong, and rendered it impossible to argue that "we are getting on well enough".

Mr. Burns rests in the progress under the Guardians' administration during the last sixty years. "In-door pauperism has dropped from 62 to 26 per 1000, out-door pauperism from 54 to 16, and child pauperism from 26 to 7 per 1000," while "the cost per head of in-door paupers has risen from £7 18s. to £13 5s. and out-door pauperism from £3 11s. to £6 1s. 5d." Striking figures, but they do not alter the facts which the inquiries of the Commissioners have brought to light. There are still workhouses which are hot-beds of corruption; there are still thousands of children brought up under pauper influences, which the boasted education for a few hours a week in an elementary school cannot stem; there are still feeble-minded people of both sexes who, for want of care, increase the number of lunatics and criminals; there are still thousands of children who cannot be properly clothed or fed on the pittance of out relief; there are still strong men and women, stirred by a deterrent system to become enemies of society, and to defy, by idleness, the authority which would, by severity, force them to work. Let any one whose mind Mr. Burns's figures satisfy dip into the pages of the Poor Law Commission Report, and certainly his heart will be indignant.

"No greater indictment" it has been truly said, "has ever been published against our civilization."

Progress indeed cannot be judged by comparative figures. In 1850 it would have marked a great change if pauperism had dropped from 62 to 26 per 1000, but in 1910 it may be that 26 per 1000 constitutes as heavy a burden. Truth depends on relation. The social conscience has become much more sensitive. This generation cannot brook wrongs which previous generations brooked. Our self-respect is wounded by the thought of poverty which our care might remove. Poverty itself is recognized to be something worse than want of food. Every citizen is necessary, not only that he may work for the commonwealth, but that he may contribute by his thoughtful interest to make government efficient and human. The standard by which individual value is judged has been raised. Figures are not by themselves measures of progress, because every unit in the course of years changes its value, and to-day, as compared with sixty years ago, each man, woman and child may be said to have a worth which has increased tenfold. Official figures do not recognize worth and are therefore irritating; they increase and do not allay bitterness.

Something then must be done, and the debate in the House of Commons suggests something which might be done immediately. The Prime Minister and the Government might at once adopt certain recommendations on which there is general agreement, and which would not involve the immediate substitution of a new body of administration in the place of the Guardians. It might, for instance, 1. establish compulsory continuation schools; 2. make adequate provision for the feeble-minded; and 3. develop some method of training for the able-bodied and able-minded who have lost their way in the industrial world.

There is general agreement as to the treatment of the feeble-minded, as to the training of the young, and as to the way of discipline for the unemployed.

The public has hardly recognized what is involved in the neglect of the measures recommended for the care of the feeble-minded. They do not know how much crime, how much poverty, and how much drunkenness may be traced to this cause, or they would not expect the laws which assume strong-mindedness to be effective. What effect can prison have on characters too feeble to resolve on reformation? What appeal to independence can have weight with those who cannot reason? Evidence abounds in the pages of Reports, and the best thought of the times has agreed on the recommendations. If these recommendations were put into a Bill and adopted a reform would be achieved which would cut deeply into the burden of unemployment and vice under which the nation now labours.

Then again as to the training of the young. Compulsory continuation schools might be established.

It is grievous to reflect that while the country is expending £23,000,000 on education, there should be a large body of men and women without any resource other than that of the mechanical use of their hands and without any interest to satisfy their minds. It may be that something is wrong in our elementary schooling, but it is hard to realize how the boy who leaves school to-day, a good reader and writer, and of clean habits, can become the dull, ignorant, and almost helpless man of thirty or thirty-five who stands among the unemployed at the table of the Relief Committee. Nevertheless it is so, and the tale of his descent has been often told. The boy, free of school, throws off school pursuits as childish things. He will have no more to do with books or with learning. He takes a situation where he can get the largest wages, and where least call is made on mental effort. He has money to spend and he spends it on the pleasures which give the most excitement. At the age of eighteen or twenty he is no longer wanted as a boy, and he has no skill or intelligence which would fit him for well-paid work as a man. He becomes a casual labourer, or perhaps gets regular employment in some mechanical occupation. Before he is forty, he is very frequently among the "unemployed," his hands capable only of doing one sort of work, and his head incapable of thinking out ways or means. His schooling has been practically wasted and he is again a burden on the community.

All inquiry goes to show that neglected boyhood is the chief source of "the unemployed". Care in securing good places for boys when they leave school, and offers of technical teaching may do something, but these means do not serve to create the intelligent labourer, on whom, more than on the skilled artisan, the wealth of the country depends. "No skilled labourer," Mr. Edison is reported to have said, "is better than the English, and no unskilled labourer is worse." The intelligent labourer is one who does common work so as to save money; one who can understand and repeat instructions; one who can rise to an emergency; one who serves others' interests and finds others' interests.

Our labourers have not this intelligence because the boy's mind, just opened at school, has been allowed to close; he has been taken away from learning just when it was becoming interesting. The obvious remedy is compulsory continuation schools, and these have been recommended again and again by investigators and committees.

Let it be enacted that young persons under eighteen cannot be employed unless their employers allow time for attendance at such schools on three days a week, and receive a certificate of attendance—let it be made obligatory on all young persons engaged in industrial work that they attend such schools. Great employers like Messrs. Cadbury have found it in their interest to make such attendance compulsory on the young persons they employ. A Departmental Committee would soon discover the best way of enforcing compulsion, and the Government by this simple means would do much to stop unemployment and poverty at its source.

Some method of training the able-bodied and able-minded unemployed might be developed.

These form a distinct class. They cannot be helped by relief, and they are demoralized by relief works. They passed through boyhood without getting the necessary equipment for life; they have, in a sort of way, a claim for such equipment, and failing such they must be a burden to the community. There are some ready to respond at once; there are others who, by long neglect, have become indolent and defiant. The first need to be put on farms or in shops where they will receive training.

Hollesley Bay is an example of such a farm, though the experiment has unfortunately been confused by the introduction of men who receive simple doles of work. But among the hundreds of married men with decent homes, and bearing good reports from employers, there are many in whom capacity is dormant. Pathetic indeed is their appeal, as worn in body and mind, ragged in clothing, they tell of work lost "because motors have taken the place of horses," "because machinery has been introduced," because "boys do men's work"; pathetic is the appeal of men who, having lost their way in life, can see nothing before them but endless casual jobs, in which they will lose any strength they gain by the fresh air and food of Hollesley. If only they could be told that by learning to work and use their brains, they would be given a chance on the land or in the Colonies. If only they could realize that they might, as others have done, become fit to occupy one of the cottages on the estate, how surely they would throw their hearts into the work and feel the joy of seeing things grow under their hands. There is no need of controversial legislation. Training farms or shops could be provided, and if the decision be deferred as to whether the control of the training farm or shops should be local or national, it might be agreed that the experiment should be made by the Board of Trade or the Board of Agriculture.

If the latter department took charge of the Colony, admitted only unemployed men fitted for agriculture, trained them, and put them in the way of taking up holdings, an experiment would be tried of immense value for future legislature.

Then, as to the other able-bodied and able-minded unemployed who have become idle and almost enemies of society. It has long been agreed that it is necessary to detain them for periods of three or four years, during which they would be given the opportunity of learning to work. The place of detention would not be a prison, but a School of Industry, in which their capacities would be developed and their self-respect encouraged. The organization of such a place of discipline might involve thought, but its establishment need involve the Government in no long controversy. The Poor Law Commission and the Vagrancy Commission are at one in urging the necessity, and it must be obvious to anyone that until some means is discovered for removing from "the unemployed" the "idle and vagrant class," the public mind will never AGREE TO WISE DEALING WITH THE PROBLEM.

Here then is something possible, something which even a Government so burdened as the present might accomplish. The direct effect would be great, if boys were checked on their way to the ranks of the unemployed; if some untrained men and women were taken from the streets and restored trained to the labour market; if the feeble-minded and the idle were removed from unwise sympathy and unfair abuse. The indirect effect would also be great, as the conviction would spread that the Government was indeed taking a matter in hand which has been year by year postponed. There would be more hope of peace and good-will between rich and poor. When so much is at once possible, is it reasonable that nothing should be done till a complete scheme has been devised?

It does not seem to be over-sanguine to believe that there are earnest men among the younger M.P.'s who, putting party aside, will agree to do what has been shown to be possible for the young people, the feeble-minded, and the unemployed.

SAMUEL A. BARNETT.

CHARITY UP TO DATE.[1]

By Canon Barnett.

February, 1912.

[1] From "The Contemporary Review". By permission of the Editor.

THE tender mercies of the thoughtless, as of the wicked, are often cruel, and charity when it ceases to be a blessing is apt to become a curse; A Mansion House fund we used in old days to count among the possible winter horrors of East London. The boldly advertised details of destitution, the publication of the sums collected, the hurried distribution by irresponsible and ignorant agents, and the absence of any policy, stirred up wild expectation and left behind a trail of bitterness and degradation. The people were encouraged in deception, and were led on in the way which ends in wretchedness.

In 1903 a Committee was formed which used a Mansion House fund to initiate a policy of providing honourable and sufficiently paid work which would, at the same time, test the solid intention of unemployed and able-bodied applicants. The report of that Committee has been generally accepted, and has indeed become the basis of subsequent action and recommendations. It seemed to us East Londoners as if the bad time had been passed, and that henceforth charitable funds would flow in channels to increase fruitfulness and not in floods to make devastation.

The hope has been disappointed. Funds inaugurated by newspapers, by agencies, or by private persons have appeared in overwhelming force, and have followed in the old bad ways. The heart of the public has been torn by harrowing descriptions of poverty and suffering, which the poor also read and feel ashamed. The means of relief are often miserably inadequate. A casual dinner eaten in the company of the most degraded cannot help the "toiling widows and decent working-men," "waiting in their desolate homes to know whether there is to be an end to their pains and privations". Two or three hours spent in fields hardly clear of London smoke, after a noisy and crowded ride, is not likely to give children the refreshment and the quiet which they need for a recreative holiday.

Much of the charity of to-day, it has to be confessed, is mischievous, if not even cruel, and to its charge must be laid some of the poverty, the degradation, and the bitterness which characterize London, where, it is said, eight million sterling are every year given away. Ruskin, forty years ago, when he was asked by an Oxford man proposing to live in Whitechapel what he thought East London most wanted, answered, "The destruction of West London". Mr. Bernard Shaw has lately, in his own startling way, stated a case against charity, and we all know that the legend on the banner of the unemployed, "Curse your charity," represents widely spread opinion.

But—practically—what is the safe outlet for the charitable instinct? The discussion of the abolition of charity is not practical. People are bound to give their money to their neighbours. Human nature is solid—individuals are parts of a whole—and the knowledge of a neighbour's distress stirs the desire to give something, as surely as the savour of food stirs appetite. But as in the one case the satisfaction of the appetite is not enough unless the food builds up the body and strength, so in the other case the charity which relieves the feelings of the giver is not enough unless it meets the neighbour's needs. Those needs are to-day very evident, and very complex. Our rich and ease-loving society knows well that a family supported on twenty shillings a week cannot get sufficient food, and that even forty shillings will not provide means for holidays—for travel or for study. There will be children whose starved bodies will never make strong men and women; and there will be men and women who live anxious and care-worn lives, who cannot enjoy the beauties and wonders of the world in which they have been placed.

There are ghastly facts behind modern unrest, which are hardly represented by tales of destitute children and the sight of ragged humanity congregated around the free shelters. The needs are obvious, and they are very complex. The man whose ragged dress and haggard face cries out for food, has within him a mind and a soul fed on the crumbs which fall from the thoughts of the times, and he is a member of society from which he resents exclusion. Relief of a human being's need must take all these facts into account. It must not give him food, at the expense of lowering his self-respect; it must not provide him with pleasure at the expense of degrading his capacity for enjoying his higher calling as a man, and it must not be kind at the expense of making independence impossible. The man who is stirred by the knowledge of his neighbour's needs must take a deal of trouble.

The only safe outlet for the charitable instinct is, it may be said, that which is made by thinking and study. The charity which is thoughtless is charity out of date. It is always hard to be up to date, because to be so involves fresh thinking, and it is so much easier to say what has been said by previous generations, and to imitate the deeds of the dead benefactors. They who would really serve their neighbour's needs by a gift must bring the latest knowledge of human nature to bear on the applicant's character, and treat it in relation to the structure of society as that structure is now understood. They must be students of personality and of the State. They must consider the individual who is in need or the charitable body which makes an appeal, as carefully as a physician considers his case; they must get the facts for a right diagnosis, and bring to the cure all the resources of civilization. The great benefactors of old days were those who thought out their actions—as, for instance, when Lady Burdett-Coutts met the need of work by building amid the squalor of East London a market beautiful enough to be a temple, or as Lord Shaftesbury when he inaugurated ragged schools—but new ages demand new actions, and the spiritual children of the great dead are not they who act as they acted, but those who give thought as they gave thought.

The charity which does not flow in channels made by thought is the charity which is mischievous. People comfort themselves and encourage their indolence by saying they would rather give wrongly in ten cases than miss one good case. The comfort is deceptive. The gift which does not help, hinders, and it is the gifts of the thoughtless which open the pitfalls into which the innocent fall and threaten the stability of society. Such gifts are temptations to idleness, and widen the breach between rich and poor. When people of good-will, in pursuit of a good object, do good deeds which are followed by cries of distress and by curses there is a tragedy.

Charity up to date, whether it be from person to person or through some society or fund, must be such as is approved by the same close thinking as business men give to their business, or politicians to their policy. The best form of giving must always, I think, be that from person to person. Would that it were more used—would that those whose feelings are stirred by the sight of many sick folk were content to try and heal one! There are always individuals in need at our own door—neighbours, workpeople, relatives, servants; there is always among those we know some one whose home could be made brighter, or whose sickness could be lightened; there are tired people who could be sent on holiday, boys or girls who could be better educated. Gifts which pass from person to person are something more than ordinary gifts. "The gift without the giver is bare," and when the giver's thought makes itself felt, the gift is enriched. The best form of charity, therefore, is personal, and if for some reason this be impossible, then the next best is that which strengthens the hands of persons who are themselves in touch with neighbours in need, such as are the almoners of the Society for the Relief of Distress, the members of the Charity Organization Committees, or the residents in Settlements.

The personal gift, inspired by good-will and directed by painstaking thought, is the best form of charity, but people who have learnt what organizations and associations can do will not be content unless those means also are applied to the relief of their neighbours. The consequence is the existence of numberless societies for numberless objects. "Which of them may be said to represent charity up to date?" The answer I submit is, "Those which approve themselves to thoughtful examination".

Appeals which touch the feelings of the readers, with well-known names as patrons and hopeful forecasts, should not be sufficient to draw support. The would-be subscriber must leisurely apply his mind, and weigh the proposals in the light of modern knowledge. The giving a subscription involves a large responsibility; it not only withdraws from use money which, as wages, would have employed useful labour, but it may actually be a means of doing mischief. As one familiar with the working of many charities, I would appeal for more thoughtfulness on the part of all subscribers. People must think for themselves and judge for themselves; but perhaps, out of a long experience, I may suggest a few guiding principles.

I. Charities should aim at encouraging growth rather than at giving relief. They should be inspired by hope rather than by pity. They should be a means of education, a means of enabling the recipient to increase in bodily, mental, or spiritual strength. If I spend twenty shillings on giving a dinner or a night's lodging to twenty vagrants, I have done nothing to make them stronger workers or better citizens, I have only kept poverty alive; but if I spend the same sum in sending one person to a convalescent hospital, he will be at any rate a stronger man, and if during his stay at the hospital his mind is interested in some subject—in something not himself—he will probably be a happier man. Societies which devote a large income to providing food and clothing do not in the long run reduce the number of those in want, while Societies which promote the clearing of unhealthy areas, the increase of open space about town dwellings, greater accessibility to books and pictures, gradually raise people above the need of gifts of food and clothing. Hospitals which do much in restoring strength to the sick would do more if they used their reputation and authority to teach people how to avoid sickness, and to make a public opinion which would prevent many diseases and accidents. The distinguished philanthropist who used to say she would rather give a poor man a watch than a coat was, I believe, wiser than another philanthropist who condemned a poor woman for spending her money on buying a picture for her room. It is more important to raise self-respect and develop taste than just to meet physical needs.

Charities intruding themselves upon the intimacies of domestic life have by their patronage often dwarfed the best sort of growth. Warnings against patronizing the poor are frequent, but many charities are by their very existence "patronizing," and many others, by sending people to collect votes, by requiring expressions of their gratitude, and by the attitude of their agents, do push upon the poor reminders of their obligations. They belong to a past age, and have no place in the present age, where they foster only a cringing or rebellious attitude. It has been well said that, "a new spirit is necessary in dealing with the poor, a spirit of humility and willingness to learn, rather than generosity and anxiety to teach". This is only another form of saying that charities must be educational, because no one can educate who is not humble. Our schools, perhaps, will have further results when the teachers cease to call themselves "masters!"

II. Charities should, I think, look to, if not aim at, their own extinction. Their existence, it must be remembered, is due to some defect in the State organization or in the habits of the people. Schools, for instance, were established by the gifts of good-will to meet the ignorance from which people suffered, and when the State itself established schools the gifts have been continued for the sake of methods and experiments to meet further needs which the State has not yet seen its way to meet. Charities, in this case, have looked, or do look, to their own extinction when the State, guided by their example, may take up their work. They have been pioneers, original, daring by experiment to lead the way to undiscovered good. Relief societies have, in like manner, shown how the State may help the poor by means which respect their character, by putting work within their reach, by emigrating those fit for colonial life, by giving orphan children more of the conditions of a family home. There are others which have looked, or still look, to their extinction, not in State action, but in co-operation with other societies with which they now compete. Competition may be the strength of commerce, but co-operation is certainly the strength of charity, and wise are those charities which are content to sink themselves in common action and die that they may rise again in another body. The Charity Organization Societies in some of the great cities have in this way lost themselves, to live again in Social Welfare Councils and Civic Leagues. There are, finally, other charities which, by their own action, tend to make themselves unnecessary. The Children's Country Holiday Fund, for instance, by giving country holidays to town children, and by making the parents contribute to the expense, develop at once a new desire for the peace and beauty of the country and a new capacity for satisfying this desire. When parents realize the necessity of such holiday and know how it can be secured, this Fund will cease to have a reason for existence.

Charities are many which fulfil this condition, but charities also are many which do not fulfil it. They seem to wish to establish themselves in permanence, and go on in rivalry with the State and with one another. There is waste of money, which might be used in pioneer work, in doing what is equally well done by others; there is competition which excites greed and imposition, and there is overlapping. Very little thought is wanted to discover many such charities which now receive large incomes from the public.

A wise observer has said: "A charity ought every twenty-five years to head a revolution against itself". Only by some such means can it be brought into adjustment with the new needs of a new time, only by some such means will it clear off excrescences and renew its youth. But, failing such power of self-reform, it is worthy of consideration whether every twenty-five years each charity should not be compelled to justify its existence before some State Commission.

III. Charities should keep in line with State activities. The State—either by national or by municipal organization—has taken over many of the duties which meet the needs of the people. Ignorance, poverty, disease and dullness have all been met, and the means by which they are being met are constantly developed. The Church, it may be said, has so far converted the State, and a cheerful payer of rates may perhaps deserve the same Divine commendation as the cheerful giver. But State organizations, however well considered and well administered, will always want the human touch. They will not, like the charities, be fitful because dependent on subscribers and committees, but they will not, like charities, temper their actions to individual peculiarities and feelings. Charities, therefore, I think, do well when they keep in line with State activities. They may, for instance, working in co-operation with the Guardians, undertake the care of the families when the bread-winner is in the infirmary, or superintend the management of industrial colonies to which the unemployed may be sent, or provide enfeebled old people with pensions until the age when they are eligible for the State pension. They may, in connexion with the School and Education authorities, support the Care Committees who look after the interest of children in elementary schools, or, like Mrs. Humphry Ward's society, give guidance in play during the children's leisure hours. They may also, in conjunction with the Sanitary Authorities, work for the increase of health and the wiser use of playgrounds and means of recreation. Men and women of good-will may, I believe, find boundless opportunities if they will serve on Municipal bodies or on the Committees appointed by such bodies to complement their work.

It may, indeed, be a further indictment against charities that much of the good-will which might have improved and humanized State action has by them been diverted. If, for instance, the passion of good-will which now finds an outlet in providing free shelters and dinners for the starving, or orphanages for destitute children, had gone to improve Casual Wards and Barrack Schools, many evils would have been prevented. At any rate, it may be said that charities working alongside of the State organizations would become stronger, and State organizations inspired by the charities would become more humane. It costs more, doubtless, to work in co-operation with others, and to subject self-will to the common will as a member of a Board of Guardians, than to be an important member of a charitable committee, but in charity it is cost which counts.

Charity—to sum up my conclusion—represents a very important factor in the making of England of to-morrow. The outbreak of giving, of which there has been ample evidence this Christmas, may represent increased good-will and more vivid realization of responsibility for those afflicted in mind, body, or estate, or it may represent the impatience of light-hearted people anxious to relieve themselves and get on to their pleasures. Society is out of joint because the wealth of the rich and the poverty of the poor have been brought into so great light. It seems intolerable that when wealth has to invent new ways of expenditure, there should be families where the earnings are insufficient for necessary food, where the children cannot enjoy the gaiety of their youth, where the boys and girls pass out through unskilled trades to pick up casual labour and casual doles. The needs are many, but the point I wish to urge is that charity which intends to help may hinder. No gift is without result, and some of the gifts are responsible for the suffering, carelessness, and bitterness of our times. Charity up to date is that which gives thought as well as money and service. The cost is greater, and many who will even deny themselves a pleasure so as to give a generous cheque cannot exercise the greater denial of giving their thought. "There is no glory," said Napoleon, "where there is no danger;" and we may add, there is no charity where there is no thought, and thought is very costly.

SAMUEL A. BARNETT.

WHAT LABOUR WANTS.[1]

By Canon Barnett.

May, 1912.

[1] From "The Daily News". By permission of the Editor.

WORKING men have become, we are often told, the governing class. They form a large part, perhaps the majority, of the electorate, and theirs is the obligation of making the laws and directing the policy on which depend the safety and honour of the nation. They have come into an inheritance built up at great cost, and on them lies the responsibility for its care and development.

Working-men, in order that they may fulfil their obligation and deliver themselves of their responsibility, may rightly, I think, urge a moral claim on the community for the opportunities by which to fit themselves for the performance of their duties. They enjoy by the sacrifice of their ancestors the inestimable privilege of freedom, but the value of freedom depends on the power to take advantage of its possibilities: the right to run in a race is all very well, but it is not of great use if the runner's legs and arms are crippled. Freedom, in fact, implies the capacity to do or enjoy something worth doing or enjoying. The working classes, who, as members of a free nation, have been entrusted with the government of the nation, cannot do what is worth doing or what they are called to do if their bodies are weakened by ill health and their minds cribbed and cabined by ignorance. How can they whose childhood has been spent in the close, smoky, and foetid air of the slums, whose bodies have been weakened in unhealthy trade, take their share in the support or defence of the nation? How can they who have learned no history, whose minds have had no sympathetic training, whose eyes have never been opened to the enjoyment of beauty, understand the needs of the people or grasp the mission of the Empire? Working men have thus a moral claim that they shall have the opportunity to secure health and knowledge, sanitary dwellings, open spaces, care in sickness and the prevention of disease, schools, university teaching, and easy access to all those means of life which make for true enjoyment.

But when such opportunities have been provided, poverty often prevents their use. This excuse does not, indeed, hold universally, and it is much to be wished that the Labour Press and other makers of Labour opinion would more often urge the importance of taking advantage of the provided means for health and knowledge. They may have reason for stirring men against the unfairness of an economic system and uniting them in a strike against the ways of capital, but success would be of little value unless the men themselves become stronger and wiser. Many workmen—for example, those engaged in the building trades—have abundant leisure during the winter. It would be well, if they, as well as those who consume hours in attending football matches, would spend some time in developing their capacities of mind and body. Labour indeed needs a chaplain who will preach that power comes from what a man is, and not only from what a man has. The Labour Press, with its voice reiterating complaints, and its eyes fixed on "possessions," makes reading as dreary as the pages of a society or financial journal.

But this is digression, and the fact remains that poverty does in the case of thousands and hundreds of thousands of families prevent the possibility of using the means necessary for the development of their capacities. A wage of 20s. a week cannot permit schooling for the children up to the age of fifteen; it will not, indeed, provide sufficient food for the healthy life even of a small family. It can give no margin for the little recreations by which the powers of the mind are renewed, and does not allow for the leisure during growing years which is necessary to the making of the mind. It leaves the breadwinner fretted by anxiety lest in days of sickness or unemployment the wolf may enter the door and destroy the home.

The mass of labourers are, in a word, too poor to be healthy or wise; they are not fit to take a part in government, and they have not the opportunity to make themselves fit. Their work is often costly though it is cheap, and their votes are worthless though gained by much canvassing. Wages which are not a living wage unfit workmen for their duty in the government of the nation.

Does this fact justify a moral claim for a living wage to be fixed and enforced by the community? Ought a wage sufficient for the support of manhood to be a first charge on the product of labour and capital? The answer has in effect been given by the establishment of Wages Boards. There are now four trades in which a wage judged by a representative committee to be a living wage is enforced, and the same principle has lately been applied to the mining industry. The extension to other trades—if the experiment succeeds—can only be a matter of time. The claim of labour has been admitted, and the immediate question is, what is likely to be the result. Employers who are forced to give a higher wage will certainly require a higher standard of work. From one point of view this is all to the good. The acceptance of low-class work is as costly to the nation as it is degrading to the worker; it is a common loss when workers make constant mistakes for want of intelligence, and prove themselves to be not worthy a living wage. Every one is the better for the discipline which is required by the service of men; it is likely to make the nation richer and the workers more self-respecting, if they are free to fit themselves to take their part in government. It will, in economic language, probably tend to decrease the cost of production, and therefore the cost of living.

But there is another point of view. The raising of the standard of work will at once throw out the less able, the unskilful, the ignorant, and the lazy. Is this for good or for evil? "For good," is the answer I offer. It is well to face facts. Legislation and philanthropy have often done mischief by treating the unemployed as one class. If they are recognized as those not worth a living wage then it is clear that either they must be fitted to earn such a wage, or be segregated in colonies where their labour will be subsidized. They have a claim on such treatment. Some by the want of care in their youth, or by some change of fashion, have no marketable skill. It seems only fair that they should have the chance of acquiring some other skill. Some, because they are lazy and work-shy, are inclined to prey upon their poor working neighbours. It seems only fair that they should be taken off the market and shut up till they learn habits of industry. Some, because they are weak in body or mind, can never earn sufficient for their upkeep. It seems only fair that they should be kept, not in workhouses or on inadequate out relief, but in colonies where their labour would go towards their own support, and sympathetic guardianship, by necessary subsidies, prevent them from starving.

Labour has a moral claim that labourers be given the opportunity of becoming free men—free to use and enjoy their manhood. English people made great sacrifices to secure freedom for the negroes, and religious people, to accomplish this object, dared to interfere in politics. The position to-day is more serious when those who are not free are called on to be governors of the nation, and religious people may again do well to interfere in politics to secure that working men may have the opportunity of developing the capacities which they have received for the service of mankind.

SAMUEL A. BARNETT.

OUR PRESENT DISCONTENTS.[1]

By Canon Barnett.

February, 1913.

[1] From "The Nineteenth Century and After". By permission of the Editor.

"HISTORY," we are told, "has often been the record of statesmen's illusions," and to one into whose mind over thirty years' memories of East London have been burnt, it seems as if this generation concerning itself about foreign aggression, and the grouping of European Powers, were walking in the vain shadow of such an illusion. It is spending millions annually on armaments against a possible enemy, and grudges a comparatively small sum against the evils which are even now eating into the strength of the nation.

Strikes and rumours of strikes are shaking the foundations of the wealth by which our Dreadnoughts are built and our great Empire secured—political apathy and indifference to the commonwealth mock fervid appeals for patriotic self-sacrifice—railing accusations are hurled by the rich that workmen loaf and drink, and by the tyranny of trades unions ruin trade; and the equally railing accusations are urged by workmen that the rich in their luxury are content to plunder the poor and live in callous indifference to the wrongs they see; and to crown all the other evidences of discontent, violent speeches and lawless conduct are weakening the old calm confidence in the stability of the social structure which has been built up by the elaborate care of many generations.

An enemy has got a footing in the heart of the Empire, and is causing this disturbance. He has evaded our fleet and our forts, and he has the power to destroy our power. The nation, like a dreamer awakening, is shaking itself as it becomes conscious of another danger than that of foreign fleets and armies. It is beginning to be anxious about its social condition and is asking somewhat fitfully, What is to be done? What is the cause of the present discontent? What are the remedies?

Many causes are suggested. It may be that education, having developed the people's capacities for enjoyment, has increased the area of discontent, and those who used to sit placidly in the shadow now demand a ray of the abundant sunshine. It may be that the frantic pace at which the modern world moves has stimulated the demand for excitement and made men impatient for change; it may be that the popular philosophy of the street and the Press, eclipsing older philosophies of the Church and the chair, impels men and nations to put their own interests before other interests—to retaliate blow for blow, and to become proud of pride. When nations, classes, or individuals seek first to protect themselves, then the other things, greed, panic, suspicion, and strife, are soon added.

All these causes may operate, but they would not, I think, be dangerous, if it were not for the fact of poverty. Ideas, philosophies, and feelings have only stirred mankind when they have been able to appeal to facts, and agitators would now agitate in vain if conditions did not agitate more eloquently. Mean streets and ailing bodies jar upon the more widely spread sense of joy, and the long hours of labour and the small wages stir an anger which becomes ready to upset society in order that the greater number might profit in the scramble. Poverty, as far as I can see, is the root cause of the prevailing discontent, the door by which the enemy enters and the fortress from which he sends out suspicion and strife to compass the nation's ruin. Poverty! And our national income is £1,844,000,000, and the nation's accumulated wealth is the almost inconceivable sum of £13,762,000,000.

The voice of the times—would that it had a Gladstone for its interpreter—is one that calls every one, be he patriot or business man, or even a pleasure-lover, to set himself to help in the eviction of poverty. If there be any fighting spirit—any chivalry left, here is the object for its attack; if there be any enlightened selfishness, here is the field for its exercise. Poverty, if it be not destroyed, will destroy the England of our hopes and our dreams.

The curious thing is that the public mind which speaks through the Press hardly realizes what is meant by poverty. There is much talk on the subject—numberless volumes are issued, and charities are multiplied, but what is in the minds of speakers, writers, and givers is obviously destitution. They think of the ragged, broken creatures kept waiting outside the doors of the shelter, and they have mental pictures of squalid rooms and starving children. Many and many a time visitors have come to Whitechapel expecting to see whole streets occupied by the ragged and the wretched, and they have been almost disappointed to find such misery the exception. There are, indeed, many thousands of people destitute, but they form only a fraction of the poor, and could, as the Poor Law Commissioners have shown, be lifted out of the condition by action at once drastic and humane. Why that action has not even been attempted is one of the many questions which the Local Government Board has to answer. But my present point is that, if all the destitute were removed, the poverty which is at the back of our present discontent would remain.

Mr. Seebohm Rowntree, whose opinion has been supported by subsequent social explorers and by scientific research, concludes that 3s. a week for an adult and 2s. 3d. for a child is necessary to keep the body in physical repair, the food being chosen simply to get the most nutrition for the least money, without any regard to appetite or pleasure. The rent for a family, even if one room be considered sufficient, can hardly be less than 4s. a week in a town, and if household sundries are to include fuel, light, and clothing for a family of five persons, 4s. 11d. is a moderate sum. It thus seems as if the smallest income on which it would be possible for an average family to exist is 21s. 8d. a week.

Mr. Charles Booth, Mr. Rowntree, and other subsequent investigators have shown that 30 per cent. of the town population have an income below or hardly above that sum, and as the wages of agricultural labourers average in England 18s. 3d. a week, in Scotland 19s. 3d., and in Ireland 10s. 11d., it is fair to conclude that the estimate of the towns may be applied to the whole kingdom, and that at least 12,000,000 of the 45,000,000 people are living on incomes below the poverty line.

Mr. Chiozza Money, in his "Riches and Poverty" approaching the subject from another side, justifies the conclusion. He shows that a population amounting to 39,000,000 persons is dependent on incomes of less than £160 a year—say 60s. a week, and absorbs £935,000,000 of the national income; that 4,100,000 persons depend on incomes between £160 and £700 per annum, and absorb £275,000,000 of the national income; and that the comparatively small number of 1,400,000 dependent on incomes over £700 a year absorb the mighty sum of £634,000,000. In other words, more than one-third of the entire income of the United Kingdom is enjoyed by one-thirtieth of its people.

In the light of these facts it is not incredible that 30 per cent of the population live in the grip of actual poverty. "The United Kingdom contains," it may be said in truth and shame, "a great multitude of poor people veneered with a thin layer of the comfortable and rich."[2]

The broad fact which stands out of these figures is that, when 21s. 8d. is taken as the sum necessary so that an average family may keep body and soul together, 12,000,000 people must give up in despair, and many other millions, depending on wages of 30s. or even 40s. a week, live anxious days. And this despair or anxiety is not on account of life, in all its multitudinous aspects, but only as to the maintenance of simple physical efficiency.

2 These and other figures are put together very lucidly by Mr. Will Reason in a little shilling book, "Poverty" published by Headly Bros., which I commend to all as a good introduction to the subject.

Let us, says Mr. Rowntree, clearly understand what physical efficiency means. A family living upon the scale allowed for in this estimate must never spend a penny on railway fare or omnibus. They must never go into the country unless they walk. They must never purchase a halfpenny newspaper or buy a ticket for a popular concert. They must write no letters to absent children, for they cannot afford to pay the postage. They must never contribute anything to their church or chapel or give any help to a neighbour which costs them money. They cannot save nor can they join sick clubs or trade unions, because they cannot pay the necessary subscriptions. The children must have no pocket-money for dolls, marbles, and sweets. The father must smoke no tobacco and must drink no beer. The mother must never buy any pretty clothes for herself or for her children. Should a child fall ill, it must be attended by the parish doctor; should it die, it must be buried by the parish. Finally, the wage-earner must never be absent from his work for a single day.

A few parents of heroic mould may have succeeded in bringing up children to healthy and useful manhood and womanhood on small wages. Tales of such are repeated in select circles, but these families generally belong to a generation less open to temptation than the present. There are now few, very few, parents who, with an uncertain wage of 30s. a week, never spend a penny for the sake of pleasure, taste, or friendship. The result is that their own or their children's physical health and well-being are sacrificed. The boys are rejected when they offer themselves as soldiers, the infant mortality is high, and the girls unprotected are more ready to become the victims of vice. The saddest of all experiences of life among the poor is the gradual declension of respectable families into the ranks of the destitute, when loss of work finds them without resources in body or skill.

It is the poverty of the great multitude of the working people and not the destitution of the very poor which is the force of the present discontent. This is not realized even by Mrs. George Kerr, whose book, "The Path of Social Progress," seems to me one of the best of those lately published on the subject. She speaks of Dr. Chalmers as having advocated a policy "which still holds the field," and is the "only scheme which actually did diminish poverty". But this policy aimed at diminishing a poverty which was practically destitution, and its method was to strengthen the people in habits which would enable them to live independent lives on wages of 20s. a week. Mrs. Kerr herself talks of the importance of a wife averaging her husband's wages, so that if her husband as a painter earns 36s. a week for four months the family expenditure ought to be limited within 18s. a week, and she evidently condemns as waste the purchase of a perambulator or bicycle. The methods she advocates by which character may be raised and strengthened are admirable, and the lead given by Dr. Chalmers cannot be too closely followed, but they have reference to destitution and not to the poverty from which working people suffer whose wages reach a more or less uncertain 30s. or 40s. a week.

Destitution, in the crusade against which philanthropists and Poor Law reformers are so well engaged, does not indeed affect the present discontent, except in so far as the presence of the destitute is a warning to the workman of his possible fate. A mechanic is, perhaps, earning 30s. a week, or even more; he, by great frugality on his own part, or by almost miraculous management on his wife's part, just succeeds in keeping his family in health; he sees the destitute in their wretchedness, he hears of many who are herded in the prison-like workhouses, and he feels that if he loses his work, if illness overtakes him or his wife, their fate must be his fate. The destitute may be a burden to the nation, but they are also a danger, in so far as they by their examples rouse a dangerous mood in thousands of workpeople whose wages hardly lift them out of the reach of poverty, and give them no opportunity by saving to make the future secure.

The cure of destitution, necessary though it be on humane and economic grounds, is not the remedy for the present discontent. If all people incapable of earning a living were cared for under the best conditions, if by careful selection according to the straitest sect of the eugenists all the people engaged in work were fit for their work, if by better education and more scientific physical training every child were fully developed, or if by moral and religious impulse all citizens were to become frugal and self-restrained, there would still be the poverty which is the source of danger so long as the share of the national income which comes to the workers is so small. The greatest need of the greatest number is a larger income.

It is, I think, fair to say that on their present income the majority of our people can neither enjoy themselves rationally nor give an intelligent vote as joint governors of the nation. They have not the freedom which takes pride in self-government.

There are, it must be evident, few signs of rational enjoyment in the vastly increased pleasure-seeking of to-day. The people crowd into the country, but only a few people find anything in nature which is theirs. They pass by the memorials of great men and great events, and seldom feel a thrill of national pride. They wander aimlessly, helplessly through museums and picture-galleries, the things they see calling out little response in their minds. They have a limited and often perverted taste for music, and have so little conversation that on holidays they are silent or shout senseless songs. They get a short-lived excitement out of sport, so that for a whole countryside the event of a year is a football match and the chief interest of a Press recording the affairs of the Empire is the betting news. The recreations of the people and their Bank Holiday pleasures, at a time when the universal mind is stirring with a consciousness of new capacity, and the world is calling more loudly than ever that its good things should be enjoyed, give cause for some anxiety. Where there is no rational enjoyment there is likely to be discontent and mischief.

The people cannot enjoy themselves so as to satisfy their nature because of poverty. They began to work before they had time to enjoy learning and before they had become conscious of their capacities and tastes. They have been crushed from their youth upwards by the necessity of earning a livelihood, and have never had the leisure to look at the beautiful world in which they have been placed. They have from their childhood been caught in the industrial machine, and have been swept away from the things which as men and women they were meant to enjoy. They have been too poor to find their pleasure in hope or in memory, enough for them if they have been able to snatch at the present and passing excitement.

Poverty is the enemy of rational enjoyment, and it also prevents the freedom which has pride in self-government. The people cannot be said to be keen to take a part in the government of their country, they are almost ready to accept a despot if they could secure for themselves more health and comfort. There is evident failure to grasp great principles in politics, and a readiness to accept in their stead a popular cry. Parties are judged by their promises, and national interests are often put below private interests; motives which are untrue to human nature are charged against opponents, and the "mob spirit" has an easy victory over individual judgment. The votes of the people may be at any moment fatal to the commonwealth.

Poverty is to a large extent the cause of this weakness in self-government and of the consequent danger to the nation. People whose minds have been crushed under the daily anxiety about the daily bread have little thought for any object but "how to live," and thus they are apt to lose the power of vision. They see money as the only good, and they are disposed to measure beauty, tradition, and work in its terms. The pictures of "the happy homes of England" and the tales of her greatness have for them little meaning. "What are our homes that we should fight for them?" "What has England done for us?" The welfare of the nation is nothing alongside that of their own class; their chief want is security from starvation.

Some conception of the nation as a whole is necessary to kindle interest in self-government, and modern poverty is gradually blotting out the old conception which grew up when people loved the countryside, where the fields laughed and sang with corn and the cottages nestled in gardens, and when they had leisure to enjoy the tales of their fathers' great deeds. Some knowledge is also necessary if those who give votes have to decide on policies which affect international relations, and hold firmly to principles in dark as well as in bright times. But how can the men and women have such knowledge who have been driven by the poverty of their homes to go to work as children, and have had no leisure in which to read history or to dream dreams? Of course they vacillate and of course they fall victims to shallow philosophy.

The people, in a word, because of poverty, are not free. They are "cogs in a great machine which uses human lives as the raw stuff out of which to fashion material wealth". They are by fear of starvation compelled to be instruments of production almost as much as if they were under a law of slavery. They do not live for an end in themselves, but for an end for which others desire to use them.

The poverty of the multitude of workpeople, which limits their capacities for enjoyment and for self-government, and is divided only by a very thin partition from the destitution of squalor and starvation, is, I believe, the chief source of our present discontent, and of the bitterness which makes that discontent dangerous. The "cares of this life" equally with "the deceitfulness of riches" are apt to choke that communion with an ideal which is the source of healthy progress.

Schemes of relief and charity do not aim to reach this poverty. What, then, is to be done? "Give more education, and better education," is the reply of the best reformers. "Let there be smaller classes in the elementary school, so that each child's personality may be developed by the teacher's personality." "Let more attention be given to physical training." "Let compulsory continuous education prevent the appalling wastage which leaves young people to find their interests in the excitement of the street." Yes, a system of more and of better education would send out men and women stronger to labour and more fit both for the enjoyment and business of life. But poverty still stands in the way of such a system of education. The family budget of the mass of the people cannot keep the boy or girl away from work up to the age of fifteen or sixteen, nor can it allow the space and leisure necessary for study, for reading, and for intellectual recreation.

What, then, is to be done? The answer demands the best thought of our best statesmen. There are, doubtless, many things possible, and no one thing will be sufficient. But by some means or other the great national income must be so shared that the 39,000,000 of poor may have a larger proportion.

We have lately been warned against careless talk about rights. It may, therefore, be inaccurate to say that 39,000,000 out of 45,000,000 citizens have a right to more than half of the eighteen hundred million pounds of income. But it is as inaccurate to say that 6,000,000 citizens have a right to the half of the eighteen hundred million pounds which they now receive. What are called "rights" have been settled by law on principles which seemed to the lawmakers of the time the best for the commonwealth. It is law made by our ancestors by which it is possible to transfer the property of the dead to the living, providing thereby a foundation on which stands the mighty accumulation of £13,762,000,000. It is, indeed, by such laws that the capitalist who has saved a small sum is able to go on increasing that sum to millions. There is no natural right by which the poor may be said to have a claim on wealth or the rich to possess wealth.

Law which has determined the lines which the present distribution of the national income follows might determine others which would make the poor richer and the rich poorer. Law has lately, by a system of insurance and pensions, given some security for illness, old age, and unemployment; it has in some trades fixed a minimum wage.

This principle might be extended. The consequent better organization of labour and its improved capacity would secure larger wages for efficient workers and probably reduce the cost of production for the benefit of consumers, but doubtless the number of the unemployed would be increased. Their inefficiency would not earn the minimum wage. For these, training or a refuge would have to be provided in farm colonies, industrial schools, or detention colonies, in accordance with the suggestion of the Poor Law Commissioners.

The law might, by taxing the holders of the accumulated wealth of the nation, subsidize education, so that no child by want of food and clothing should be driven from school before the age of fifteen or sixteen. It might, by securing for the poor as well as for the rich an abundant provision of air-space and water for the healthy and adequate care and attention for the sick, reduce the death-rate among the 39,000,000 poor people to the level of that which now obtains among the 6,000,000 richer people. "Health before all things" has long been on the banner of politicians, and though much has been done much more remains to be done. There is no reason why the death-rate of a poor district should be higher than that of a rich district.

Law, to offer one other example, might do more "to nationalize luxuries". In an article on "Practicable Socialism," which, as the first-fruits of an experience gained by my wife and myself in ten years of Whitechapel life, the Editor of this Review accepted in April, 1883, I suggested that legislation might provide for the people not what they *want* but what they *need*. Much has been done in this direction during the last thirty years; but still there is not the free and sufficient provision of the best music in summer and winter, of the best art, of the best books—there is not even the adequate supply of baths and flower-gardens, which would bring within the reach of the many the enjoyments which are the surest recreations of life.

It is thus possible to give examples of laws which would bring to the poor the use of a larger share of the national income. It is not easy to frame laws which, while they remove the burden and the danger of poverty, may by encouraging energy and self-respect develop industrial resourcefulness. But it ought not to be beyond statesmen's power to devise such measures.

The point, however, which I desire to make clear is that if the poor are to become richer the rich must become poorer. Increase of production followed by an increased national income has under the present laws—as has been shown in the booming trade of recent years—meant that the rich have become richer. The present income is sufficient to assure the greater health and well-being of the whole population, but the rich must submit to receive a smaller proportion.

This proposition rouses much wrath. Its advocates are charged with preaching spoliation and robbery, with setting class against class, and with destroying the basis on which national prosperity is settled. The taxation which compels the rich to reduce their expenditure on holidays and luxuries may seem hard, and the fear lest the tax which this year takes 5 per cent of their income will be further increased may induce panic among certain classes; but it is harder for the poor to go on suffering for want of the means of life, and there is more reason for panic in the thought that the mass of the people remain indifferent to the national greatness. The tax, it must be remembered, which reduces the expenditure of the rich on things which perish in their using—on out-of-season foods, on aimless locomotion, and the excitements of ostentation—and at the same time makes it possible for the poor to spend more on food and clothing, increases the work of working people. The millions of money, for example, taken from the rich to supply pensions for the poor have enabled the old people to spend money on food and clothing, which has been better for the nation's trade than money spent on luxuries. It is a striking fact that if the people used what is held to be a bare sufficiency of woollen and cotton goods, the demand for these goods would be increased threefold to sixfold. The transference, therefore, of more of the national income from the few rich to the many poor need not alarm patriots.

The tax-collectors' interference with the use of the accumulated wealth, now controlled by a comparatively small number of the people, is much less dangerous to the national prosperity than the discontent which arises from poverty. A proposition which offers security for the nation at the cost of some sacrifice by a class should, it might be expected, be met to-day by the more powerful members of society as willingly as in old days the nobles met the call to battle. But the powerful members of modern society hate the doctrine of taxation, and the hatred becomes a sort of instinct which draws them towards any alternative policy which may put off the evil day. If they give, their gifts are generous, frequently very generous, but often unconsciously they have regarded them as a sort of ransom which they threaten they will not pay if taxes are imposed, doing thereby injustice to their generosity. The rich do not realize the meaning of poverty, its wounds to human nature, or its dangers to the nation.

Poverty, I would submit is at the root of our present discontent, not the poverty which the Poor Law and charity are to relieve, but the poverty of the great mass of the workers. Out of this poverty rises the enemy which threatens our peace and our greatness, and this poverty is due not to want of trade or work or wealth, but to the want of thought as to the distribution of our enormous national income. When the meaning of poverty is realized, the courage and the sacrifice which in the past have so often dared loss to avert danger will hardly fail because the loss to be faced is represented by the demand-note of the tax-collector. Gifts cannot avert the danger, repression will increase the danger, and the preachers who believe in the coming of the Kingdom must for the old text, "God loveth a cheerful giver," substitute as its equivalent, "God loveth a cheerful taxpayer".

SAMUEL A. BARNETT.

SECTION V.

SOCIAL SERVICE.

Of Town Planning—The Mission of Music—The Real Social Reformer—Where Charity Fails—Landlordism Up-to-date—The Church and Town Planning.

OF TOWN PLANNING.[1]

By Mrs. S. A. Barnett.

January, 1911.

<u>1</u> From "The Cornhill Magazine". By kind permission of the Editor.

MUCH has been said lately about town planning. Conferences have been held, speeches have been made, articles have been written, papers have been read, and columns of newspaper-notices have appeared, and yet I am daring to occupy eleven pages of the CORNHILL MAGAZINE to try and add a few more remarks to what has already been so well and so forcibly put forth.

But in apology for the presumption, it can be said that what I want to say does not entrench upon the province of the architect, the surveyor, or the artist. The questions of traffic-congestion, density of population, treatment of levels, arrangement of trams, water or gas, relation of railway termini or docks to thoroughfares, organization of periodic excess of street usage, relative positions of municipal buildings, harmony of material and design, standardization of streets and road grading, appreciation of scale; on these matters I will not write, for on them contributions, interesting, dull, suggestive, or learned, have been abundantly produced, and "are they not written in the Book of the Chronicles" of the great Conference held last month under the auspices of the Royal Institute of British Architects? And are not their potentialities visible beneath the legal phraseology of Mr. John Burns' Town-planning Act of last Parliament?

It is so delightful to realize that some of the best brains of this and other countries are turning their thoughts to the solution of what Mr. T. S. Horsfall (who for many years was a voice crying in the wilderness) demanded as the elemental right of every human being, "the conditions of a healthy life". It is comforting to know that others are doing the thinking, especially when one is old, and can recall one's passionate, youthful indignation at the placid acceptance of stinking courts and alleys as the normal homes for the poor, when the memory is still vivid of the grand day when one portion of the network of such courts, in St. Jude's parish, was swept away, and a grave, tall, carefully planned tenement building, erected by the public-spirited kindness of the late Mr. George M. Smith, arose in its stead, "built to please Barnett as an experiment".

Some five-and-twenty years ago, when old Petticoat Lane was pulled down, my husband sent in to the Local Authority a suggestion of laying the area out so that Commercial Road should be continued right through to Bishopsgate; the letter and plans were merely acknowledged and the proposal ignored. Five years ago we filled one of the rooms in the Whitechapel Exhibition with plans of how East London might be improved, but it elicited only little interest, local or otherwise; and now last month, but a few years later, all the walls of Burlington House were covered with town-planning exhibits, drawings, plans, and designs, and its floor space amply supplied with models from all parts of the world.

And the thought given is so fresh, so unconventional, and so full of characteristics, that one came away from a careful study of that great Exhibition with a clear sense of the individualities of the various nations, as they had stated their ideals for their towns. Some in broad avenues, great piazzas, parallel streets, careful to adopt Christopher Wren's ideal, that "gardens and unnecessary vacuities . . . be placed out of the town". Some in fairy cities, girt with green girdles of open space, tree-lined roads, parks designed for quiet as well as for play, waterways used for pleasure locomotion as well as for business traffic, contours considered as producers of beauty, the view as well as the shelter planned for. Some with scrupulous care for the history of the growth of the city, its natural features, the footmarks left by its wars, each utilized with due regard to modern requirements and the tendencies of the future. Some glorying in the preservation of every scrap which could record age or civic history, others blatantly determined to show that the old was folly, and that only of the brand-new can it be said "the best is yet to be".

The imagination is stirred by the opportunities which the Colonies possess, and envy is mixed with gratitude that they will have the chance of creating glorious cities warned by the Old Country's mistakes, and realizing by the progress of economic science that the flow of humanity is ever towards aggregation. The "Back-to-the-land" cry falls on ninety irresponsive ears to ten responsive ones, for the large majority of human beings desire to live in juxtaposition with mankind. It behoves thinkers all the more, therefore, to plan beautiful cities, places to live as well as to work in, and enough of them to prevent a few becoming so large as to absorb more than a healthy share of national life and wealth.

But if all of us may think imperially, it is given to most of us only to act locally, and, therefore, I will convey your minds and mine back from the visions of town planning amid the plains of Canada, the fiords and mountains of British Columbia, the high lands and broad velds of Africa, the varied beauties of wood, hill, and sea of Australia and New Zealand, back from the stimulating, almost intoxicating, vision of the work lying before our great Colonies, to the sobering atmosphere of a London or a Manchester suburb, with its miles of mean streets already built, or its open fields and new-made roads, laid out as if under the ruler of the office-boy.

Whoever undertakes the area to be laid out, whether it is the municipality or a public land company, should see that the planning is done on a large scale. The injury wrought to towns hitherto has been often due to the narrowness of personal interests and the limitation of the acres dealt with, both of which dim the far sight. The almost unconscious influence of dealing with a wide area is shown in existing schemes, which have been undertaken by owners of large estates, whether the area be planned for an industrial village, such as Mr. Lever's at Port Sunlight, or for a housing-reform scheme like Mr. Cadbury's at Bournville; or to accommodate the leisured, as the Duke of Devonshire's at Eastbourne, or the artistic, as Mr. Comyns Carr's at Bedford Park; or to create a fresh commercial city, as conceived by Mr. Ebenezer Howard at Letchworth; or to house all classes in attractive surroundings as at the Hampstead Garden Suburb. Whatever be the purpose, the fact of a large area has influenced them all. It has had, as it were, something of the same effect as the opportunity of the Sistine Chapel had on Michael Angelo. The population to be accommodated was large enough to require its own places of worship, public halls, or clubs, its schools, and recreation-grounds. So the lines were drawn with a generous hand, and human needs considered, with a view to their provision within the confines of the estate, instead of being treated as the organ-grinder, and advised to seek satisfaction in the next street—or accommodation on neighbouring land.

The idea of town or suburb planning has not yet found its way into the minds which dominate local Public Authorities, but a few examples will doubtless awaken them to the benefits of the Act, if not from the æsthetic, yet from the economic point of view, and then borough or ward boundaries will become as unnoticeable for town-planning purposes as ecclesiastical parish ones now are for educational administration.

Foremost among the problems will be the allotment of different positions of the area under consideration to different classes of society, or perhaps it would be better to say different standards of income.

No one can view with satisfaction any town, whether in England, America, or the Colonies, where the poor, the strenuous, and the untutored live as far as possible removed from the rich, the leisured, and the cultivated. The divorce is injurious to both. Too commonly is it supposed that the poor only suffer from the separation, but those who have the privilege of friendships among the working-people know that the wealthy lose more by not making their acquaintance than can possibly be computed.

"I often advise you to make friends," said the late Dr. Jowett to a body of undergraduates assembled in Balliol Hall to hearken to my husband and Mr. C. S. Loch, as they spoke of the inhabitants of East or South London in the early 'seventies, but "now I will add further advice: Make some of your friends among the poor."

Excellent as the advice is, it is hardly possible to follow when certain classes live at one end of the town, and other classes dwell in the extreme opposite district. It may be given to the few to create artificial methods of meeting, but to the large mass of people, so long as they live in separate neighbourhoods, they must remain ignorant of each other to a very real, if undefinable, loss—the loss of understanding, mutual respect, and that sense of peace which comes when one sits in the parlour and knows the servants are doing their best, or works in the kitchen and knows that those who govern are directed by a large-hearted sympathy. Again and again in 1905-6, when the idea of provision being made for all classes of society in the Hampstead Garden Suburb was being submitted to the public, I was told that the cultivated would never live voluntarily in the neighbourhood of the industrial classes, but I was immensely surprised when I laid the scheme before a leading workman and trade-unionist to be told:—

"It is all very nice as you say it, Mrs. Barnett, but I'm mistaken if you will find any self-respecting workman who cares to bring his family to live alongside of the rich. They're a bad example with their pleasure-loving sons and idle, vain daughters, always thinking of dressing, and avoiding work and natural duties as if they were sins."

The acceptance of society newspaper paragraphs and divorce reports as accurate and exhaustive accounts of the lives of the leisured, even by thinking workmen, serves as an additional evidence of the need of common neighbourhood to correct so dangerous and disintegrating a view.

There can be no doubt but that Part III of the Housing Act of 1890 is, in so far as it affects recent town development, responsible for much of this lamentable ignorance, for under its powers provision can only be made to house the industrial classes, and thus whole neighbourhoods have grown up, as large in themselves as a small provincial town occupied by one class, or those classes the range of whose difference is represented by requiring two or three bedrooms, a "kitchen," or a "parlour cottage".

That this segregation of classes into distinct areas is unnecessary as well as socially dangerous, is evidenced by many small English towns, such as Wareham, Godalming, Huntingdon, where the grouping together of all sorts of people has taken place under normal conditions of growth, as well as in the Garden Suburb at Hampstead, where the areas to house people of various degrees of income were clearly defined in the original plan, and have been steadfastly adhered to. In that estate the rents range from tenements of 3s. 3d. a week to houses standing in their own gardens of rentals to £250 a year, united by cottages, villas, and houses priced at every other figure within that gamut. The inhabitants can dwell there as owners, or by renting their dwellings, or through the welcoming system and elastic doors of the co-partners, or as weekly tenants in the usual way. No sort of difficulty has arisen, and the often-expressed fears have proved groundless. Indeed, the result of the admixture of all classes has been a kindlier feeling and a richer sympathy, as people of varied experience, different educational standards, and unequal incomes feel themselves drawn together in the enjoyment of good music, in the discussion of social problems, in the preparation by their children of such a summer's day festival as the "Masque of Fairthorpe," or to enjoy the unaffected pleasure of the public open spaces and wall-less gardens.

In England we have not yet reached the gorgeous, riotous generosity of the Americans, who plan parks by the mile, and cheerfully spend, as Boston did, £7,500,000 for a girdle of parks, woods, meadows, sea and lake embankments; or vote, as Chicago did, £3,600,000 for the creation of a connected system of twenty-two parks; but we in humbler England have some ground for congratulation, that, as a few years ago a flowerless open space was counted adequate, now a well-kept garden is desired; but on the definition of their uses and the difficulties of their upkeep something has yet to be said.

Every one has seen derelict open spaces, squares, crescents, three-angled pieces of ground deliberately planned to create beauty, but allowed to become the resting places of too many weary cats or disused household utensils, the grass neither mown, protected, nor re-sown. "The children like it kept so," people say, but I doubt if they do. In Westminster there are two open spaces, one planted and cared for, the other just an unkept open space. Both face south, both overlook the river, both are open free, but the children flock into the garden, leaving the open space drearily empty. It is to be regretted, for their noise, even when it is happy shouting and not discordant wrangling, is disturbing to those whose strenuous lives necessitate that they take their exercise or rest without disturbance. But, on the other hand, the children are entitled to their share of the garden, and those "passionless reformers," order, beauty, colour, may perhaps speak their messages more effectually into ears when they are young.

The solution of the difficulty has been found by the Germans in their thoughtful planning of parks, and few things were more delightful in the Town-planning Exhibition than the photographs of the children paddling in the shallow pools, making castles (I saw no sign of fortifications!) in the sand, playing rough running games on gravel slopes, or quieter make-believes in the spinneys, all specially provided in specially allocated children's areas. Isolated instances of such provision are existent in our English parks, but the principle, that some people are entitled to public peace as well as others to public play, is not yet recognized, and that there should be zones in which noise is permitted, and zones in which silence must be maintained is as yet an inconceivable restriction. So the children usually shout, race, scream, or squabble amid the grown-ups, kept even in such order as they are by the fear of the park-keeper, whom their consciences encourage them to credit with supernatural powers of observation. He is usually a worthy, patient man, but an expensive adjunct, and one who could sometimes be dispensed with if the children's "sphere of influence" were clearly defined. The promiscuous presence of children affects also both the standard of cost of the upkeep of open spaces, although the deterioration of their standard is more often due to the lapse of the authority who created them.

It is because the changes of circumstances so frequently affect disastrously the appearance of public spaces that I would offer for consideration the suggestion that they should be placed under the care of the municipality, under stringent covenants concerning their uses, purposes, maintenance, and reservation for the inhabitants of special dwellings. This step would not, of course, be necessary where the owner or company still holds the land, but in cases where the houses for which the square or joint garden was provided have each strayed into separate ownership, and their ground-rents treated only as investments, then everyone's duty usually becomes no one's duty, and the garden drops into a neglected home for "unconsidered trifles". I could quote instances of this, not only in East London, but in Clifton, Reading, Ventnor, York, or give brighter examples of individual effort and enthusiasm which have awakened the interest of the neighbours to take pride in the appearance, and pay towards the upkeep, of their common pleasance.

The arguments in favour of the municipality having the care of these publicly enjoyed or semi-private open spaces would be the advantages of a higher gardening standard, the economy of interchange of roots, seeds, and tools, the benefit of a staff large enough to meet seasonal needs, the stimulating competition of one garden against another, and the additional gift of beauty to the passers-by, who could thus share without intrusion the fragrance of the flowers and the melody of symphonies in colour.

"But how can the public enjoy the gardens when they are usually behind walls?" I hear that delightful person, the deadly practical man, murmur; and this brings me to another question, "Are walls round open spaces necessary?"

English people seem to have adopted the idea that it is essential to surround their parks and gardens with visible barriers, perhaps because England is surrounded by the sea—a very visible line of demarcation; but, in the stead of a dancing joy, a witchful barrier, uniting while it separates, they have put up grim hard walls, ugly dividing fences, barriers which challenge trespass, and make even the law-abiding citizen desire to climb over and see what is on the other side.

It is extraordinary how firmly established is the acceptance of the necessity of walls and protection. Nearly thirty-five years ago, when the first effort was made to plant Mile End Road with trees, and to make its broad margins gracious with shrubs and plants, we were met by the argument that they would not be safe without high railings. I recall the croakings of those who combated the proposal to open Leicester Square to the public, and who of us has not listened to the regrets of the landowner on the expense entailed by his estate boundary fences?

If you say, "Why make them so high, or keep them up so expensively, as you do not preserve your game? Why not have low hedges or short open fences, over which people can see and enjoy your property?" he will look at you with a gentle pity, thinking of you as a deluded idealist, or perhaps his expression will change into something not so gentle as it dawns on him that, though one is the respectable wife of a respectable Canon, yet one may be holding "some of those—Socialist theories".

Not long ago I went at the request of a gentleman who owned property, with his agent to see if suggestions could be made to improve the appearance of his estate and the happiness of his tenants. The gardens were small enough to be valueless, but between and around each were walls, many in bad repair.

"The first thing I should do would be to pull down those walls, and let the air in; things will then grow, self-respect as well as flowers," I said.

"What!" exclaimed the agent, "pull down the walls? Why, what would the men have to lean against?" thus conjuring up the vision one has so often seen of men leaning listlessly against the public-house walls, a sight which the possession of a garden, large enough to be profitable as well as pleasurable, ought to do much to abolish.

It is difficult to find arguments for walls. In many towns of America the gardens are wall-less, the public scrupulously observing the rights of ownership. In the Hampstead Garden Suburb all the gardens are wall-less, both public and private. The flowers bloom with the voluptuous abundance produced by virgin soil, but they remain untouched, not only by the inhabitants, which, of course, is to be expected, but by the thousands of visitors who come to see the realization of the much-talked-of scheme, and respect the property as they share its pleasures.

In town-planning literature and talk much is said about houses, roads, centre-points to design, architectural features, treatment of junctions, and many other items both important and interesting; but the tone of thought pervading all that I have yet read is that it is the healthy and happy, the respectable and the prosperous, for whom all is to be arranged. It takes all sorts to make a world, and the town planner who excludes in his arrangements the provision for the lonely, the sick, the sorrowful, and the handicapped will lose from the midst of the community some of its greatest moral teachers.

The children should be specially welcomed amid improved or beautiful surroundings, for the impressions made in youth last through life, and on the standards adopted by the young will depend the nation's welfare. A vast army of children are wholly supported by the State, some 100,000, while to them can be added nearly 200,000 more for whom the public purse is partly responsible. In town planning the needs of these children should be considered, and the claims of the sick openly met.

Hospitals are intended to help the sick poor, so, in planning the town or its growth, suitable sites should be chosen in relation to the population who require such aid; but in London many hospitals are clustered in the centre of the town, are enlarged, rebuilt, or improved on the old positions, though the people's homes and workshops have been moved miles away; thus the sick suffer in body and become poorer in purse, as longer journeys have to be undertaken after accidents, or when as out-patients they need frequent attention.

The wicked, the naughty, the sick, the demented, the sorrowful, the blind, the halt, the maimed, the old, the handicapped, the children are facts—facts to be faced, facts which demand thought, facts which should be reckoned with in town planning—for all, even the first-named, can be helped by being surrounded with "whatsoever things are pure, whatsoever things are lovely, and whatsoever things are of good report".

Every one who has been to Canada must have been struck with the evidence of faith in educational appreciation which the Canadians give in the preparation of their vast teaching centres.

"What impressed me greatly," said Mr. Henry Vivian in his speech at the dinner given in his honour on his return from the Dominion, "was the preparation that the present people have made for the education of the future people," and he described the planning of one University, whose buildings, sports-grounds, roads, hostels, and gardens were to cover 1300 acres. Compare that with the statement of the Secretary of a Borough Council Education Authority, who told me the other day, with congratulatory pleasure, that long negotiations had at last obtained one acre and a quarter for the building of a secondary school and a hoped-for three acres some distance off for the boys' playground.

The town planning of the future will make, it is to be hoped, generous provision for educational requirements, and not only for the inhabitants of the immediate locality. As means of transit become both cheaper and easier, it will be recognized as a gain for young people to go out of town to study, into purer air, away from nerve-wearing noise, amid flowers and trees, and with an outlook on a wider sky, itself an elevating educational influence both by day and night.

The need of what may be called artificial town addition can only concern the elder nations, who have, scattered over their lands, splendid buildings in the centre of towns that have ceased to grow. As an example, I would quote Ely. What a glorious Cathedral! kept in dignified elderly repair, its Deans, Canons, Minors, lay-clerks, and choir, all doing their respective daily duties in leading worship; but, alas! there the population is so small (7713 souls) that the response by worshippers is necessarily inadequate—the output bears no proportion to the return. Beauty, sweetness, and light are wasted there and West Ham exists, with its 267,000 inhabitants, its vast workshops and factories, its miles of mean streets of drab-coloured "brick boxes with slate lids"—and no Cathedral, no group of kind, leisured clergy to leaven the heavy dough of mundane, cheerless toil.

If town planning could be treated nationally, it might be arranged that Government factories could be established in Ely. Army clothiers, stationery manufacturers, gunpowder depôts would bring the workers in their train. A suitable expenditure of the Public Works Loans money would cause the cottages to appear; schools would then arise, shops and lesser businesses, which population always brings into existence, would be started; and the Cathedral would become a House of Prayer, not only to the few religious ones who now rejoice in the services, but for the many whose thoughts would be uplifted by the presence in their midst of the stately witness of the Law of Love, and whose lives would be benefited by the helpful thought and wise consideration of those whose profession it is to serve the people.

Pending great changes, something might perhaps be done if individual owners and builders would consider the appearance, not only of the house they are building, but of the street or road of which it forms a part. A few months ago, in the bright sunshine, I stood on a hill-top, facing a delightful wide view, on a newly developed estate, and, pencil in hand, wrote the colours and materials of four houses standing side by side. This is the list:—

No. 1 HOUSE.—Roof, grey slates; walls, white plaster with red brick; yellow-painted woodwork; red chimneys.

No. 2 HOUSE.—Roof, purpley-red tiles; walls, buff rough cast; brown-painted woodwork; yellow chimneys.

No. 3 HOUSE.—Roof, orangey-red tiles; walls, grey-coloured rough cast; white-painted woodwork; red chimneys.

No. 4 HOUSE.—Roof, crimson-red tiles; walls, stone-coloured rough cast; peacock-blue paint; red chimneys.

This bare list tells of the inharmonious relation of colours, but it cannot supply the variety of tones of red, nor yet the mixture of lines, roof-angles, balcony or bow projections, one of which ran up to the top of a steep-pitched roof, and was castellated at the summit. The road was called "Bon-Accord". One has sometimes to thank local authorities for unconscious jokes.

My space is filled, and even a woman's monologue must conclude some time! But one paragraph more may be taken to put in a plea for space for an Open-air Museum. It need not be a large and exhaustive one, for there is something to be said for not making museums "too bright and good for human nature's daily food". There might be objects of museum interest scattered in groups about the green girdle which the young among my readers will, I trust, live to see round all great towns; or an open-air exhibit on a limited subject might be provided, as the late Mr. Burt arranged so charmingly at Swanage; or the Shakespeare Gardens, already started in some of the London County Council parks, might be further developed; or the more ambitious schemes of Stockholm and Copenhagen intimated; but whichever model is adopted the idea of open-air museums (which might be stretched to include bird sanctuaries) is one which should find a place in the gracious environment of our well-ordered towns when they have come under the law and the gospel of the Town-planning Act.

Henrietta O. Barnett.

THE MISSION OF MUSIC.[1]

By Canon Barnett.

July, 1899.

[1] From "International Journal of Ethics". By permission of the Editor.

"WE must have something light or comic." So say those who provide music for the people, and their words represent an opinion which is almost universal with regard to the popular taste. The uneducated, it is thought, must be unable to appreciate that which is refined or to enjoy that which does not make them laugh and be merry.

Opinions exist, especially with regard to the tastes and wants of the poor, by the side of facts altogether inconsistent with those opinions. There are facts within the knowledge of some who live in the East End of London which are sufficient, at any rate, to shake this general opinion as to the people's taste in music.

In Whitechapel, where so many philanthropists have tried "to patch with handfuls of coal and rice" the people's wants, the signs of ignorance are as evident as the signs of poverty. There is an almost complete absence of those influences which are hostile to the ignorance, not, indeed, of the mere elements of knowledge (the Board Schools are now happily everywhere prominent), but to the ignorance of joy, truth, and beauty. Utility and the pressure of work have crowded house upon house; have filled the shops with what is only cheap, driven away the distractions of various manners and various dresses, and made the place weary to the body and depressing to the mind.

Nevertheless, in this district a crowd has been found willing, on many a winter's night, to come and listen to parts of an oratorio or to selections of classical music. The oratorios have sometimes been given in a church by various bodies of amateurs who have practised together for the purpose; the concerts have been given in schoolrooms on Sunday evenings by professionals of reputation. To the oratorios men and women have come, some of them from the low haunts kept around the city by its carelessly administered charity, all of them of the class which, working for its daily bread, has no margin of time for study. Amid those who are generally so independent of restraint, who cough and move as they will, there has been a death-like stillness as they have listened to some fine solo of Handel's. On faces which are seldom free of the marks of care, except in the excitement of drink, a calm has seemed to settle and tears to flow, for no reason but because "it is so beautiful!" Sometimes the music has appeared to break gradually down barriers that shut out some poor fellow from a fairer past or a better future than his present: the oppressive weight of the daily care lifts, other sights are in his vision, and at last, covering his face or sinking on his knees, he makes prayers which cannot be uttered. Sometimes it has seemed to seize one on business bent, to transport him suddenly to another world, and, not knowing what he feels, has forced him to say, "It was good to be here". A church filled with hundreds of East Londoners, affected, doubtless, in different ways, but all silent, reverent, and self-forgetful, is a sight not to be forgotten or to be held to have no meaning. To the concerts have crowded hard-headed, unimaginative men, described in a local paper as being "friends of Bradlaugh". These have listened to and evidently taken in difficult movements of Beethoven, Schumann, and Chopin. The loud applause which has followed some moments of strained, rapt attention has proclaimed the universal feeling.

With a knowledge of the character of the music, the applications for admission have increased, and the announcement of a hope that the concerts might be continued the following winter, and possibly also extended to weekday evenings, has brought from some of those present an expression of their desire for other high-class music. The poor quarters of cities have been too long treated as if their inhabitants were deficient in that which is noblest in human nature. Human beings want not something which will do, but the best.

If it be asked what proof there be that such music has a permanent effect on the hearers, the only answer is that people do not always know how they have been most influenced. It is the air unconsciously breathed which affects the cure much more often than the medicine so consciously taken. Music may most deeply and permanently affect those who themselves can express no appreciation with their words or show results in their lives. Like the thousand things which surrounds the child and which he never notices, music may largely serve in the formation of character and the satisfaction of life. That the performance of this music in the East End is not followed by expressions of intelligent appreciation or by immediate change of life is no proof of its failure to influence. The fact that crowds come to listen is sufficient to make the world reconsider its opinion that the people care only for what is light or laugh-compelling. There is evidently in the highest music something which finds a response in many minds not educated to understand its mysteries nor interested in its creation. This suggests that music has in the present time a peculiar mission.

"Man doth not live by bread alone," expresses a truth which even those will allow who profess themselves careless about present-day religion. There is in human beings, in those whom the rich think to satisfy by increased wages and improved dwellings, a need of something beyond. The man who has won an honourable place, who by punctuality, honesty, and truthfulness has become the trusted servant of his employer, is often weary with the very monotony of his successful life. He has bread in abundance, but, unsatisfied, he dreams of filling quite another place in the world, perhaps as the leader daring much for others, perhaps as the patriot suffering much for his class and country, or perhaps as the poet living in others' thoughts. There flits before him a vision of a fuller life, and the vision stirs in him a longing to share such life. The woman, too, who in common talk is the model wife and mother, whose days are filled with work, whose talk is of her children's wants, whose life seems so even and uneventful, so complete in its very prosaicness, she, if she could be got to speak out the thoughts which flit through her brain as she silently plies her needle or goes about her household duties, would tell of strange longings for quite another sort of life, of passions and aspirations which have been scarcely allowed to take form in her mind. There is no one to whom "omens that would astonish have not predicted a future and uncovered a past".

Beyond the margin of material life is a spiritual life. This life has been and may still be believed to be the domain of religion, that which science has not known and can never know, which material things have not helped and can never help. It has been the glory of religion to develop the longing to be something higher and nobler by revealing to men the God, Who is higher than themselves.

Religion having abdicated this domain to invade that of science has to-day suffered by becoming the slave of æsthetic and moral precepts. Her professors often yield themselves to the influence of form and colour or boast only of their morality and philanthropy.

It is no wonder, therefore, that many who are in earnest and feel that neither ritualism nor philanthropy have special power to satisfy their natures, reject religion. But they will not, if they are fair to themselves, object to the strengthening of that power which they must allow to have been a source of noble endeavour and of the very science whose reign they acknowledge. The sense of something better than their best, making itself felt not in outward circumstance but inwardly in their hearts, has often been the spring of effort and of hope. It is because the forms of present-day religion give so little help to strengthen this sense, that so many now speak slightingly of religion and profess their independence of its forms. Religion, in fact, is suffering for want of expression.

In other times men felt that the words of the Prayer Book and phrases now labelled "theological" did speak out, or at any rate did give some form to their vague, indistinct longing to be something else and something more; while the picture of God, drawn from the Bible history and Bible words, gave an object to their longing, making them desire to be like Him and to enjoy Him for ever.

In these days, however, historical criticism and scientific discoveries have made the old expressions seem inadequate to state man's longings or to picture God's character. The words of prayers, whether the written prayers of the English Church or that rearrangement of old expressions called "extempore prayer," do not at once fit in with the longings of those to whom, in these later days, sacrifice has taken other forms and life other possibilities. The descriptions of God, involving so much that is only marvellous, jar against minds which have had hints of the grandeur of law and which have been awed not by miracles but by holiness. The petitions for the joys of heaven do not always meet the needs of those who have learnt that what they are is of more consequence than what they have, and the anthropomorphic descriptions of the character of God make Him seem less than many men who are not jealous, nor angry, nor revengeful.

Words and thoughts alike often fail to satisfy modern wants. While prayers are being said, the listless attitude and wandering gaze of those in whose souls are the deepest needs and loftiest aspirations, proclaim the failure. Religion has not failed, but only its power of expressing itself. There lives still in man that which gropes after God, but it can find no form in which to clothe itself. The loss is no light one. Expression is necessary to active life, and without it, at any rate, some of the greater feelings of human nature must suffer loss of energy and be isolated in individuals. Free exercise will give those feelings strength; the power of utterance will teach men that they are not alone when they are their best selves.

The world has been moved to many a crusade by a picture of suffering humanity, and the darkness of heathenism calls forth missionaries of one Church and another. Almost as moving a picture might be drawn of those who wanting much can express nothing. Here are men and women, bone of our bone, flesh of our flesh: they have that within them which raises them above all created things, powers by which they are allied to all whom the world honours, faculties by which they might find unfailing joy. But they have no form of expression and so they live a lower life, walking by sight, not by faith, giving rein to powers which find their satisfaction near at hand, and developing faculties in the use of which there is more of pain than joy. The power which has been the spring of so much that is helpful to the world seems to be dead in them; that sense which has enabled men to stand together as brothers, trusting one another as common possessors of a Divine spark, seems to be without existence. A few may go on walking grimly the path of duty, but for the mass of mankind life has lost its brightness. Dullness unrelieved by wealth, and loneliness undispersed by dissipation, are the common lot. In a sense more terrible than ever, men are like children walking in the night with no language but a cry. He that will give them the means once more to express what they really are and what they really want will break the bondage.

The fact that the music of the great masters does stir something in most men's natures should be a reason for trying whether music might not, at any rate partially, express the religious life of the present day.

There is much to be said in favour of such an experiment. On the one side there is the failure of existing modes of expression. The prettinesses of ritualism and the social efforts of Broad Churchism, even for the comparatively small numbers who adopt these forms of worship, do not meet those longings of the inner life which go beyond the love of beauty and beyond the love of neighbours. The vast majority of the people belong to neither ritualism nor Broad Churchism; they live, at best, smothering their aspirations in activity; at worst, in dissipation, having forsaken duty as well as God. Their morality has followed their religion. In the East End of London this is more manifest, not because the people of the East are worse than the people of the West, but because the people of the East have no call to seem other than they are. Amid many signs hopeful for the future there is also among East Londoners, unblushingly declared at every street-corner, the self-indulgence which robs the young and weak of that which is their right, education and protection; the vice which saps a nation's strength is boasted of in the shop and flaunted in the highways, and the selfishness which is death to a man is often the professed ground of action.

Morality for the mass of men has been dependent on the consciousness of God, and with the lack of means of expression the consciousness of God seems to have ceased. On this ground alone there would be reason for making an experiment with music, if only because it offers itself as a possible means of that expression which the consciousness of God supports. And, on the other side, there is the natural fitness of music for the purpose.

In the first place, the great musical compositions may be asserted to be, not arrangements which are the results of study and the application of scientific principles, but the results of inspiration. The master, raised by his genius above the level of common humanity to think fully what others think only in part, and to see face to face what others see only darkly, puts into music the thoughts which no words can utter and the descriptions which no tongue can tell. What he himself would be, his hopes, his fears, his aspirations, what he himself sees of that holiest and fairest which has haunted his life, he tells by his art. Like the prophets, having had a vision of

God, his music proclaims what he himself would desire to be, and expresses the emotions of his higher nature.

If this be a correct account of the meaning of those great masterpieces which may every day be performed in the ears of the people, it is easy to see how they may be made to serve the purpose in view. The greatest master is a man with much in him akin to the lowest of the human race. The homage all pay to the great is but the assertion of this kinship, the assertion of men's claim to be like the great when the obstructions of their mal-formation and mal-education shall be trained away. Men generally will, therefore, find in that which expresses the thoughts of the greatest the means of expressing their own thoughts. The music which enfolds the passions that have never found utterance, that have never been realized by the ordinary man, will somehow appeal to him and make him recognize his true self and his true object. Music being itself the expression of the wants of man, all who share in man's nature will find in it an expression for longings and visions for which no words are adequate. It will be what prayers and meditations now so often fail to be, a means of linking men with the source of the highest thoughts and efforts, and of enabling them to enjoy God, a joy which so few now understand.

More than this, the best existing expression of that which men have found to be good has been by parables, whose meanings have not been limited to time or place but are of universal application. Heard by different people and at different times, parables have given to all alike a conception of that which eye cannot see nor voice utter; each hearer in each age has gained possibly a different conception, but in the use of the same words all have felt themselves to be united. The parable of the prodigal son has represented the God who has been won to love by the sacrifice of Christ and also the God who freely forgives. Such forms of expression it is most important to have in an age when movement is so rapid that things become old as soon as they are new, separating to-morrow those who have stood together to-day, and when at the same time the longing for unity is so powerful that the thought of it acts as a charm on men's minds.

In some degree all art is a parable, as it makes known in a figure that which is unknown, revealing the truth the artist has felt to others just in so far as they by education and surroundings have been qualified to understand it. Titian's picture of the Assumption helped the mediæval saint to worship better the Virgin Mother, and also helps those of our day to realize the true glory of womanhood.

But music, even more than painting and poetry, fulfils this condition. It reveals that which the artist has seen, and reveals it with no distracting circumstance of subject, necessary to the picture or the poem. The hearer who listens to a great composition is not drawn aside to think of some historical or romantic incident; he is free to think of that of which such incidents are but the clothes. Age succeeds to age; the music which sounded in the ears of the fathers sounds also in the ears of the children. Place and circumstance force men asunder, but still for those of every party or sect and for those in every quarter of the world the great works of the masters of music remain. The works may be performed in the West End or in the East End—the hearers will have different conceptions, will see from different points of view the vision which inspired the master, but will nevertheless have the sense that the music which serves all alike creates a bond of union.

Music then would seem fitted to be in this age the expression of that which men in their inmost hearts most reverence. Creeds have ceased to express this and have become symbols of division rather than of unity! Music is a parable, telling in sounds which will not change of that which is worthy of worship, telling it to each hearer just in so far as he by nature and circumstance is able to understand it, but giving to all that feeling of common life and assurance of sympathy which has in old times been the strength of the Church. By music, men may be helped to find God who is not far from any one of us, and be brought again within reach of that tangible sympathy, the sympathy of their fellow-creatures.

There is, however, still one other requisite in a perfect form of religious expression. The age is new and thoughts are new, but nevertheless they are rooted in the past. More than any one acknowledges is he under the dominion of the buried ages. He who boasts himself superior to the superstitions of the present is the child of parents whose high thoughts, now transmitted to their child, were intertwined with those superstitions. Any form of expression therefore which aims at covering emotions said to be new must, like these emotions, have associations with the past. A brand new form of worship, agreeable to the most enlightened reason and surrounded with that which the present asserts to be good, would utterly fail to express thoughts and feelings, which, if born of the present, share the nature of parents who lived in the past. It is interesting to notice how machines and institutions which are the product of the latest thought bear in their form traces of that which they have superseded; the railway carriage suggests the stage-coach, and the House of Commons reminds us of the Saxon Witanagemot. The absolutely new would have no place in this old world, and a new form of expression could not express the emotions of the inner life.

Music which offers a form in which to clothe the yearnings of the present has been associated with the corresponding yearnings of the past, and would seem therefore to fulfil the necessary condition. Those who to-day feel music telling out their deepest wants and proclaiming their praise of the good and holy, might recognize in the music echoes of the songs which broke from the lips of Miriam and David, of Ambrose and Gregory, and of those simple peasants who one hundred years ago were stirred to life on the moors of Cornwall and Wales.

The fact that music has been thus associated with religious life gives it an immense, if an unrecognized power. The timid are encouraged and the bold are softened! When the congregation is gathered together and the sounds rise which are full of that which is and perhaps always will be "ineffable," there float in, also, memories of other sounds, poor perhaps and uncouth, in which simple people have expressed their prayers and praises; the atmosphere, as it were, becomes religious, and all feel that the music is not only beautiful, but the means of bringing them nearer to the God after Whom they have sought so long and often despaired to find.

For these reasons music seems to have a natural fitness for becoming the expression of the inner life. The experiment, at any rate, may be easily tried. There is in every parish a church with an organ, and arrangements suitable for the performance of grand oratorios; there are concert halls or schoolrooms suitable for the performance of classical music. There are many individuals and societies with voices and instruments capable of rendering the music of the masters. Most of them have, we cannot doubt, the enthusiasm which would induce them to give their services to meet the needs of their fellow-creatures.

Money has been and is freely subscribed for the support of missions seeking to meet bodily and spiritual wants; music will as surely be given by those who have felt its power to meet that need of expression which so far keeps the people without the consciousness of God. Members of ethical societies, who have taught themselves to fix their eyes on moral results, may unite with members of churches who care also for religious things. Certain it is that people who are able to realize grand ideals will be likely in their own lives to do grand things, and doing them make the world better and themselves happier.

SAMUEL A. BARNETT.

THE REAL SOCIAL REFORMER.[1]

By Canon Barnett.

January, 1910.

[1] From "The Manchester Weekly Times". By permission of the Editor.

THE world is out of joint. Reformers have in every age tried to put it right. But still Society jerks and jolts as it journeys over the road of life. The rich fear the poor, the poor suspect the rich, there is strife and misunderstanding; children flicker out a few days' life in sunless courts, and honoured old age is hidden in workhouses; people starve while food is wasted in luxurious living, and the cry always goes up, "Who will show us any good?"

The response to that cry is the appearance of the Social Reformer. Philanthropists have brought forward scheme after scheme to relieve poverty, and politicians have passed laws to remove abuses. Their efforts have been magnificent and the immediate results not to be gainsaid, but in counting the gains the debit side must not be forgotten. Philanthropists weaken as well as strengthen society; law hinders as well as helps. When a body of people assume good doing as a special profession, there will always be a tendency among some of their neighbours to go on more unconcerned about evil, and among others to offer themselves as subjects for this good doing. The world may be better for its philanthropists, but when after such devotion it remains so terribly out of joint the question arises whether good is best done by a class set apart as Social Reformers.

There is an often-quoted saying of a monk in the twelfth century: "The age of the Son is passing, the age of the Spirit is coming". He saw that the need of the world would not always be for a leader or for a class of leaders, but rather for a widely diffused spirit.

The present moment is remarkable for the number of societies, leagues, and institutions which are being started. There never were so many leaders offering themselves to do good, so many schemes demanding support. The Charities Register reveals agencies which are ready to deal with almost any conceivable ill, and it would seem that anyone desiring to help a neighbour might do so by pressing the button of one of these agencies. The agencies for each service are, indeed, so many, that other societies are formed now for their organization, and the would-be good-doer is thus relieved even from inquiring as to that which is the best fitted for his purpose.

The hope of the monk is deferred, and it seems as if it were the leaders and not the spirit of the people which is to secure social reform. The question therefore presses itself whether the best social reformers are the philanthropists. Specialists always make a show of activity, but such a show is often the cover of widely spread indolence. Specialists in religion—the ecclesiastics—were never more active than when during the fifteenth century they built churches and restored the cathedrals, but underneath this activity was the popular indifference which almost immediately woke to take vengeance on such leaders. Specialists in social reform to-day—the philanthropists—raise great schemes, but many of their supporters are at heart indifferent. It really saves them trouble to create societies and to make laws. It is easier to subscribe money—even to sit on a committee—than to help one's own neighbour. It is easier to promote Socialism than to be a Socialist. Activity in social reform movements may be covering popular indifference, and there is already a sign of the vengeance which awakened indifference may take in the cry dimly heard, "Curse your charity".

Better, it may be agreed, than great schemes—voluntary or legal—is the individual service of men and women who, putting heart and mind into their efforts, and co-operating together, take as their motto "One by One"; but again the same question presses itself in another form: Should the individual who aspires to serve his generation separate himself from the ordinary avocations of Society, and become a visitor or teacher? Should the business man divide his social reforming self from his business self, and keep, as he would say, his charity and his business apart?

The world is rich in examples of devoted men and women who have given up pleasure and profit to serve others' needs. The modern Press gives every day news of both the benefactions and the good deeds of business men who, as business men, think first, not of the kingdom of heaven, but of business profits. This specialization of effort—as the specialization of a class—has its good results; but is it the best, the only way of social reform? Is it not likely to narrow the heart of the good-doer and make him overkeen about his own plan? Will not the charity of a stranger, although it be designed in love and be carried out with thought, almost always irritate? Is it not the conception of society, which assumes one class dependent on the benevolence of another class, mediæval rather than modern? Can limbs which are out of joint be made to work smoothly by any application of oil and not by radical resetting? Is it reasonable that business men should look to cure with their gifts the injuries they have inflicted in their business, that they should build hospitals and give pensions out of profits drawn from the rents of houses unfit for human habitation, and gained from wages on which no worker could both live and look forward to a peaceful old age? Is it possible for a human being to divide his nature so as to be on the one side charitable and on the other side cruel?

The question therefore as to the best Social Reformer, still waits an answer. Before attempting an answer it may be as well to glance at the moral causes to which social friction is attributed. Popular belief assumed that the designed selfishness of classes or of individuals lies at the root of every trouble. Bitter and fiery words are therefore spoken. Capitalists suspect the aspiring tyranny of trade unions to be compassing their ruin, workmen talk of the other classes using "their powers as selfish and implacable enemies of their rights". Rich people incline to assume that the poor have designs on their property, and the poor suspect that every proposal of the rich is for their injury. The philosophy of life is very simple. "Every one seeketh reward," and the daily Press gives ample evidence as to the way every class acts on that philosophy. But nevertheless experience reveals the good which is in every one. Mr. Galsworthy in his play, "The Silver Box," pictures the conflict between rich and poor, between the young and the old. The pain each works on the other is grievous, there is hardness of heart and selfishness, but the reflection left by the play is not that anyone designed the pain of the other, but that for want of thought each misunderstood the other, and each did the wrong thing.

The family whose members are so smugly content with the virtue which has secured wealth and comfort, whose charities are liberally supported, and kindness frequently done, where hospitality is ready, would feel itself unfairly charged if it were abused because it lived on abuses, and opposed any change which might affect the established order. The labour agitator, on the other hand, feels himself unfairly charged when he is attacked as designing change for his own benefit and accused of enmity because of his strong language. It may be that his words do mischief, but in his heart he is kindly and generous. There are criminals in every class, rich men who prey on poor men, and poor men who prey on rich men, but the criminal class is limited and the mass of men do not intend evil. The chief cause of social friction is, it may be said, not designed selfishness so much as the want of moral thoughtfulness. The rogue of the piece is not the criminal, but—you—I—every one.

The recognition of this fact suggests that the best Social Reformer is not the philanthropist or the politician so much as the man or the woman who brings moral thoughtfulness into every act and relation of daily life.

There is abundance of what may be called financial thoughtfulness, and people take much pains, not always with success—to inquire into the soundness of their investments and the solvency of their debtors. The Social Reformer who feels the obligation of moral thoughtfulness will take as much pains to inquire whether his profits come by others' loss. He may not always succeed, but he will seek to know if the workers employed by his capital receive a living wage and are protected from the dangers of their trade. He will look to it that his tenants have houses which ought to make homes.

There is much time spent in shopping, and women take great pains to learn what is fashionable or suited to their means. If they were morally thoughtful they would take as much pains to learn what sweated labour had been used so that things might be cheap; what suffering others had endured for their pleasure. They might not always succeed, but the fact of seeking would have its effect, and they would help to raise public opinion to a greater sense of responsibility.

Pleasure-seekers are proverbially free-handed, they throw their money to passing beggars, they patronize any passing show which promises a moment's amusement; greater moral thoughtfulness would not prevent their pleasure, but it would prevent them from making children greedy, so that they might enjoy the fun of watching a scramble, and from listening to songs or patronizing shows which degrade the performer. Gwendolen, in George Eliot's "Daniel Deronda," did not realize that the cruelty of gambling is taking profit by another's loss, and so she laid the foundation of a tragedy. Pleasure-seekers who make the same mistake are responsible for some of the tragedies which disturb society.

The Social Reformers who will do most to fit together the jarring joints of Society are, therefore, the man and woman who, without giving up their duties or their business, who without even taking up special philanthropic work are morally thoughtful as to their words and acts. They are, in old language, they who are in the world and not of the world. If any one says that such moral thoughtfulness spells bankruptcy, there are in the examples of business men and manufacturers a thousand answers, but reformers who have it in mind to lead the world right do not begin by asking as to their own reward. It is enough for them that as the ills of society come not from the acts of criminals who design the ills, but from the thousand and million unconsidered acts of men and women who pass as kindly and respectable people, they on their part set themselves to consider every one of their acts in relation to others' needs.

The real Social Reformer is therefore the business man, the customer, the pleasure-seeker, who in his pursuits thinks first of the effect of those pursuits on the health and wealth of his partners in such pursuits. The spirit of moral thoughtfulness widely spread among rich and poor, employers and employed, better than the power of any leader or of any law, will most surely set right a world which is out of joint.

Samuel A. Barnett.

WHERE CHARITY FAILS.[1]

By Canon Barnett.

January, 1907.

[1] From "Pearson's Weekly". By permission of the Editor.

I DO not think that anyone will dispute the fact that our charity, taken as a whole, is administered in a somewhat wasteful and haphazard fashion. At the same time, however, I question whether the public is alive to the full extent of the evil arising from the utter lack of system in our administration of charity.

For it is not merely the question of the waste of the public's money, though that is bad enough; it is the far graver matter of the depreciation of our greatest national asset, character, by injudicious and indiscriminate philanthropy.

Owing to the absence of any supreme charitable board or authority, and the lack of co-operation between charitable bodies, it is very tempting to a poor man to tell a lie to draw relief from many sources. He gets his food and loses his character.

Indeed, I have no hesitation in saying that the present system directly encourages mendacity and mendicity, and, unless remedied, must inevitably affect the moral fibre of the nation.

The want of co-operation already alluded to is, of course, at the root of the evil, so far as waste of money is concerned, and I am often asked why charitable bodies will not co-operate. My answer is that it is very often a case of pride in results. Officials do not wish to share the credit of their work; they want to be able to claim to their subscribers that they have spent more money or relieved more cases than their rival round the corner, just as hospitals are led to regard the number of patients they treat as the criterion of their usefulness.

However, although I hold that hospitals might well extend their sphere from the cure to the prevention of disease, by taking more part in teaching people the laws of health and influencing them to keep such laws in their homes, I am not concerned with that question here, and mention hospitals only to introduce my first suggestion for charity reform.

The operations for the King's Hospital Fund have shown what can be done to check waste by bringing about a saving of £20,000 a year in the hospitals' bills for provisions, etc.

Until the King's Hospital Fund was instituted there was no general knowledge of the comparative expenditure of hospitals on food, etc., with the result that some paid exorbitant prices for certain articles and some for others. The action of the King's Fund has equalized expenditure, with the result I have stated.

Now it occurs to me that another board like the King's Hospital Fund would be able to bring about a similar saving in the administration of other charities which now compete to the loss of money subscribed by the public for the public, and, as I have said, to the detriment of character.

Such a Board would check waste and extravagance engendered by competition, and it could be brought into being as swiftly and effectively as was the King's Hospital Fund.

So much for an immediate measure, but I suggest as a more certain method that every twenty-five years or so there should be an inquiry by some authority, either national or local, into every philanthropic institution.

The terms of reference of such inquiry might be: firstly, the economic and business-like character of the management; secondly, the way in which co-operation was welcomed, and whether something more could not be done for further co-operation; and lastly, the institution might be tried by the standard of its usefulness to its surroundings. For, remember, every charity which really exists for the public good ought to test itself by this question, "Is our aim that of self-extinction?" The truest charity, that is to say, should aim to remove the causes, not the symptoms of evil.

But many shirk this self-inquisition, and linger on breeding mendicity, after their place has been taken by State or municipal organizations, or after they have ceased to fulfil any useful purpose.

It may be that this public authority I suggest would not at once effect very much, but a public inquiry provides facts for public opinion to work upon, and thus inevitably brings reform.

My final words, however, must again be as to the mischief liable to be done to character by thoughtless charity. People should think most carefully and solemnly before they give, lest they do more harm than good, and until our charity is properly organized and supervised, I fear that much money will be wasted on undeserving cases and in unnecessary and extravagant expenses of administration.

SAMUEL A. BARNETT.

LANDLORDISM UP TO DATE.[1]

By Canon Barnett.

August, 1912.

[1] From "The Westminster Gazette". By permission of the Editor.

"The position of landlord and tenant is often one of opposing interests." This remark from the first number of the "Record" of the Hampstead Garden Suburb must commend itself as true to all readers of the daily Press. The "Record," however, in two most interesting articles, shows that with landlordism up to date it need no longer be true. The Hampstead Garden Suburb Trust, of which Mr. Alfred Lyttelton is president, and Mrs. S. A. Barnett hon. manager, is the landlord of 263 acres—shortly to be increased by another 400 acres, most of which will be worked in conjunction with the Co-Partnership Tenants. To meet the needs of the 25,000 people who will ultimately be housed on this unique estate the whole has been laid out with a view to the comfort of the people, including in the idea of "comfort" not only well-built houses with gardens, but also the opportunities for the interknowledge of various classes which alike enriches the minds of rich and poor. A visit to the estate suggests the multitudinous interests which have been considered. The houses are grouped around a central square, on which stand the church, the chapel, and the institute, and it is so planned that from the cottages at 5s. 6d. a week, as from the mansions with rentals of from £100 to £250 a year, the inhabitants alike enjoy beauty either of gardens, tree-planted streets, public open spaces, or glimpses over the distant country.

The Hampstead Garden Suburb Trust, as the leading article in the "Record" says, "has done what any other far-seeing and enlightened landlord has done," with the difference that its pecuniary interest in the financial success of the scheme is limited by a self-obtained Act of Parliament to 5 per cent. In a summary, which it is well to quote, the doings of this up-to-date landlord are gathered together:—

"As a landlord the Trust has laid out and maintains the open spaces, the tennis courts, the wall-less gardens with their brilliant flowers, the restful nooks, the village green, which, with the secluded woods, can be enjoyed in common by rich and poor, simple and learned, young and old, sources of 'joy in widest commonalty spread'.

"As a landlord the Trust has given the sites for both the Established Church and the Free Church, each standing on the Central Square in equally prominent positions, worthy of the beautiful buildings their respective organizations have erected.

"As a landlord the Trust has given the site for the elementary school, and has spared no pains to obtain a building adapted to the best and most carefully thought-out methods of modern education.

"As a landlord the Trust has built the first section of the Institute, with the conviction that their hope of bringing into friendly relations all classes of their tenants will be furthered by the provision of a centre where residents and neighbours can be drawn together by intellectual interests. Although the Institute is not yet two years old, the Trust has already organized and maintained many activities, a full report of which is to be found in subsequent pages of the 'Record'.

"As a landlord the Trust has built three groups of buildings which they counted necessary towards the completion of their civic ideal: (*a*) Staff cottages, so that the men employed on the estate should be housed suitably and economically; (*b*) a group of homes where the State-supported children and others needing care and protection should live under suitable and adequate administration, and share the privileges and pleasures of the suburb; (*c*) motor-houses, with dwellings for the drivers, so that the richer people may have their luxury, and the poorer their habitations near their work.

"As a landlord the Trust conceives ideas for the public good and presses them on companies and others in the hope of their achievement. It was thus that the Improved Industrial Dwellings Company, Limited, built (from Mr. Baillie Scott's designs) the beautiful quadrangle of Waterlow Court, where working ladies find the advantages of both privacy and a common life.

"As a landlord the Trust is pushing forward negotiations with a view to obtaining a first-rate Secondary School, the directors believing that the provision of high-class education meets a need not usually considered when an estate is being developed, and that the school site should not be limited to the minimum necessary ground subsequently bought at an inflated price.

"As a landlord the Trust welcomes the public spirit and civic generosity of any of their tenants, taking special pride, perhaps, in the beautiful shops, the 'Haven of Rest' for the old and work-weary, and the club house (so admirably planned and alive with social and pleasurable activities), the tennis courts, the bowling greens, the children's gardens, the skating rink— each and all established and held for co-operative pleasure and joint use by their chief tenants, the co-partners."

This record of what has already been done prepares the reader to read with new interest the second article, "An Ideal—and After," by Mr. Raymond Unwin, who now stands at the head of "town-planners". He shows the great principles which have to be considered in planning town extensions, which principles have generally been forgotten in the growth of London suburbs. He then gives a plan of the 412 acres which lie between the Finchley and the Great North Road, and are about to be incorporated in the Hampstead Garden Suburb. He shows what direction the roads should take so as to secure readiness of access to the railway stations, and at the same time leave the Central Square with its fine buildings dominating and giving beauty to the whole neighbourhood. He shows also how other heights should be occupied by churches or public buildings, and he proposes that another centre (and another will be needed when it is remembered that the estate is nearly four miles long) "should approximate more nearly to the Market Place or Forum, where the main lines of traffic will meet, and to which access from all parts will be made easy". The articles make fascinating reading and lay hold of that pioneer instinct which has helped to make Englishmen such good Colonists. If the reading arouses some indignation at the lost chances of London, the fact that Mr. Unwin, on behalf of the Trust, and the co-partnership tenants are dealing with this great estate, in conjunction with the Finchley District Council, gives some hope. In years to come our children will see that the Hampstead Garden Suburb Trust as a pioneer landlord did notable work in avoiding current mistakes and in pointing the way for other metropolitan districts to follow. Out of eighty-two authorities in Greater London only twenty-seven have so far started to avail themselves of the powers of the Housing and Town-Planning Act, and meanwhile the jerry-builder is at large, uncontrolled, and very actively at work.

SAMUEL A. BARNETT.

THE CHURCH AND TOWN PLANNING.[1]

By Canon Barnett.

August, 1912.

[1] From "The Guardian". By permission of the Editor.

EVERY year we are told that so many churches have been added to London. Every year a volume is published by the Bishop of London's Fund with pictures of these churches—buildings of conventional character, showing in their mean lines and sterile decoration the trail of the order to limit their cost to £8000 or £9000. Every year we see London extending itself in long straight ranks of small houses, where no tower or spire suggests to men the help which comes of looking up, and no hall or public building calls them to find strength in meeting together.

Town-planning is much discussed, and the discussion has taken shape in an Act of Parliament; but meantime the opportunities are being lost for doing what the discussions and the Act declare to be necessary for health and happiness. Hendon is probably the most highly favoured building land nearest to London. It has undulating ground, where gentle hills offer a wide prospect towards the west; it has fine trees whose preservation might secure grace and dignity to the neighbourhood; and it has also a large sheet of water, the reservoir of the Brent, whose banks offer to young and old recreation for body and for spirit. A few years ago town-planning might have secured all these advantages, and at the same time provided houses and buildings which would have helped to make social life a fair response to the physical surroundings. But while talk is spent on the advantages of variety in buildings, of the importance of securing a vista which street inhabitants may enjoy, and of the value of trees and open spaces, straight roads are being cut at right angles across the hills, trees are being felled, and nothing has been done to prevent what will soon become slum property extending alongside the lake. Willesden, as it may be seen from Dollis Hill—a chess-board of slate roofs—is an object lesson as to the future of London if builders and owners and local authorities go on laying out estates with no thought but for the rights of private owners.

What, however, it may be asked, can the Church do? "Agitate—protest?" Yes, the Church, familiar with the lives of inhabitants of mean streets, can speak with authority. It can tell how minds and souls are dwarfed for want of outlook, how pathetic is the longing for beauty shown in the coloured print on the wall of the little dark tenement, how hard it is to make a home of a dwelling exactly like a hundred other dwellings, how often it is the dullness of the street which encourages carelessness of dirt and resort to excitement—how, in fact, it is the mean house and mean street which prepare the way for poverty and vice. The voice of joy and health is not heard even in the dwellings of the righteous. The Church might help town-planning as it might help every other social reform, by charging the atmosphere of life with unselfish and sympathetic thought. But the question I would raise is whether the Church is not called to take more direct action in the matter of town-building. Its policy at present seems to build a church for every 4,000 or 5,000 persons as they settle on the outskirts of London. The site is generally one given by a landlord whose interests do not always take in those of the whole neighbourhood. The building itself aims primarily at accommodating so many hundreds of people at a low cost per seat, and outside features are regarded as involving expenses too great for present generosity. This policy which has not been changed since Bishop Blomfield set the example of building the East London district churches, is, I believe, prejudicial to Church interests, as it certainly is to the dignity of the neighbourhood in which they stand.

The Church might help much in town-planning if it would change its policy, and, instead of dropping unconsidered and trifling buildings at frequent intervals over a new suburb, build one grand and dominant building on some carefully chosen site to which the roads would lead. The Directors of the Hampstead Garden Suburb as a private company have shown what is possible. They have crowned the hill at the base of which 20,000 people will soon be gathered, with the Church, the Chapel, and the public Institute. This hill dominates the landscape for miles round, and is the obvious centre of a great community of people. The Church by adopting a like policy would at once give a character to a new suburb, the convergence of roads would be marked, and order would be brought into the minds of builders planning out their different properties. The architects would be conscious of the centre of the circle in which they worked, and the houses would fall into some relation with the central building. Every one would feel such a healthy pride in the grandeur of the central church that it would be more difficult for things mean and unsightly to be set up in its neighbourhood. The church buildings in the City of London, or those which are seen towering over some of the newer avenues in Paris, or those familiar in our country towns and in villages, often seem as if they had brought together the inhabitants and were presiding over their lives. They look like leaders and suggest that the world is a world of order. The Bishop of London's Fund, or the authorities who direct the principal building policy, and spend annually thousands of pounds in its pursuit, have thus a great opportunity of giving direction to the expansion of London. They might by care in the selection of sites, and by generous expenditure at the direction of a large-visioned architect, do for the growing cities or towns of to-day what the builders of the past did for the cities and towns of their time. The Church by its direct action might thus give a great impetus to town planning, the need of which is in the mouths of all reformers.

But it may be asked whether the Church ought to contribute to the making of beauty at the cost of its own efficiency. Has not the State one duty and the Church another? Without answering the question it is I think easy to show that a new policy would cost less money, and be more efficient in promoting worship. It is obviously no more costly to build one magnificent building for £25,000 or £30,000 than to build three ordinary buildings at £8000 or £9000 each, while the maintenance of the three, with the constant expense of repairs, must be considerably greater.

And if it be asked whether one grand and generous and dignified building will attract more worshippers than three of the ordinary type, my answer is "Yes, and the worshippers will be assisted to a reverent mind and attitude". I speak what I know as a vicar for thirty years of a district church in East London. The building was always requiring repair, its fittings were oppressively cheap, and there were twelve other churches within much less than "a Sabbath day's journey". There is no doubt that the people preferred and were more helped by worship in the finer and better served parish churches. I used to feel what an advantage it would have been if the parish church, endowed and glorified with some of the money spent on the district churches, could have been the centre of a large staff of clergy, and have offered freely to all comers the noblest aids to worship. A feeling of patronage is incompatible with a feeling of worship, and the district church, with its constant need of money and its mean appearance, is always calling for the patronage of the people. The grandly built and imposing building, which gives the best and asks for nothing, provokes not patronage but reverence. There is, I believe, great need for such places of worship, as there is also need for meeting halls where in familiar talk and with simple forms of worship the clergy might lead and teach the people; but I do not see the need for the cheap churches, which are not dignified enough to increase habits of reverence, and often pretend to an importance which provokes impertinence.

The Church has been powerful because it has called on its members to put their best thought and their best gifts into the buildings raised for the worship of God. It owes much to the stately churches and sumptuous cathedrals, for the sake of which men of old made themselves poor; and to-day the hearts of many, who are worn by the disease of modern civilization, are comforted and uplifted as in the greatness of these buildings they forget themselves. The Church is as unwise as it is unfaithful when it puts up cheap and mean structures. It is not by making excuses—whether for its members who keep the best for their own dwellings or for itself when it takes an insignificant place in the streets—that the Church will command the respect of the people. It must prove its faith by the boldness of its demand. But I have said enough to show that the Bishop of London's Fund would serve its own object of providing the best aid to worship, if it would respond to the call of the present and seize the opportunity of taking a lead in town-planning. Church policy—as State policy—is often best guided by the calls which rise for present needs, and if our leaders, distrusting "their own inventions," would set themselves to assist in town-planning it might be given them to do the best for the Church as well as for the health and wealth of the people.

SAMUEL A. BARNETT.

SECTION VI.

EDUCATION.

The Teacher's Equipment— Oxford University and the Working People, *two articles*—Justice to Young Workers—A Race between Education and Ruin.

THE TEACHER'S EQUIPMENT.[1]

By Canon Barnett.

March, 1911.

[1] From "The Westminster Gazette". By permission of the Editor.

LIBERALS must be somewhat disappointed that a Liberal Government has done so little for education. The reforms for which they stand—their hopes for the nation—depend on the increase of knowledge and intelligence among the people. The establishment of Free Trade, wise economy and wise expenditure, and the support of the statesmanship which makes for peace, all presuppose an instructed electorate. But the present Government has passed no measure to strengthen the foundation on which Liberalism rests; attempts, indeed, were made to settle the religious difficulty, but ever since those attempts were wrecked by the House of Lords, Ministers have been content to do nothing, although outside the religious controversy they might have launched other attempts laden with important reforms and safe to reach their port. The administration of the law as it stands has doubtless been vigorous; able and public-spirited officials have seen that everything which the law requires has been done, and every possible development effected, but the Liberal Government has done nothing to improve the Law. Minister of Education succeeds Minister of Education, years of opportunity roll by, while children still leave school at an age when their education has hardly begun, while compulsory continuation schools still wait to be started, while great—not to say vast—endowments are absorbed in the objects of the wealthier classes, while the provision for the equipment of teachers is unsatisfactory.

The equipment of the teachers is confessedly the most important item in any programme of education, as it is upon the teacher rather than upon the building or the curriculum that the real progress of education depends. That equipment, as far as elementary schools are concerned, is now given in training colleges, and especially in residential colleges. Young men and women, that is to say, who have been through a secondary school, and also shown some aptitude for teaching, receive, largely at Government expense, two years' instruction and training in colleges which are managed either by religious denominations or by local educational authorities. In the colleges the staff is mostly occupied in giving the knowledge which forms part of a general education, and very little time is spent in training or in the study of problems of the child life.

TRAINING COLLEGES.

The system is unsatisfactory on many grounds. (1) The rivalry between denominational and undenominational colleges stirs the keenest partisanship. When in his annual statement Mr. Runciman began to talk about the number of students in the different colleges he had, he said with some irony, "to drop the subject, knowing how far the religious controversy is likely to interest this House". (2) The system is most costly, and every year, including building grants, an amount of something like half a million of money is paid for the training—or, to speak more accurately, for the ordinary education of young men and women who may feel no call for teaching and cannot be really bound to take it up for their life's work. (3) It breeds a feeling of indignation among those who do not get employment, and there is now an agitation because the State does not find work for those whom it has selected to receive a special training, and bound, even though it be by an ineffective bond, to follow a particular calling. (4) It brings together a body of students whose outlook to the future is identical, it encourages, therefore, narrow views, and breeds the exclusive professional spirit in a profession whose usefulness depends on its power to assimilate the thought of the time and to sacrifice its interest for wider interests. The training college system as a means of equipping teachers for their work is not satisfactory, and the Archbishop of Canterbury was well justified when he said: "The thing which mattered most in the educational work in England to-day was the question of the training colleges".

THEIR REFORM OR THEIR ABOLITION.

The reforms suggested generally follow the lines of further expenditure on buildings or on staff, but such expenditure would not remove the objections. The money annually spent is very large—equal to the gross income of Oxford University—and if more were spent there is no very effective way of securing that the best among the teachers so trained would remain in the profession; the men would still take up more remunerative work, and the women would still marry. The rivalry between denominational and undenominational would continue, and the protest of conscientious objectors—religious or secular—as each further expense was proposed would increase difficulties. If the number turned out of the training colleges were larger there would be a more widely spread sense of wrong among the unemployed, who would with difficulty recognize that something else was wanting in a teacher than the certificate of a training college. But most fatal of all to the proposed extension or improvement of the system, is the objection that the more and the stronger the colleges become, the more deeply would the professional spirit be entrenched, and the more powerful would be the influence of the teaching class in asserting its rights.

SUBSTITUTION OF A BETTER WAY OF TRAINING.

The reform might, I submit, follow the line of restriction and proceed towards the ultimate abolition of the residential colleges in their present form. The way is comparatively simple. Let the children from elementary schools be helped—as, indeed, they now are—by scholarships to enter secondary schools, and go on to University colleges, or to the Universities. Equal opportunity for getting the best knowledge would thus be open to children of all classes. Let any over the age of nineteen who have passed through a college connected with some University, or otherwise approved as giving an education of a general and liberal character, be eligible to apply for a teachership, and if, after a period of trial in a school—say for three or six months—they, on the report of the inspector and master, have shown an aptitude for teaching, then let them, at the expense of the State, be given a year's real training in the theory and practice of teaching. Teachers are, it must be remembered, born and not made. One man or woman who, without any experience, is placed over a class will at once command attention, while another with perhaps greater ability will create confusion. Those who are not born to it may indeed learn the tricks of discipline, and, like a drill-sergeant, command obedience and keep order. Many of the complaints which are heard about the unintelligence and the want of interest in children who have come from schools where to the visitor's eye everything seems right are due, I believe, to the fact that the teachers have not been born to the work. They have trusted to the rules they have learnt and not to the gift of power which is in themselves. They teach as the scribes and not with authority. Let, therefore, the men and women who have this power be those whom the State will train; let it give them not, as at present, a few weeks in a practising school, but experience in a variety of schools in town and in country, and under masters with different systems; let them be made familiar with the last thoughts on child life, and with all the many different theories of education. The State will in this way draw from all classes in the community the men and the women best fitted to teach, and it will give them a training worthy the name. The teachers will have the best equipment for their work.

The advantages of this proposal to get rid of the training colleges as they now are may be summarized: (1) There will be an end of the religious difficulty where at present it is most threatening. The children with scholarships will go to the schools and University colleges they elect just as do the children who are aiming at other careers. The State in the training it provides will have nothing to do with the special training required for giving religious knowledge—as such training would naturally be given by the different denominations at their own expense. (2) The half million of money annually spent on training colleges would not be required for the training now proposed. It cannot, however, be said that the money would be returned to the taxpayers; education—if the nation is to be saved—must become more and more costly, but it may be said that the greater part of this sum and the existing buildings would be used for the general education of persons taken from all classes of the community and preparing to walk in all sorts of careers. (3) There would be no body of men and women with the grievance that, having been selected at an early age, trained as teachers, and bound to a profession, no work was provided. Every one would have had the best sort of education for any career, and only one year, after a fair time for choice and probation, would have been given to special training. (4) The danger of professionalism would be lessened. Men and women educated in schools and colleges alongside of other students with other aims, would, by their association, gain a wider outlook on life, and would be freed from the influences which tend now to force them into an organization for the defence of their rights. If afterwards they did join such organizations they would do so with a wider consciousness of their relation to a body larger than their own, and to a knowledge greater than they themselves had acquired.

A substantial number of young persons do even under present conditions spend their three years with the Government scholarship at Universities or University colleges, and the experience thus gained illustrates the advantage to intending students of mixing with persons intended for other careers.

Here, then, I submit, is a way of reform in what is confessedly the most important part of our system of education. It might be undertaken at no extra expense, and with small dislocation of existing institutions. The one thing necessary is zeal for education among our political leaders. The best students of the social problem tell us the remedy for the unrest is education, and anyone considering the signs of the times in England will say also that there must be more education if employers and employed, if statesmen and people, if the pulpit and the pew are to understand one another. The chief Minister in any Government, the Minister on whose zeal and ability all the others depend for the ultimate success of their work, is the Minister of Education. If he is zealous he will find a way of equipping the teachers.

SAMUEL A. BARNETT.

OXFORD UNIVERSITY AND THE WORKING PEOPLE.[1]

By Canon Barnett.

First Article.

February, 1909.

[1] From "The Westminster Gazette". By permission of the Editor.

Oxford last year invited seven working men to act with seven members of the University on a Committee appointed to consider what the University can do for the education of working people. The step is notable—Oxford and Cambridge have long done something to make it possible for the sons of workmen, by means of scholarships, to enter the colleges, to take degrees, and, as members of the University, to climb to a place among the professional classes. Oxford, in appointing this Committee, has taken a new departure, and aimed to put its resources at the disposal of people who continue to be members of the working classes.

The report of the Committee, of which the Dean of Christ Church was Chairman, and Mr. Shackleton, M.P., Vice-Chairman, forms a most interesting pamphlet, which may be obtained for a shilling from any bookseller or the Clarendon Press. It tells of the purpose, the history, and the endowments of the University, and it also gathers together evidence of the demand which is being raised by working people for something more than education in "bread and butter" subjects. This evidence is summed up in the following report:—

The ideal expressed in John Milton's definition of education, "that which fits a man to perform justly, skilfully, and magnanimously, all the duties of all offices," is one which is, we think, very deeply embedded in the minds of the working classes, and we attribute part of the failure of higher education among them in the past, to the feeling that, by means of it their ablest members were being removed to spheres where they would not be available for the service of their fellows. What they desire is not that men should escape from their class, but that they should remain in it and raise the whole level. The eleven millions who weave our clothes, build our houses, and carry us safely on our journeys demand university education in order that they may face with wisdom the unsolved problems of their present position, not in order that they may escape to another. . . . To-day in their strivings for a fuller life, they ask that men of their own class should co-operate as students with Oxford in order that, with minds enlarged by impartial study, they in their turn may become the public teachers and leaders, the philosophers and economists of the working classes. The movement, which is thus formulated in a report signed by seven representative workmen, is fraught with incalculable possibilities.

The sum of happiness in the nation might be vastly increased, and politics might be guided by more persistent wisdom. The great sources of happiness which rise within the mind and are nourished by contact with other minds are largely out of reach of the majority of the people. These sources might be brought within their reach. The working classes whose minds are strengthened by the discipline of work, might have the knowledge which would interest them in the things their hands make; they might, in the long monotonies of toil, be illuminated by the thoughts of the great, and inspired by ideals; they might be introduced to the secrets of beauty, and taught the joy of admiration. They might be released from the isolation of ignorance, so that, speaking a common language, and sharing common thoughts, they would have the pleasure of helping and being helped in discussions with members of other classes on all things under the sun.

The workman knows about livelihood; he might know also about life, if the great avenues of art, literature, and history, down which come the thoughts and ideals of ages, were open to him. He might be happy in reading, in thinking, or in admiring, and not be driven to find happiness in the excitement of sport or drink. The mass of the people it is often said are dumb, so that they cannot tell their thoughts; deaf, so that they cannot understand the language of modern truth; and blind, so that they cannot see the beauty of the world.

The speaker, in Mr. Lowes Dickenson's dialogue, condemns this generation when he says, "their idea of being better off is to eat and drink to excess, to dress absurdly, and to play stupidly and cruelly".

The majority of the people, it must be admitted, cannot have the best sort of happiness, that which comes from within themselves, from the exercise of their own thoughts, and from the use of their own faculties. For want of knowledge the sum of happiness is decreased, and for want of the same knowledge the dangers of war and social troubles are increased. The working people have now become the governing class in the nation. Up to now, the acting governors—the majority which controls the Government—have cajoled them by party cries, by appeals to passion, and by the familiar blandishments of expert canvassers, to fall in with their policy. But every year working people are forming their own opinions, and making their opinions felt, both in home and foreign policy. They will break in upon the international equilibrium, so delicately poised amid passions and prejudices; they will decide the use of the Dreadnoughts and the armies of the world; they will settle questions of property and of tariff; they will form the authority which will have to control individual action for the good of the whole. How can they possibly carry this responsibility if they have no wider outlook on life, no greater knowledge of men, no more power of foresight, no more respect for tradition than that which they already possess?

How shortsighted is the policy which spends millions on armaments, and leaves them to become destructive in ignorant hands. How important for national security is a knowledge "in widest commonalty spread". Oxford, to a large extent, possesses this knowledge and the means of its distribution.

"The national Universities, which are the national fountainheads of national culture," as one workman has said, have been regarded as the legitimate preserves of the leisured class. They have helped the rich to enjoy and defend their possessions, they have given them out of their resources the power to see and to reason; they have made them wise in their own interests; they have given to one class, and to the recruits who have been drawn to that class from the ranks of the workman, the knowledge in which is happiness and power. The question arises, should Oxford, can Oxford, give the same gifts to working people while they remain working people? The answer of the report is an unequivocal "Yes".

In the first place the University has inherited the duty of educating the poor. Its colleges have in many cases been founded for poor scholars, and its tradition is that poverty shall be no bar to learning.

In the next place its long-established custom, of bringing men into association in pursuit of knowledge, is one which peculiarly fits it to help workmen, whose strength lies in that power of association which has covered some districts of England with a network of institutions—industrial, social, political, and religious. Men who have joined in the discussions of the workshop, been members of the committee of a co-operative store, and acted as officials of a friendly society, have had in some ways a better preparation for absorbing the teaching of the University on life, than is given in the forms and playing field of a public school. The tutor of a class of thirty-nine working people at N—— who read with him, the regular session through, a course of Economic History, reports that the work was excellent, and a visitor from Oxford was impressed "by the high level of the discussion and the remarkable acumen displayed in asking questions".

In the last place, the University has the money. The total net receipts of the Universities and colleges—apart from a sum of £178,000 collected from the members of the Universities and colleges—is £265,000. Of this sum, £50,000 is given in scholarships and exhibitions to boys who for the most part have been trained in the schools of the richer classes, and of this sum £34,000 is given yearly without reference to the financial means of the recipient. The report does not analyse the expenditure of this large income, except in so far as to suggest that some of the scholarship and fellowship money might be diverted to the more direct service of working people's education. Common sense, however, suggests that there must be many possible economies in the management of estates, in the overlapping of lecturers, and in the expense on buildings. The experience of the Ecclesiastical Commission has shown how much may be gained if estates are removed from the care of many amateur corporations, and placed under a centralized and efficient management. The knowledge, too, that some colleges have ten times the income of others, without corresponding difference in the educational output, suggests that money may be saved.

Oxford seems to be compelled, both by its traditions, its customs, and its money to do something for the education of the working people. The question whether it can do so, is answered by the scheme which the report recommends; that a committee be formed in Oxford, consisting of working-class representatives, in equal numbers with members of the University; that this Committee should draw up a two years' curriculum, select the tutors, who must also have work in Oxford, and settle the localities in which classes shall be held; that students at these classes be admitted to the diploma course; that half of the teachers' salary be paid by the University, and the other half by the Committee of the locality in which the classes are held. The report, with a view to bringing working people under the influence of Oxford itself, further recommends that colleges be asked to set aside a number of scholarships or exhibitions, to enable selected students from the tutorial classes to reside in Oxford, either in Colleges, in University Halls, as non-collegiate students, or at Ruskin Hall.

These recommendations have certain advantages and certain shortcomings, the consideration of which must be deferred to another article.

SAMUEL A. BARNETT.

OXFORD UNIVERSITY AND THE WORKING PEOPLE.[1]

By Canon Barnett.

Second Article.

February, 1909.

<u>1</u> From "The Westminster Gazette". By permission of the Editor.

THE points in the scheme which Oxford proposes to adopt for bringing its resources to the services of working people are: The appointment of representative workmen on the Committee responsible for the object. The offer of a working University tutor to a locality where a class of thirty workpeople has been formed, willing to adopt one of the two years' courses which the committee has approved. The recognition of the students of these classes as eligible for a diploma in Economics, Political Science, etc. The open door, so that students selected from the classes may be able to enter and to reside in the University.

Two questions arise: Will the scheme attract workmen? Will it get the sympathetic, if not the enthusiastic, support of the University?

1. Will it attract workmen? Workmen, apart from the demand that they, as a class, should share in the joy and the power of knowledge, have learnt that they must have educated men of their own class to direct their own organizations. There are 1,153 trade unions, 389 friendly societies, 2,646 co-operative societies, and many other councils or congresses, most of which employ paid officers who are daily discharging duties of the utmost responsibility and delicacy, and which make demands on their judgment of men and knowledge of economic and political principles, as great or greater than those made on the Civil servant in India or in this country. Workmen want officials who, familiar with their point of view, will have the knowledge and experience to convince educated opponents of the justice of their contentions. The education which Oxford can give by broadening a man's knowledge and strengthening his judgment, would make him a more efficient servant of his own society, and a more potent influence on the side of industrial peace.

Will workmen accept the offer which Oxford makes? Much shyness and prejudice have to be overcome. Oxford is often associated with opinions foreign to the democratic ideal. The manners of University men sometimes suggest that they are superior persons, and a reputation for expensive trifling is widely spread. Workmen are afraid that their young men in the University atmosphere may be alienated from their class, grow ashamed of their belongings, and put on artificial manners. They doubt whether the teaching may not be of a kind directed in the interest of property, and they fear lest there may be too many temptations to idleness and to play. They do not want, as one Labour leader has said, "good democratic stuff spoiled by Oxford lecturers, who may give our people a shoddy notion of respectability, and a superficial idea of things which can be shown by the airs and graces of book learning".

Oxford is thus suspect; but, on the other hand, the place has immense attraction, as is proved by the fact that so many Trade Unions send their men to study at Ruskin College.

"What," it was asked of one of their students, "do you get here you could not have got in a college in your own town?"

"I get Oxford," was his reply; and it is evident in much talk that, even when Oxford is "suspect," it has a great hold on the workman's mind. There may be shyness, but it is only shyness that may be overcome by trust.

The place of workmen, therefore, on the University committees must be an assured place, and not one allowed as a favour or on sufferance. Their voices must be heard as to the subjects to be taught, and as to the teachers who are chosen; they must be able to make their influence felt in the University, which, as it is national, is their University. The local centres where classes are given must, in the same way, be locally controlled and independent of University control. The committees of these centres must have full choice of the place and time of their meetings, select from the list the courses of study to be followed, and approve the tutor. They must, indeed, have the same character as club or co-operative classes, while, through the Oxford tutor, the course of studies and the examination, light is let in from the University. The life must be in the local centres, but it must draw its air from Oxford.

The problem as to the admission of working people to residence is more difficult. The proposal is that, by means of scholarships, they should be enabled to live in colleges or in halls, or as non-collegiate students. The difficulty would be got over if enough students could come to be a support to one another. There must always be a fear lest, if they be few in number, they may either lose their independence or else go to the extreme of protest. The University can, however, get over this difficulty by providing sufficient money to bring up a sufficient number of men, who will strengthen one another and influence the corporate life of the place. The question whether students should reside in colleges, in halls, or in lodgings may be left to solve itself. If they are to reside in colleges, the present system of erecting new buildings, with suites of expensive rooms, might well be checked. Simpler buildings, adapted to the needs of workmen students, would save money, bring together types of men in one community, and not detract from the beauty of the city.

The schemes will, I believe, attract workmen if the University takes pain to subordinate itself, and trusts to truth rather than to power. Workmen, if once their suspicion—justified, it must be allowed—be allayed, will find that there is in Oxford more sympathy with their point of view than can possibly be found in any other English community. Oxford men have, as a rule, open minds, and many of their younger Fellows are close and devoted students of social questions. Many working men have already experienced what Mr. Crooks experienced when, at a meeting in a college hall, having hurled some stinging sentences at the superiority which University men assumed, his remarks were received, "not with boot-jacks, but with cheers" Friendships between working men and members of the University are soon formed—both are used to living in associations, both have a love of free discussion, both, to a larger extent than other Englishmen, are believers in equality. The scheme, if the University wishes it, will attract workmen.

2. The other question is, Will the scheme win the support of the University? A statute has already been passed appointing a committee consisting of working-class representatives, and it has been agreed that tutorial-class students may be admitted to the diploma course. The University can hardly do more. It cannot alter its constitution, which to a large extent leaves the government in the hands of college nominees, with an ultimate appeal to members of the University, scattered throughout the country. Its total income is only £24,000 a year, and it has no power to enforce adequate contributions from the colleges, although their total income from endowments is £265,000 a year. The University itself, unless it be reformed by Act of Parliament, or unless the colleges voluntarily endow it with the power and the means, can do very little to carry out the scheme.

Will the Colleges act in the matter? Will they pass over to the control of the University a fair portion of the money they now spend either on scholarships and fellowships confined to boys from a few schools, or on the maintenance of choirs and tutors, or on new buildings? It is not enough that one or two colleges make a grant to support some workmen's centre. Workmen will resent the patronage of a college. The money must be transferred to the University, the tutors must have a University standing, and the scholarships, which enable men to reside in Oxford, must be both ample and numerous. The University has, so far as it can, acted on the recommendation of the report. Will the Colleges rise to the opportunity, and enable Oxford to give the people the knowledge they need, for the satisfaction of their own lives and the security of the nation?

The Colleges as yet have given little sign of a will to do anything but strengthen their own independence, and make provision for students prepared in the public schools. In one or two instances, fellowships have been given to men who have become lecturers under the University Extension Scheme, but the example has not been followed.

For many years pupil teachers from the elementary schools have come to Oxford for their training; one or two colleges have given scholarships; but again the example has not spread, and the inspector has had to complain of the scant provision which has been made for the men's advantage.

A plan was once initiated by which parties of teachers and others were accommodated in colleges during the long vacation, and tasted some of the advantages of Oxford life and teaching. The plan worked excellently; it removed the reproach that for six months in the year the greatest educational capital of the nation is allowed to lie idle. But there was little enthusiasm; the energy of the few residents who were responsible was, after a few years, worn out, if not by opposition, by apathy.

The colleges have as yet shown little power of adapting themselves to the education of the new governing class. It may be that they will be roused by this report, and that something adequate may be done.

The point I would urge is that the something be adequate—a few classes scattered about the country, a few men admitted to Oxford, will court a failure, and justify condemnation of the attempt.

The colleges have their opportunity, but beyond the colleges is my friend Bishop Gore, now Bishop of Oxford, with his demand for a Commission, and beyond the Bishop is the rising power of labour, with its tendency, if it be not checked by University influence, to use all national endowments for material rather than spiritual ends.

The Bishop's case for a commission is broadly based on the impossibility of working the present constitution of the University for its efficient government; on the mischievous waste which spends the resources of fine minds and unique surroundings on boys, many of whom are capable of doing little more than play; on the folly of subsidizing with scholarships and fellowships one set of schools, and one or two types of knowledge; on the expensive habits which the system fostered. The case was not answered, and cannot be answered. The report of the committee is the first response to its call, and, as the Bishop said in a speech at Toynbee Hall, it has given him a hope for which he has long waited.

The next response ought to be an appeal from the University itself for a Commission which will enable it to order the resources of Oxford as a whole, and apply its powers so as to carry out fully the recommendations of the report.

SAMUEL A. BARNETT.

JUSTICE TO YOUNG WORKERS.

By Canon Barnett.

8 November, 1909.

THIRTY years ago the "bitter cry" of the poor disturbed the public mind. Housing has since been improved. Technical teaching has since been established. The expenditure on the Poor Law has been greatly increased. General Booth has raised the money for his social scheme. Philanthropy has redoubled its efforts, and taken new forms. But still the "bitter cry" is raised. The number of the unemployed is greater than ever. There is more vagrancy, which the Prison Commissioners complain is adding to the inmates of the prisons, and the amount spent on poor relief goes up by leaps and bounds. Royal Commissions, Departmental Committees, philanthropic conferences, scientific professors have been facing the problem which every year becomes more threatening to the national welfare. Their recommendations are many. The striking fact is that in one recommendation they all concur. The one thing which they agree to be necessary is further training for young people between the ages of thirteen and seventeen.

The report of the Consultative Committee of the Board of Education, lately published, gives the final word on the subject. The reports begin by showing that out of the 2,000,000 children in England and Wales who have passed their fourteenth birthday, and are still under seventeen years of age, only one in four receives on week-days any continued education. "The result is a tragic waste of early promise." The children go out of the elementary schools, which have been built up at immense expense, and before they reach the age of seventeen, when the technical schools may be entered, many have acquired desultory habits, and lost the power of study. Released from school, they become idle and lawless, or they enter "blind alley" employments, and for the sake of high immediate wages, miss the chance of ultimate responsible employment. The Committee agree with the Poor Law Commissioners, "that the results of the large employment of boys in occupations which offer no opportunity of employment as men are disastrous," and go on to quote the Minority Report: "The nation cannot long persist in ignoring the fact that the unemployed, and particularly the under-employed, are thus being daily created under our eyes out of bright young things, for whose training we make no provision".

The Committee having brought out this extravagant waste of money and effort and young life, sets itself to consider a remedy. It suggests improvements in the day schools by giving a larger place in the curriculum to subjects which train the hand and eye, and develop the constructive powers. It further suggests that steps should be taken to prolong the school life of children, and it will be a surprise to many readers that under the age of thirteen years 5,300 every year pass out of school, and that the extension of the age to fourteen would involve the addition of 150,000 children to the registers. These numbers do not include the scholars now partially exempted from school attendance by the wisdom or unwisdom of managers, who may be estimated as numbering some 48,000 children, between thirteen and fourteen years of age. The Committee add their opinion that the law which permits half-time in the textile districts should be materially changed, and it goes on to recommend that "no children under sixteen should be allowed to leave the day school unless they could show to the satisfaction of the local education authority that they were going to be suitably occupied, and that such exemptions should only continue so long as they remained in suitable employment".

This recommendation follows on evidence of how large a proportion of boys and girls enter forms of employment "which discourage the habit of steady work, lessen the power of mental concentration, and are economically injurious to the community, and deteriorating in their effect on individual character". Employment or apprenticeship Committees have been formed, whose members spare no pains in advising the older scholars, and the parents of such scholars, in the choice of an occupation. They have done enough to show how much more might be done could the advice be driven home with more system and authority. If the recommendation were made the law, no child under sixteen would be allowed to enter upon industrial life without sufficient guidance, both as to the choice of a place, and as to continued education.

"Continued education," whatever be the improvements in the day school or the laudation of exemption from attendance, comes thus to be regarded as the one thing necessary. "It is clear to the Committee that the lack of continued educational care during the years of adolescence is one of the deeper causes of national unemployment."

Continuation schools have greatly developed during late years. They are more frequent, they offer teaching which is more attractive and more adapted to the social needs of the neighbourhoods in which they have been opened. Educational authorities and private organizations have taken pains to commend the schools and make them known. Employers have in some cases required attendance at continuation schools as a condition of employment, and in other cases have encouraged attendance by giving off-time, by payment of fees, and by the offer of prizes. Workpeople have taken pleasure in visiting the schools, and when they are represented on the management, get rid of some suspicions, often to become enthusiastic supporters.

Continuation schools may thus be said to have passed the period of experiment, and it is now recognized that the curriculum should neither be that of the old night-school, nor of the modern recreation evening. It should aim rather at providing a good general education, to equip men and women for intelligent citizenship, as well as to supply workers with technical knowledge, and with that adaptability which is one of the most valuable possessions of workpeople under modern conditions. It cannot too often be repeated that the aim of education is not to make machines, but to make men and women. People who know how to think and to reason, who have capacities for enjoyment which do not need the stimulus of excitement, will be more valuable citizens, and when they lose one form of work, will more readily take to another.

The right sort of continuation school is now known. Such schools increase yearly in number, and the attendances also increase, but the Committee has been led to the conclusion that voluntary methods alone will not solve the problem. There must be recourse to compulsory powers. In many districts the authorities are apathetic, in other districts voluntary methods are powerless against the ignorance and indifference of the people. The majority of employers, moreover, are indifferent, failing to recognize that closer care for the educational interest of their young employés would enhance their own profit, and the pupils are often too tired to attend any school. The law at present says, "Children are compelled to attend school till the age of thirteen," it therefore creates the impression that at the age of thirteen the obligation ceases. The law alone can remove this impression, and it must in the future say: "Young people are compelled to attend continuation schools till the age of seventeen".

The Committee, in coming to the conclusion that a compulsory system is necessary, has been confirmed in the conclusion by the elaborate organization of day and evening schools (continuation) in Germany and Switzerland, and by the movement in France for the extension of educational opportunities during the years following the conclusion of the day-school course. The Committee has also discovered signs of the growth of opinion in England in favour of such a course, and this Government has already adopted it in the Scotch Act of 1908. Out of eighty-nine witnesses examined on this question sixty declared themselves in favour of this compulsion, and of the twenty-nine who objected, many modified their objections. The Committee felt themselves justified in recommending that the example of the Scotch Act be followed, and that every local education authority should be required to establish suitable continuation classes, and that attendance should be made compulsory for all young persons under seventeen, when the local education authority make by-laws to that effect.

The obligation for the satisfactory working of the compulsion would be thrown primarily on the employer. Every employer would be bound to supply the officer of the education authority with the names of young people in his employ; to arrange the hours of work so as to make it possible for them to attend classes on certain days or nights without causing the overstrain of their bodies; it would be his duty to inspect the attendance cards of pupils at the classes; and he would be forbidden under penalties to keep in his employment anyone not in regular attendance.

The local authority would be called on to draw up its by-laws with due regard to the character of the employment in various districts, so as to cause as little inconvenience as possible to trade, and avoid any physical overstrain to pupils. All street selling by boys and girls under seventeen would be prohibited, except in the case of those who were formerly licensed, and this licence would be forfeited unless the holders' attendance card proved the necessary attendance at the continuation school.

The Committee make special suggestions as to girls in urban districts, and generally as regards rural districts. Various needs demand various provisions. The point, however, which stands out most clearly is that after all needs have been weighed, and after all objections have been considered, a system of compulsory continuation classes is recommended both in the interests of the young people, who, for want of such classes, miss the fruit of their education, and in the interest of the community, who have to bear the burden of the unemployed.

Germany and Switzerland have established compulsory continuation schools; Scotland has now followed their example. The Consultative Committee has now shown that England is ready, and has suggested a practicable scheme. Will the men and women whose hearts are torn, and whose national pride is wounded by the sight of so many workers unable to earn a living wage, and whose reason tells them that their unemployed are often incompetent, because their training stopped and licence began at thirteen years of age, and whose minds have now been informed by figures that it is for want of care during the most critical period of their lives that loafers and vagrants are made—will the men and women who thus feel and know make the Government understand that this one thing it is necessary shall be taken in hand without further delay?

SAMUEL A. BARNETT.

A RACE BETWEEN EDUCATION AND RUIN.[1]

By Canon Barnett.

March, 1912.

[1] From "The Westminster Gazette". By permission of the Editor.

I.

"Twenty years too late" is the reflection suggested by the report of the success of the Universities' Experiment of Tutorial Classes for Working People. The present industrial situation needs, it may be agreed, a working-class able to take large and generous views, capable of shaping not only a class but a national policy, trained to separate the essential from the unessential, and to act consistently on principles tried and proved in the history of the past. The old Universities have the resources for giving the people this equipment. They have wealth; they have teachers penetrated by the traditions accumulated in Oxford and Cambridge; they exist, we are told, to give liberal culture a broader outlook, a historical perspective. The Universities, roused by the Workers' Education Association, have, by means of the Tutorial Classes, achieved notable success. They have offered to groups of twenty or thirty working people in the great towns means by which they might enter a larger life, feel the years which are behind, and get a grasp of eternal principles. The means have been seized with surprising eagerness. Men after a hard day's work have been found week after week at the tutors' tables for the study of economics, political philosophy, or history; they have kept up attendance for three years, and they have learnt, to quote the words of some who attended a summer meeting in Balliol College, "the wonderful development which has taken place in my mind" now "that my prejudices have been dispelled and mental horizon widened"—that "study is a pleasure rather than a task".

The students, in a word, receive a share of that larger education which the Universities exist to give. But success over so small an area, affecting only a few thousand men, but serves to show what might have been if the movement had commenced twenty years earlier.

The working people have now come into power, and they have many wrongs to put right. The anxious question is, Will they use their power more wisely and more generously than the capitalist class? There is not much sign of a wide and generous outlook in a policy which assumes that war is the necessary attitude of employed and employers. There is not much evidence of an inspiring vision of society when there is so little recognition of the interdependence of all sorts and conditions of men. There is not much grasp of principle among those who begin a strike, which must involve untold suffering, as if it were a holiday. The working people may have wrongs to bear, they may have splendid qualities of faithfulness to comrades and endurance under hardships, but they can hardly be said to have that knowledge of humanity which makes them humble before the best, with a capacity for judgment and a standard by which to apply it.

The race in all nations seems to be one between Education and Ruin. The Universities who are especially responsible for national education have too late begun to share their resources with working people, and the success of their long-delayed start has only served to encourage the formation of the rival Central Labour College. This College is thus described by Mr. Rowland Kenney: "It makes no pretence of giving a 'broad' education. . . . Its teaching is frankly partisan. History is dealt with as a record of the struggles which have taken place in social groups, because of the conflicting interests of the various classes that have from time to time divided society. . . . Its key to the interpretation of Sociology is class interest; dividing the social groups into the owners and non-owners of property, it points out the common interest of all those who work for wages. . . . It absolutely cuts out any idea of conciliation as a final solution of labour problems." The College, in the name of education, appears to be using its forces to block the way to peace and goodwill which it is largely the object of education to keep open. It preaches a class war, treats every member of the middle class as "suspect," and bitterly opposes the Workers' Education Association because its Council includes University men. This College is said to supply the brains behind the labour revolt.

The Universities, hating to be reformed, and allowing the misuse of their resources by undergraduates, sometimes described by Rhodes scholars as "British babes," have been unable to do their part for the nation. They have stood aside from elementary education, only coldly tolerating the establishment of training colleges in their neighbourhood, and only timidly following a few of their members when they have led the way in the extension of University teaching. It may almost be said that they have lost influence over public opinion, and that their mission of raising the tone of democracy, of clarifying human sympathies and elevating human preferences have passed to other hands. A recent visitor to India remarked on his return that many of its difficulties seemed due to its government by "unreformed Oxford," and reflecting on the strike, one is led to say that some of its most disturbing features are due to unreformed Universities.

II.

There is something more needed, if not demanded, than a rise of wages. A few more shillings a week would soon be absorbed by men whose first use of leisure is in the enjoyment of somewhat sordid forms of sport. The men are hardly to be blamed for what are condemned as low tastes and brutal pleasures. They are what their environment has made them, and a mining village is not likely to develop a love of home-making, a taste for beauty, or any joy in the use of the higher faculties of admiration, hope, and love. The long, grimy rows of houses, without any distinctive features by which a man might recognize and become proud of his home. The absence of gardens which would call him to enjoy nature and be its fellow-worker; the want of a bathroom other than a tub in the sitting-room, by which to feel clean from the dirt of the day; the meanness of such public buildings as are provided—the church, the library, or the meeting-hall—do not provoke his soul to admiration or stir up a thirst for knowledge; such surroundings are likely to make the miner content with his pigeons, his dogs, and his football matches. Why, it may be asked, have not more owners done what some owners have done, and make a Bournville or a Port Sunlight for the workpeople. If out of the average 10 per cent profits, it is impossible to provide an appreciable addition to the men's weekly wages, it is not impossible to provide better and pleasanter housing. Why is it that owners and managers, who by many acts have shown themselves to be people of goodwill, have been content that workmen should live under conditions which unfit them to enjoy the best things: why is it that with all their charity they miss their opportunity? The fault lies, I believe, largely with the Church—Established and Free. The Church has too often gone on preaching a mediæval system, it has not moved with the times, and does not recognize that goodwill to-day must find other ways of charity than those trodden by our fathers, when they built almshouses and provided food or clothing. It has allowed a business man to be hard in his business, if he is easy in response to charitable appeals. But times have changed, and we no longer hope for a society in which rich people are kind to poor people; we rather think of a society where employers and employed share justly the profits of work; where there is no dependent class, and all find pleasure in the gifts of character which follow the full growth of manhood in rich and poor. If the Church recognized some such conception of society it would aim to humanize business relations and teach investors to ask, as Bishop Stubbs (whose "Social Creed," lately published in the "Times," well repays study) suggests, "Not only whether a business is *safe* to pay, but whether the business *deserves* to pay". Coal-owners, under the Church's influence, might substitute for such villages as Tonypandy, villages such as Earswick, and then every increase of wages would mean that widening of human interests which helps to satisfy the individual and to increase the stability of the nation.

The strike is doing vast mischief, as it dislocates trade, spreads poverty, and embitters class relationships. But all its mischief may be outweighed if it forces people to think. Our prosperity, the triumphs of machinery, the daily provision of opinions by an ubiquitous Press, have encouraged a self-satisfied and easy-going spirit. We do not take pains to make up our minds; we do not try to think our rivals' thoughts; employers do not put themselves in the men's place, and the men do not put themselves in the employers' place; none of us put ourselves in the Germans' place when they are angry at our policy. The greatest danger of the time is the forgetfulness of danger, the light-heartedness of the people, and the want of seriousness which prefers enjoyment to study, and the carelessness which, for example, goes on refusing to consider the Insurance Act, saying, "It will never come into force". People will not think. The Tariff Reform agitation has done untold good in making, at any rate, a few people think out the meaning of Free Trade. The strike will do good if it makes people—masters and men—think out the interdependence of trade—whence it is that profits come—what is the relation between home and foreign trade—what is the duty which a trade bears to the State—what is the justification for a strike or a lock-out which cripples the State—and what are the calls for State interference. Professor William James declares that the secret and glory of our English-speaking race "consists in nothing but two common habits carried into public life—habits more precious, perhaps, than any that the human race has gained. . . . One of them is the habit of trained and disciplined good temper towards the opposite party when it fairly wins its innings. The other is that of fierce and merciless resentment towards every man or set of men who break the public peace." The strike and its sufferings will not be in vain if by making us think it strengthens our hold on those heirlooms.

SAMUEL A. BARNETT.